STRESS RESPONSE SYNDROMES

Stress Response Syndromes

MARDI JON HOROWITZ, M.D.

Professor of Psychiatry
Langley Porter Neuropsychiatric Institute
University of California

JASON ARONSON, INC. • New York

ISBN: 0-87668-215-8

Library of Congress Catalog Number: 75-34708

Manufactured in the United States of America

For Nancy, Ariana,
Jordan and Joshua

Acknowledgments

While written as a theoretical essay, this book is based on ten years of clinical and experimental research on cognitive and emotional responses to stress. This work was made possible by grants from the National Institute of Mental Health in the form of a Research Career Development Award and, later, Research Scientist Development Awards (K3 MH-22573), and a six year grant for stress research (MH-24341). This support over an eight-year period made it possible to receive simultaneous training and practice in psychoanalysis and psychiatric research. On this route I was guided by many persons associated with the Career Awards Program, but wish to particularly acknowledge my gratitude to the late Bert Boothe as well as Betty Pickett, Mary Haworth, David Hamburg, Frederick Worden, and Ernest Haggard.

Jurgen Ruesch and Enoch Callaway were my first teachers in psychiatric research. They, and Mr. Toon, chemistry teacher at Fairfax High School, gave me the gift of science. That process was continued by Ransom Arthur, Edward Weinshel, Harold Sampson, and Robert Wallerstein. Help in putting these concepts into practical operation was also provided by Alexander Simon and Leon Epstein. I am also indebted to Jack Block, Jerome Singer, Richard Lazarus, Irving Janis, Leo Goldberger, Morton Reiser, Eric Erikson, Sheldon Korchin, Herbert Schlesinger, Paul Ekman, George Klein, Peter Ostwald, and

Jerome Motto, for significant consultations with me at important turning points.

I would like to especially acknowlege Emanuel Windholz as teacher. I had the privilege of co-teaching courses with Dr. Windholz on cognition and emotion in personality disorders at the San Francisco Psychoanalytic Institute. Many of the concepts about personality differences in this book stem from his ideas in those seminars. Even beyond this debt, I have been his student in one way or another since 1959 and learned from him the basic route to clinical understanding: to observe, review, repeat, and reconsider until a pattern emerges with clarity. My other psychoanalytic teachers, especially Allan Roos, Emmy Sylvester, Joseph Weiss, Stanley Goodman, and William Barrett reinforced the power of this path to knowledge.

My work has been nurtured by space, research money, and spiritual support from the personnel of Mount Zion Medical Center and Langley Porter Neuropsychiatric Institute of the University of California in San Francisco. Langley Porter provided the opportunity for me to form and direct the Stress Research Unit. The faculty of that unit has included Seymour Boorstein, Alan Skolnikoff, Richard Lieberman, James Kennedy, Nancy Kaltreider and George Kaplan. Useful additional consultations have been provided by Cliff Attkisson, William Hargreaves, John Hess, and Herbert Peterson. All have provided valuable ideas during our case discussions, and these have been abstracted to form this text. Trainees contributed an equal amount and I look forward to the extension of this type of clinical work by John Bebelaar, Frederick Parris, Richard Olsen, Stephen Schane, Nick Kanas, Robert Nadol, Robert Hammer, Wayne Sanders, Eric Gann, and Ronald Krasner.

The person who has made the Stress Research Unit "go" has been my research associate, Nancy Wilner. Her intelligence, commitment, and hard work are only exceeded by her warmth. She has contributed to, edited, and helped evolve this manuscript. Catherine Schaefer, Kenneth Sher, and Susan Dunham, provided additional moral support, as well as numerous hours in typing, checking, and assembling references. Richard Lieberman, Eric Gann, and Jerome Oremland read the manuscript and offered helpful advice and ideas. At an earlier period, my research associate, Stephanie Becker, provided energy and intelligence in the laboratory phase of this research.

I would like to briefly indicate my scientific debts. Sigmund Freud provided the basis for this work. The collection by Mandler and Mandler "Thinking: From Association to Gestalt" provided key stimulation quite early in the development of my thinking, as did all the writings of Heinz Hartmann and David Rapaport. The cognitive point of view was encouraged by George Klein, Irving Janis, Richard Lazarus, and Emanuel Peterfreund. The writings of Heinz Kohut on narcissism, Otto Kernberg and Robert Wallerstein on defense mechanisms, David Shapiro on neurotic styles, and Roy Schafer, Robert Holt, Max Schur, and Robert Waelder on psychoanalytic metapsychology, have been profound influences.

I also thank my patients and those of the Stress Research Unit for their trust and the good they may have done others by revealing themselves. My wife and children reduced my own stress throughout this work and accepted that which I imposed on them. Dedicating this book to them provides a chance to signal my gratitude.

Classical Psychoanalysis and Its Applications:
A Series of Books
Edited by Robert Langs, M.D.

Langs, Robert—THE TECHNIQUE OF PSYCHOANALYTIC PSYCHOTHERAPY VOL. I and II

Kestenberg, Judith—CHILDREN AND PARENTS: PSYCHO-ANALYTIC STUDIES IN DEVELOPMENT

Sperling, Melitta—THE MAJOR NEUROSES AND BEHAVIOR DISORDERS IN CHILDREN

Giovacchini, Peter L.—PSYCHOANALYSIS OF CHARACTER DISORDERS

Kernberg, Otto—BORDERLINE CONDITIONS AND PATHO-LOGICAL NARCISSISM

Nagera, Humberto—FEMALE SEXUALITY AND THE OEDIPUS COMPLEX

Hoffer, Willie—THE EARLY DEVELOPMENT AND EDUCATION OF THE CHILD

Meissner, William W.—THE PARANOID PROCESS

Horowitz, Mardi J.—STRESS RESPONSE SYNDROMES

Mardi Horowitz is one of a new genre of psycho-analysts who are profoundly influencing the current psychoanalytic scene. Drawing upon his research and clinical psychoanalytic experiences, Horowitz has devoted himself to a series of investigations that have culminated in this book. His previous work in image formation, cognition, art therapy, body image, hallucinatory experiences, and thought processes has made clear his powers as both a scientific observer and astute clinician. *Stress Response Syndromes* is the crystallization of his investigations into these syndromes as a means of developing a general, information processing model of symptom formation and psychotherapy. His study of the cognitive-emotional reactions to stress events clarifies the nature of their phenomenonology and is the vehicle for the development of a new and important theory of symptom formation and a pragmatic rationale for the treatment process. Supported by extensive clinical illustrations, Horowitz offers both a practical model of therapy that takes into account individual variations in character structure, and a basic paradigm for future research into the psychotherapeutic process. The book offers original theoretical and clinical insights that are applicable to a wide range of clinical problems, and enriches both cognitive and psychoanalytic theories. Horowitz has again demonstrated the widening horizons of classical psychoanalysis and its applications.

Robert Langs, M.D.

Foreword

In 1966, in a review surveying "The Current State of Psychotherapy: Theory, Practice, Research," published in the *Journal of the American Psychoanalytic Association*, I could comfortably (that is, with little risk of effective refutation) quote the sober appraisal of a friendly (non-analyst) psychotherapy researcher, Hans Strupp, that, at least to that date, even with all the burgeoning recent growth in research inquiry into psychotherapy, that very slight influence had as yet been exerted by research upon psychotherapy theory or practice. I quoted approvingly Strupp's bold statement that, "clinical penetration and scientific rigor have varied inversely. . . . If the advances of psychoanalysis as a therapeutic technique are compared with the experimental research contributions, there can be little argument as to which has more profoundly enriched the theory and practice of psychotherapy. To make the point more boldly, I believe that up to the present, research contributions have had exceedingly little influence on the practical procedures of psychotherapy." To put Strupp's argument conversely, the overwhelming proportion of what clinicians knew and found useful in conducting clinical work came from impressionistic clinical experience and apprenticeship training and not from systematic formal psychotherapy research at all.

This book by Dr. Mardi Horowitz on the psychological understanding and the psychotherapeutic amelioration of a specifically circumscribed psychopathological entity, the Stress Response Syndrome, is an exciting and long needed investigation that reflects the creative interplay of psychotherapy, research, and practice. It is, after all, of the essence of the clinical medical and health disciplines, the so-called healing arts, of which psychotherapy partakes, that continuing advance in understanding and in practice should accrue from the effective and creative interplay of formal research, basic investigation—in theoretical structure, in experimental laboratory, or in field observation or survey—in interplay with the clinical experience and clinical reflection of the bedside, or in our instance, the consulting room. It is this creative interplay between research and practice, leading to the enhancement of *both*, which has been so underdeveloped in our "peculiar" science with its heretofore essentially one-sided development, sparked by the innovative genius of a Freud, of clinical insight and understanding without the signal benefit of concomitant growth from the formal and systematic research side of any comparable insight and understanding.

Mardi Horowitz's book is a multi-faceted model, or rather a series of models, paradigmatic of a new genre, that brings psychotherapy research meaningfully into the clinical picture; that is, where each influence furthers the other. What is the nature then of these models? There is first a model of *problem setting* and *problem delineation* in the field of psychological understanding and psychological intervention. Through a sequence (1) of typical clinical *case history* of a so-called "traumatic neurosis" in sufficient detail; (2) of equally detailed and at the same time wide-ranging *field observation* and survey drawing upon disaster and extreme circumstance, whether wartime military combat or peacetime fire or shipwreck, whether such inhumane extreme circumstances as concentration camps and nuclear holocaust or more "everyday" circumstance of rape, severe illness, death and bereavement; and (3) of equally meticulous attention to the varieties of ingenious analogies to these stress situations, to the extent that they can be ethically re-created within the *experimental laboratory* and there safely studied via controlled manipulation of critical dimensions; through this sequencing, and drawing of common threads, this book serves as a model for the use of consulting room, of field observation, and of experimental laboratory to throw complementary and therefore incremental illumination upon the essential problem of psychotherapy, the understanding and the possibilities for intervention into the psychological dysfunctions of people.

This volume is secondly a model for the rational description of the *natural history* of a psychopathological syndrome or state, a description, that is, of what Dr. Horowitz calls the "general theory," the psychological explanation of sequentially unfolding phases and the general principles of psychological management and psychotherapeutic intervention specifically and differentially appropriate to the specific developmental phase and state of the disorder. To say the least, this is a beginning effort to bring some rational order out of what so often looks like a chaotic welter of conflicting claims and competing approaches all vying for consumer acceptance in the unregulated psychotherapy marketplace. And thirdly, really as corollary to the "general theory" that accounts for the understanding and the psychotherapeutic modification of the naturally unfolding stress response syndrome, is the model for differentiated understanding and intervention based on the differing enduring character dispositions of the various *personality types or styles* (the hysterical, the obsessional, and the narcissistic, for example) as they differently mesh with the impositions and implications of the disease state and the requirements and possibilities of the intervention strategies.

And fourthly, the volume is a foretaste of a model for the imposition of *other treatment modes* (in this instance, an essay on the behavioral therapy approach) conceptualized by *its* adherents within an entirely different system of psychological suppositions and meanings, understood and given meaning here within the overall psychodynamic framework of this entire volume—written as it is by a psychoanalyst—and illustrative therefore of how such a differently conceptualized approach can interact more or less effectively with the psychopathological process and be understood (i.e. "explained") in its degree of effectiveness by us in *our* terms. Truly an ambitious program for future study is heralded here!

For that is what the entire volume is, a succession of models for a viable program of psychotherapy research that can become ultimately the labors of many successor volumes—the application to other, less circumscribed, psychopathological formations unfolding in *their* natural histories; the extension to other differentiated personality dispositions or types; the encompassing of more varying therapeutic modes (Gestalt, transactional, existential-humanistic, etc.) as they each varyingly interact with differing personality styles as caught in the web of differing illness states—all reconceptualized for their effect within the framework of psychoanalytic understanding. As such a model, or rather succession of models, this book has created, or at least systematized, methods of psychotherapy research that generate findings that do affect and meaningfully alter practice. In this sense it is a most positive response to Strupp's implied plea and in itself the vehicle of a significant shift in the role that carefully devised therapy study and carefully executed therapy research can play vis à vis the clinical therapy process.

July 1975

ROBERT S. WALLERSTEIN, M.D.
Chairman, Department of Psychiatry
University of California, San Francisco
School of Medicine

CONTENTS

PART V—CLINICAL EXAMPLES

PART VI—CONCLUDING REMARKS

Part I

INTRODUCTION

CHAPTER ONE

A Paradigm for Clinical Knowledge and Practice

THERE IS A LAG in the progressive development of dynamic psychotherapy that can be counteracted by the assemblage of clinical theories and observations within well-defined sectors of conceptualization. Such sectors will be formed by specification of the problems to be treated, the predispositions of patients, and the goals of therapy.

In psychotherapies of short duration the aim is resolution of specific problems. Characterological revision, the aim in reconstructive work such as psychoanalysis, is not attempted or else is focused on a particular conflict or trait. Nonetheless, characterological styles will be observed in brief problem centered therapy. They may function as a resistance to the process of investigation, working-through, and change.

There has been considerable work done on the management of resistances and techniques relevant to transference and therapeutic alliance in psychoanalytic therapy but little systematic effort has been devoted to relating the patient's character, habitual defenses, or cognitive style to choices and nuances of problem-centered psychotherapeutic technique.

Instead, there has been heavy reliance on "rules of thumb" derived from psychoanalytic technique, especially the principle of interpretation of defenses prior to interpretations of that which is warded off. It is important to know when this rule proves useful and when it is a waste of time, when procedures

3

other than those involving interpretations are optimally useful and when they are not.

STRATEGY

What is needed in dynamic psychotherapy is additional theory, anchored to observables, that is concerned with the relationship between a patient's habitual "style", and his current state and needs, and the rational or "ideal" form of psychotherapeutic technique. This theory would have to include these facets:

1. A clear statement of the psychopathological or maladaptive *states* under consideration.
2. A clear statement of at least some *typologies* of patient styles for the organization and processing of thought and emotion during such states.
3. A clarification of the interrelationship between the patient's style and state and various modalities and styles of *psychotherapy* (e.g., even extending to different ways to give the same interpretation). This clarification would include a theory of how interventions work and why a mode of therapy useful with one patient's style might hinder work with a different patient.

The present approach starts at the existing level of clinical understanding and treatment and works toward progressive clarification and systematization. Stress response syndromes are chosen for close study as the state of maladaption, for the following reasons:

1. The relevant external events are known and recent. Therefore, memories and fantasies can be compared to a consensual reality.
2. The general human response tendencies are also known, phasic, and recognizable. Clinical and experimental studies indicate the existence of general stress response tendencies which take two seemingly opposite forms. One is manifested by intrusive and repetitive thoughts, emotions, and behavior. The other involves ideational

denial, emotional numbing, and behavioral constriction. These general tendencies vary across persons according to cognitive, emotional, and regulatory styles but can be found in some form in patients of any diagnostic or characterologic category.

3. The course of treatment is often short and the patient's states vary during treatment, allowing clinicians to view change clearly.

4. The symptoms formed and dissipated after stress events are important throughout psychopathology. They include loss of control over thought and emotion, denial and numbing, repetitious or maladaptive behavior, assault, extremes of anxiety, general tension and impaired relationships, and psychophysiological disorders.

5. Psychotherapy, often involving some sort of working through and interpretation of defenses and meanings, is frequently the treatment of choice. Within psychoanalytically oriented psychotherapy, there have been various procedures advocated and also called erroneous if ill-timed or used with the wrong person (e.g., abreaction versus support and permitted denial). Multiple other types and theories of therapy (e.g., desensitization, guided imagery, abreaction, catharsis, gestalt techniques, psychodrama) have also been advocated and can be selectively prescribed according to the state and character style of the patient.

6. Clear questions can thus be asked of the clinical material: (a) How does the external stress event interact with the character, cognitive style, and conflicts of the person involved? Development of clear connections between observation and inference about "habitual defenses" form a vital step in this therapeutic work. (b) Where is the person blocked in terms of completing the assimilation of and accommodation to the stress event? (c) How does the relationship with the therapist's activity modify the working-through or warding-off process?

PRELIMINARY TACTICS

In support of the scientific method, Sir Francis Bacon said, "The truth will sooner come from error than from confusion."

While this may not be true in connection with dogmatic error, a tactic of clear statement will be advocated, risking the attendant problem of reductionistic thinking. A conscious effort is made to reduce the rich but confusing array of information about a patient into categories along three dimensions:

1. The current phase of his response to stress, current symptoms and/or problems, and the relation of current events to past events;
2. His disposition in terms of personality structure, habitual defenses, cognitive and coping style, behavior patterns, and the lock-in of these with his family and society;
3. The therapeutic relationship and therapy techniques currently in use or appropriate to prescribe.

To serve these ends the book is divided into sections. Part II describes the background of investigations which delineate the fundamental characteristics of stress response syndromes. Following that, Part III, a theoretical section, explains these general response tendencies, and describes the general principles of brief treatment focused on relief of stress-induced symptoms and signs.

Part IV then adds the variations on these general principles, just as there are variations in harmonies and progressions on a musical theme. Three neurotic styles are contrasted, using a single manipulated case to keep the general conflict and syndrome picture as constant as possible. The currently active concept of narcissistic personality is added to the classical patterns of hysterical and obsessional personalities. This is not so much for the purpose of spanning classical and modern dispositional variables, as it is for elucidating three important cognitive operations used to ward off emotional pain in states of stress-induced neurotic conflict.

While the emphasis is on focused, brief, psychodynamic psychotherapy, this paradigm permits conceptualization of the processes should other forms of therapy be used. As an example of this type of treatment variation, behavioral therapy techniques are selected. In Chapter 11, systematic desensitization and implosive variants of behavior therapy are examined as they might be applied to persons with hysterical or obsessional personality styles who develop stress response syndromes.

Following the description of relatively universal tendencies and stylistic variations on these tendencies, Part V presents the complexity of clinical instances in the form of six case histories. These include verbatim transcripts of sections of the psycho-therapeutic process in order to provide concrete illustrations of how personality factors and pre-existing conflicts effect the reaction of a given person to a stressful life event. In Part VI, a final chapter shows how the theory of stress response articulates with other sectors of clinical knowledge and how it may provide a paradigm that can be extended into other areas.

To avoid the confusion Sir Francis Bacon spoke of, it is necessary to curtail the field of inquiry. While attempting to formulate what is known about stress response syndromes in terms of phase of response, disposition, and therapeutic approach, it is necessary to indicate what aspects of the important topic of stress will be trimmed. There is extensive literature on cross-cultural and sociological patterns of response to stress, on somatic responses, on adult traits set in motion by childhood traumas, and on developmental variation in stress response capacity. These topics will not be discussed, so that the cognitive and emotional process by which a person assimilates psychologically stressful life experiences can be focussed on as clearly as possible.

Part II

STRESS RESPONSE SYNDROMES

CHAPTER TWO

Intrusion and Denial: A Prototypical Case History

INTRUSIVE REPETITIOUSNESS AND DENIAL are labels for two extremes of response to stressful life events. The meanings beyond these labels are the concern of this book. Since exploration of these deeper meanings involves abstract statements and generalizations, it is wise to begin with a concrete example. The case of Harry provides this referent. His unbidden images of the body of a dead girl illustrate intrusive repetition of a horrible sight, and his temporary nonacknowledgment of how moved he was by his involvement in her death, illustrates a period of denial.

His case will be described here, and then used as a model in much that follows. Harry is a fictional character. His history is true to life in that it composites in brief readable form, characteristics found in studies of real persons. The events of his life can be held constant. while his character style is molded in various ways, in order to contrast the response of different personality types to the same circumstance.

HARRY

Harry is a 40-year-old truck dispatcher. He had worked his way up in a small trucking firm. One night he took a run himself because he was short-handed. The load consisted of steel pipe carried in an old truck. This improper vehicle had armor

11

between the load bed and the driver's side of the forward compartment but did not fully protect the passenger's side.

Late at night Harry passed an attractive and solitary girl hitchhiking on a lonely stretch of highway. Making an impulsive decision to violate the company rule against passengers of any sort, he picked her up on the grounds that she was a teen-aged hippie who did not know any better and might be molested.

A short time later a car veered across the divider line and entered his lane, threatening a head-on collision. Harry pulled across the shoulder of the road into an initially clear area, but crashed abruptly into a pile of gravel. The pipe shifted, penetrated the cab of the truck on the passenger's side, and impaled the girl. Harry crashed into the steering wheel and windshield and was briefly unconscious. He regained consciousness and was met with the grisly sight of his dead companion.

The highway patrol found no identification on the girl, the other car had driven on, and Harry was taken by ambulance to a hospital emergency room. No fractures were found, his lacerations were sutured, and he remained overnight for observation. His wife, who sat with him, found him anxious and dazed that night, talking of the events in a fragmentary and incoherent way so that the story was not clear.

The next day he was released. Against his doctor's recommendations for rest and his wife's wishes, he returned to work. From then on, for several days, he continued his regular work as if nothing had happened. There was an immediate session with his superiors and with legal advisers. The result was that he was reprimanded for breaking the rule about passengers but also reassured that otherwise the accident was not his fault and he would not be held responsible. As it happened, the "no-passenger" rule was frequently breached by other drivers, and this was well known to the group.

During this phase of relative denial and numbing of emotional responses, Harry thought about the accident from time to time but was surprised to find how little emotional effect it seemed to have. He was responsible and well-ordered in his work, but his wife reported that he thrashed around in his sleep, ground his teeth, and seemed more tense and irritable than usual.

Four weeks after the accident he had a nightmare in which mangled bodies appeared. He awoke with an anxiety attack. Throughout the following days he had recurrent, intense, and intrusive images of the dead girl's body. These images, together with ruminations about the girl, were accompanied by anxiety attacks of growing severity. He developed a phobia about driving to and from work. His regular habits of weekend drinking increased to nightly use of growing quantities of alcohol. He had temper outbursts over minor frustrations, experienced difficulty concentrating at work and even while watching television.

Harry tried unsuccessfully to dispel his ruminations about feeling guilty for the accident. Worried over his complaints of insomnia, irritability, and increased alcohol consumption, his doctor referred him for psychiatric treatment. This phase illustrates the period of compulsive repetition in waking and dreaming thought and emotion.

Harry was initially resistant, in psychiatric evaluation, to reporting the details of the accident. This resistance subsided relatively quickly and he reported recurrent intrusive images of the girl's body. In a psychiatric history, the following background was found.

BACKGROUND

Harry's family lived in a middle California city of approximately 100,000 population, and practiced the Baptist faith in a nonzealous manner. His father worked as a hardware store manager throughout his career, bringing in a middle-class income. His mother married his father after graduation from high school, and has been a housewife and mother since then. There were three siblings, two older and one younger sister.

Harry's father, a strict and moralistic man, had a constricted outlook on life. He was out of work during the Depression and remained preoccupied with trying to save money. When this was not possible, he was irritated or worried. Aside from work and family, he valued his men's club activities and his hobby of trout fishing. He consistently displayed a rigorous sense of morality and was a strict disciplinarian. As will be seen, Harry internalized these standards of behavior, and this contributed to guilty feelings after the accident. He was never overtly affectionate but did praise the children when they were good. He took Harry on occasional fishing trips but remained fairly remote.

Harry's mother, a responsible and somewhat masochistic woman, doted on her husband and struggled to provide a good home for her children. She often overworked herself to make sure that the house was clean, the meals on time, and the laundry done. She sometimes cried and belittled herself when she was unable to complete these tasks. Harry felt that his mother was unappreciated by his father, and that his father did not help her enough. While the father sat in his chair during the evening, the mother continued to do quite a bit of hard work. Harry helped sporadically. Harry's mother favored him and was generally forgiving of his transgressions.

One older sister resented Harry's favored position with their mother. She periodically teased and tormented him. The other two sisters shared their mother's attitude that he was the special one. He felt especially close to the younger sister but not much attachment to the older sisters.

Harry was one of the more intelligent and gifted children in his high school class. Some teachers tried to encourage him to go to college. Meanwhile, he fell in love with a girl in his class, and they had an affair. Gradually, with considerable guilt over each new step in sexual intimacy, the relationship developed. Late in the senior year of high school, she became pregnant. They decided they were in love, should therefore get married, and have the child. Harry found a job working for a local store and this led to his gradual entry into the truck-driving field. Periodic promotions followed until he achieved the position of chief dispatcher a few years before the accident. He worked hard, valued the esteem of the men, but felt bored and limited. The resultant readiness for "something else" contributed a certain impulsiveness to his life, as in a readiness to break the rules and pick up the girl.

Harry and his wife have three children, two boys and a girl. Although Harry occasionally feels dragged down by the amount of time the children demand from him evenings and weekends, he is an attentive and loving father. He works at this, and consciously wants to be a better husband and father than his father had been. Resentment toward his wife occasionally surfaces, however, for he also wants independence from what he experiences as her demands. The associated ideas are that, if it weren't for her and the development of a family, he would have been able to go to college, develop his potential, and be involved in more interesting and remunerative work.

For a two-year period he was drafted and served in the military. His wife and family were able to accompany him to a stateside base. He remembers this as one of the happier periods of his life because of the variety of experience and the comraderie with other men. He has felt occasionally depressed since then.

When he is feeling morose, instead of coming home for dinner, Harry will go to a local bar with some of the men from work. He generally returns home three or four hours later, moderately intoxicated. His wife reacts with coldness, tears, or an angry attack. He counteracts by feeling either upset, guilty, and apologetic, or else being angry in return, criticizing his wife's faults and shortcomings. On one occasion he hit her during such an altercation, she threatened to leave him, and the physical abuse was never repeated. After the accident he feared that his wife would react to the act of picking up the girl with similar coldness, accusation and anger.

Following such outbursts between them, Harry tends to carry a grudge against his wife for several weeks. To his surprise, she recovers the same day. Her main grievance is that she feels unappreciated for all the devotion she gives as his wife and mother of the children. Although their sex life is intermittently active, she accuses him of being less interested in her, and herself of being less interesting. While Harry does not state it to her, he feels this is true. He has been sexually interested in women at work, but this has not gone beyond flirtations and kissing at office parties. His sexual fantasies were activated by seeing the girl alone on the highway.

Harry's main leisure activites are picnicking and camping with his family and trout fishing with his father. The two have developed a kind of distant but affectionate relationship around this activity. In addition, Harry likes to read. He tends to select recent novels, and has also purchased a set from a "great books" series that he is determined to read through from beginning to end.

TREATMENT

During the course of psychotherapy, Harry worked through several complexes of ideas and feelings linked associatively to the accident and his intrusive images. The emergent conflictual themes included guilt over causing the girl's death, guilt over the sexual ideas about her he fantasied before the accident, guilt that he felt glad to be alive when she had died, and fear and anger that he had been involved in an accident and her death. There was also a magical belief that the girl "caused" the accident by her hitchhiking, and associated anger with her, which then fed back into his various guilt feelings.

His symptoms gradually lessened. At first he was able to sleep better. Gradually he felt less anxious, tense, and irritable. He reduced his alcohol intake to an occasional social drink. Later, the image symptoms stopped and his relationships returned to about the same level as before the accident, except that he felt closer to his wife, who is credited with helping him through a difficult period.

Each of the complexes of ideas and feelings were activated not only by the accident but by Harry's state prior to the conflict. Friction and sexual disinterest in his wife led to fantasies about other women and activities that resulted in feelings of guilt. Such guilt was connected with his feelings after the accident, just as his anger with his wife was related to his anger with the girl hitchhiker. Thus the stress event led to a period of stress which combined internal and external elements.

These various elements and combinations will be considered in more detail in subsequent chapters. Harry will be considered in terms of variations in how therapy might be conducted. The important matter here is the concrete illustration of the signs and symptoms after the accident. Recognition of such signs as the denial period, the free interval when Harry functioned well at work after the accident, and recognition of the symptom of intrusive images, is enhanced by knowledge of a clinical theory of stress response syndromes. Without this knowledge, the free period might look like a normal adaptiveness and the intrusive images might not have been inquired about or might have been regarded as unimportant in an interview.

CHAPTER THREE

Clinical Observations and the Diagnostic Dilemma

THE MOST IMPORTANT ASSERTIONS about psychological responses to threat were advanced by Breuer and Freud (1895) in the "Studies on Hysteria." A wide variety of cognitive, emotional, and behavioral symptoms were interpreted as symbolic or disguised repetitions of prior traumatic events.

COMPULSIVE REPETITIONS

Post-traumatic conversion reactions, in which motor or sensory disturbances occurred without neurological cause, had been noted by other investigators such as Charcot and Janet (see Veith, 1965, for a review). "Railroad spine," for example, was a common disability after railway accidents. While the threat of litigation played a motivational role, it became quite clear to neurologists that conscious malingering was not the reason for much of the pain, numbness, or symptoms of paralysis that persisted long after the disasters. Post-traumatic hysterias such as "railway spine" were thought to effect men or women, but "hysteria" proper, with symptoms of dissocation as well as motor-sensory disorders, was originally seen as predominantly an illness of women (Veith, 1965: Luisada, Peele, and Pittard, 1974). When Freud presented ideas about "male hysteria" to the Vienna Medical Society, after he had studied this syndrome with Charcot, he was roundly criticized.

Freud and Breuer (1895), using the early methods of psychoanalysis, explored hysterical symptoms in terms of associated memories and fantasies. They found that prior traumas of a psychological nature provided the contents re-enacted either symbolically or directly in the symptoms. The traumatic events often involved an element of sexuality in which the person was involuntarily aroused in a situation where such excitement was both excessive and incompatible with morality. Emotions and impulses to action were strong and yet warded off by defenses such as repression, splitting or dissociating and undoing. The pressure for expression together with defensive distortions of expression was seen as the cause of symptoms that emerged long after the problematic event. Symptom relief was obtained through an emotionally charged recollection of the earlier traumatic memories. Incompatible ideas were worked through as the fended-off feelings were expressed.

In their investigations, Freud and Breuer noted the importance of psychological traumas precipitating such diverse hysterical symptoms as recurrent visual hallucinations, emotional attacks, convulsive movements, and other sensory or motor disturbances. They also noted that there was frequently a latent period between the occurrence of a stressful event and the onset of symptoms. Once symptoms formed, however, there was a remarkable tendency toward recurrence or persistence long after termination of the event and its immediate effects. In addition, there was frequently a kind of bland denial of the meaning of symptoms which was called "la belle indifference."

Freud made many theoretical revisions following the initial psychoanalytic discoveries of the traumatic basis of hysterical symptoms. He was dismayed to find that the "memories" of childhood seduction, the primary "trauma" in his theory, were not always true memories but mnemonic constructions based on fantasy elaborations of childhood situations (Jones, 1953). Thus the "traumatic event" did not always represent an external stress but also involved internal components. Also, a traumatic event might produce virtually any symptomatic picture, not just hysterical syndromes (Freud, 1920).

Through elaborations and corrections of theory, the concept of trauma became generalized. As psychoanalysis developed, trauma was regarded as the cause of various symptoms, conflicts, fixations, character traits, defenses, and adaptive and maladaptive cognitive and affective developments (Bibring, 1943; Fenichel, 1945). This generalization of trauma as an explanatory concept necessitated description of its many variations. The result was an array of terms such as multiple, strain, cumulative, screen, bad-object, fantasy, and retrospective traumas (Glover, 1929; Sears, 1936; Freud, 1937; Greenacre, 1952; Fairbairn, 1954; Stern, 1961; Furst, 1967; and Sachs, 1967). In spite of this diffusion of terminology and theory, the key findings remained quite clear to clinicians and are consensually validated: after a traumatic event there is a compulsive tendency toward repetition of some aspect of the experience (Freud, 1914, 1920; Schur, 1966).

This involuntary repetition includes recurrence in thought of stress event experiences, of feelings related to the original experience, or behavioral reenactments of aspects of the experience itself. Repetitions in thought may take many forms including nightmares, dreams, hallucinations, pseudohallucinations, recurrent unbidden images, illusions, and recurrent obsessive ideas. Harry's images of the dead body of the girl are one example. Emotional repetitions may occur with or without clear conscious awareness of their conceptual associations. Behavioral re-enactments range from compulsive verbalization of the event, through recurrent expressions of the event, in gesture, movement, or artistic productions, to patterning of interpersonal relations. That is, life patterns may be reconstructed in such a way that the "trauma" itself is repeated over and over again in equivalent or symbolic form. Finally, there are a variety of repetitive physiological responses to stress, and behavioral or cognitive repetitions may include recurrence of stress-related physiological responses such as sweating, tremor, palpitations, or other autonomic symptoms.

These repetitions may occur in spite of pronounced conscious efforts at avoidance and suppression but are not necessarily static replicas of the original experience. A series of successive revisions in content and form are frequently noted in clinical studies. Often, such repetitions may eventually lose their intrusive and involuntary nature. The change in content and reduced intrusiveness indicates that a progressive mastery of the experience has taken place. Unfortunately this is not always so, and some intrusive repetitions persist indefinitely.

DENIAL

The involuntary repetition of stress-relevant contents may stand in stark contrast to its ostensible opposite: massive ideational denial of the event and general emotional numbness. Menninger (1954) called this "hypersuppression" the most normal and the most prevalent of defenses. Warding off thoughts about the stress event, or its implications, may alternate with intrusive repetitions in a variety of phasic relationships. Denial and numbness may characterize a given time span of hours or days; this may alternate with phases of ideational intrusion and emotional pangs. Also, there may be intrusive repetitions of one aspect of a stress event, with simultaneous denial and numbing of another implication of the event (Fear-content intrusions, for example, with repression of guilt-content associations).

To recapitulate, clinical studies indicate that major stress events tend to be followed by involuntary repetition in thought, emotion, and behavior. Such responses tend to occur in phases and to alternate with periods of relatively successful warding off of repetitions as manifested by ideational denial and emotional numbness.

COMMON THEMES

Any event is appraised and assimilated in relation to the past history and the current cognitive and emotional set of the person who experiences it. Idiosyncratic responses result. But human beings are as similar as they are different, and certain conflicts between wishes and realities seem fairly universal after stress events such as accidental injuries, illness, and losses. Clinical studies reveal at least the following themes as common, albeit often unconscious, problems for the working-through process initiated by stressful life events. Such thematic contents are involved as intrusive ideas, as ideas that are warded off, as well as ideas that are deliberately contemplated.

1. *Fear of Repetition*

Any event that occurs may recur. Anticipation of repetition of painful stress events conflicts with the wish to avoid displeasure. Persons fear a real repetition and they also fear repetition in thought.

2. *Shame Over Helplessness or Emptiness*

Expectation of personal omnipotence or total control is unrealistic, but is nonetheless a universal hope and sometimes a deeply felt personal belief. The failure to prevent a stress event such as an accident, and the breakdown that may follow an event such as an illness, is regarded as a loss of control and conflicts with the wish to have power and mastery. Persons who have had a heart attack or back injury, for example, may apologize profusely because they cannot carry out garbage cans or they may even, inappropriately, carry them out to avoid a sense of shame for either shirking their duty or having become useless. A parent, after a fire has burned down the family house, may feel deflated in the eyes of his children now that things are not as comfortable as they were. Magical thinking often extends such irrational attitudes so that inability to master a stressful event is regarded as equivalent to a loss of bowel or bladder control, or a regression to infantile helplessness.

3. Rage at the Source

Rage is a natural response to frustration. As strange as it sounds, an important theme after stress events is anger at any symbolic figure who can, however irrationally, be construed as responsible. A mother who cuts her finger while slicing meat may feel an impulse to say to a nearby child, "See what you made me do." Asking "Why it happened" after a stress event is usually associated with a need to find out who is to blame, and who should be punished. Rage will commonly conflict with a sense of social morality. A common example is rage at a person who has fallen ill, a feeling that is in conflict with the recognition that it is not his fault and that he needs help, not blame.

4. Guilt or Shame over Aggressive Impulses

The rage alluded to above often extends to destructive fantasies directed toward anyone symbolically connected to the personal frustrations triggered by a stressful event. When violence is a part of the event, this, in and of itself, seems to stimulate internal aggressivity. The combined aggressivity conflicts with a sense of conscience, as above, and leads to feelings of guilt or shame. Negative feelings toward a person who has died, and reactive guilt or shame, are a common version of this type of conflict.

Another impulse that can evoke guilt or shame is the urgent need to look at a potential threat. This virtually instinctive investigative thrust would seem to be conflict-free, but that is not the case when other persons are victims. For example, there may be severe bodily damage to others in an accident, where both social convention and natural revulsion dictate looking away or covering up. Staring at bodies seems to the person who does it to be an unwarranted aggression. Memory of looking can lead to anxiety or guilt, when the person feels he was morbidly curious and fails to recognize the presence of an intrinsic need to gain information about threat.

5. Fear of Aggressivity

There is another conflict between the destructive fantasies mentioned above and a wish to remain in control. A person fears that he will impulsively act out his fantasies in an out-of-control manner. For example, a soldier traumatized by repeated combat experiences, will often fear on return to civilian life that he will physically attack persons who offer only slight frustrations.

6. Survivor Guilt

When others have been injured or killed one is relieved to realize that he has been spared. Once again, at a level of magical thinking there is a common irrational belief that destiny chooses an allotment of victims, as if to placate the primitive gods, and that if one has eluded the Fates, it is at the expense of those inevitable victims who have not been spared. The wish to be a survivor conflicts with moral attitudes, leading to an attitude of self-castigation for selfishness.

7. Fear of Identification or Merger with Victims

A complementary theme related to survivor guilt is the fear of not being separate from the victims. At a primitive level of thinking persons are not conceptualized as discretely separate. If an event has hurt another there is a primitive fear that it may have or will hurt oneself. This may set in motion a train of thought assuming the self as victim, even when this conflicts with reality.

8. Sadness in Relation to Loss

Any painful stress event has an element of loss that conflicts with the universal wish for permanence, safety, and satisfaction. The loss may be another person, an external resource, or an aspect of the self. Naturally, some losses are more symbolic than real but they are no less important. A person who has been laid off from work, not for personal reasons, but because a plant has closed, may suffer a loss of self-esteem from deprivation of his work role.

As mentioned earlier, these eight themes provide the ideational and emotional contents that are commonly warded off in periods of denial or are intrusive in periods of compulsive repetition. Any one of these themes merges the current stress event with previous conflicts over previous stress events. Guilt over aggressive impulses is too common to everyone's past history to be a theme unique to a current trauma. The current event will gain emotional association to previous guilt-aggression memories and fantasies. Such blends of themes lead to the diagnostic dilemma: how much of a given problem is due to the recent life event, however stressful; how much is due to prior developments?

DIAGNOSTIC ISSUES

When symptoms and signs persist for months or years after the stress event, some clinicians would say that these enduring syndromes signified a traumatic neurosis; others would say that the stress event or the acute stress reaction precipitated a latent neurosis. The enduring syndrome, according to the latter point of view, is a neurosis like any other and does not deserve a special designation as some sort of stress response syndrome. As mentioned above, psychodynamic investigations of syndromes occurring after stress events do demonstrate an intermingling of elements from unresolved childhood conflicts with response elements related to the recent experience (see e.g., Windholz, 1945; Greenacre, 1952; Murphy, 1961; Solomon et al., 1971).

Given that all psychological manifestations are determined by multiple causes, the question becomes one of relative weights of possible etiological factors. The crucial issue concerns the existence, nature, and etiological importance of general stress response tendencies as contrasted with idiosyncratic or person-specific types of variation in response to stress. This issue has proved so difficult that, at present, there is no diagnostic category "Traumatic Neuroses" in the official 1952 American psychiatric nomenclature (DSM-I) or in the 1968 revision (DSM-II). Neuroses that follow major external stress events are to be classified, according to presenting symptoms, as other types of neuroses (anxiety neurosis, obsessive-compulsive neurosis, hysterical neurosis, and so on).

In DSM-I, symptomatic responses to very stressful experiences could also be classified as "Gross Stress Reactions," but this category was deleted in DSM-II. In DSM-II, the system, at this writing, the appropriate categorization would be "Transient Situational Disturbances" using the subheadings of adjustment reaction of adult, adolescent, or childhood life. DSM-III will probably take cognizance of such issues as will be discussed here, and return a stress response entity to the official list of diagnoses.

In the psychiatric literature, the courtroom, and in case conferences in training institutions, the diagnosis "traumatic neurosis" is used frequently, however, and there is considerable agreement on what is meant by the term (Keiser, 1969). For example, traumatic neurosis, in Hinsie and Campbell's Psychiatric Dictionary (1960), is defined as having these essential features:

> (1) fixation on the trauma with amnesia for the traumatic situation which may be total or partial; (2) typical dream-life (dreams of annihilation, aggression dreams where the patient is the aggressor but is defeated, frustration or Sisyphus dreams, and occupational dreams in which it is the means of livelihood rather than the body-ego which is annihilated); (3) contraction of the general level of functioning, with constant fear of the environment, disorganized behavior, lowered efficiency, lack of coordinated goal activities, and profoundly altered functioning in the autonomic, motor, and sensory nervous system; (4) general irritability; and (5) a proclivity to explosive aggressive reactions." (p. 497)

Harry had a "fixation on the trauma" in the form of recurrent images of the girl and, later, in pangs of guilt. He had what could be seen as a partial amnesia in that he forgot an important conscious experience of his own. On regaining consciousness he saw the girl's body and experienced the thought that someone had to be dead. He realized it was she and not he, and felt a momentary relief. He felt badly to have such a response, and like Freud and Breuer's hysterical patients, repressed that component of the memory. He also had a frightening dream life, the contraction in functioning, irritability, and aggressivity mentioned in the Hinsie and Campbell definition.

The term "fixation on trauma" in the preceding definition refers to the same phenomena that are labeled as "repetition compulsion" in the psychoanalytic definition of traumatic neurosis:

Traumatic Neurosis: A neurosis in which overwhelming tension and painful affects, such as anxiety or guilt related to a traumatic experience, can be mastered by the usual defenses of the ego. Pathological and archaic ego mechanisms are set in motion which determine a clinical picture dominated by somatic features and a repetition compulsion forcibly bringing to mind the original trauma. Symptoms include marked emotional lability, with uncontrollable discharges of anxiety, fear, or rage; severe disturbances of sleep, with typical dreams in which the trauma is painfully re-experienced; and mental repetitions in the waking state of the traumatic situation, in whole or in part, in the form of fantasies, thoughts, or feelings. Psychological mastery of the trauma is usually accompanied by recession of the traumatic elements and increasing prominence of psychoneurotic symptoms. (Moore and Fine, 1968)

The situation is an interesting one. There is no official diagnostic categorization for a historically based and well-defined syndrome. A possible reason for the discrepancy is that as the syndrome is studied in a given person, it seems to lose its connection with an immediate stress event and gain connections to conflicts and character traits present before the event. That

is what is compressed in the statement, from the above definition, about the "recession of the traumatic elements in increasing prominence of psychoneurotic symptoms." For example,
Harry's irritability and temper outbursts at his wife after the
girl's death were not simply the results of the accident, but
were incorporated frictions present before and even contributing to the stress event.

The question of how much is predisposition and how much
is the effect of immediate stress is hard to elucidate because
every syndrome will be composed of both sources of influence.
The absence of a fixed terminology for "traumatic neurosis" in
the official nomenclature has led to an "every author for himself" effect in psychiatric textbooks. The main terminological
variants are "Gross Stress Reaction," "Traumatic Neurosis,"
and "Neurosis Following Trauma."

The lack of agreement persists even when we restrict the
issue to include only *adults* who have experienced clearly stressful *external* events and who have persisted symptomatic responses *after* removal from the external stress. There are, for
example, variances in how to group stress response syndromes
with other psychiatric syndromes. Textbook authors Redlich
and Freedman (1966) describe *"traumatic neurosis"* as part of
their section of the psychoneuroses. In Kolb's new edition
(1968) of Noyes' textbook of psychiatry, the grouping is again
with psychoneurosis, but the title is "Gross Stress Reaction,"
divided into acute reactions, exemplified by combat neuroses,
and chronic reactions, exemplified by concentration camp syndromes. Similarly, in Arieti's *American Handbook of Psychiatry*
and Kardiner's (1959) chapter entitled "The Traumatic Neuroses of War" are parts of the section on psychoneuroses. But, in
Volume III of that handbook, there is another chapter by Ross
(1966) entitled "Neuroses Following Trauma." In greater contrast, Freedman's (1967) textbook of psychiatry does not include traumatic neurosis with other neuroses but instead has a
section entitled "Personality Disorders IV: Gross Stress Reaction" which is itself divided into two chapters, one discussing

phases of response to external stress events (Weiss and Payson, 1967), and one entitled "Traumatic War Neurosis" (Brill, 1967).

The inadequacy of current classification and terminology is noted by many of the above authors. The main difficulty lies with the lack of clear phenomenological demarcation between such different kinds of stress response as:

1. The immediate or acute patterns of response to a stress event. This roughly correlates with the diagnostic terms Gross Stress Reaction" of DSM-I and "Transient Situational Disturbances" of DSM-II.
2. The extended (subacute or chronic) patterns of response to the stress event. This roughly correlates in common usage with the term "traumatic neurosis" when the symptoms or signs are relatively severe.
3. The precipitation of latent and idiosyncratic psychological conflicts and reactions by external events which may or may not be stressful to the average expectable person. This category correlates with the general idea of "precipitating stress" and "psychoneuroses that follow trauma."
4. Changes in personality as a consequence of stress events and items 1-3 above. This category would correlate, perhaps, with special syndromes such as survivor syndrome, which will be discussed later.

The foregoing separation of phases of response does not form an adequate solution to the diagnostic dilemma because the four divisions are often not distinguishable in terms of phenomenology or etiology. Certain signs and symptoms appear in every category, and this includes both intrusion and denial variants. Personality predispositions may play an important role in acute and chronic stress response patterns as well as in precipitation of neuroses and personality change. Everyone agrees that psychological responses are determined by multiple causes and factors, but there is disagreement as to the etiological valence of idiosyncratic or typological personality variables and general stress response tendencies. This disagreement peaks in discussion of chronic stress response syndromes.

Basically, the issue comes down to this: if general stress response tendencies are prime factors in causing the signs and symptoms of a chronic syndrome, then stress response syndrome is a valid nosological entity. If personality predispositions are invariably prime factors in chronic responses, then "neuroses [or other diagnostic entities] following stress" is a sufficient categorization. The debate on the greater or lesser importance of personality factors versus general stress response factors in causing post-stress symptoms can be illustrated by two exerpts from an important World War II conference on traumatic neurosis (U.S. Public Health Service, 1943).

> Dr. Abram Kardiner: I was very glad to hear Dr. Hoch's report, because it is a confirmation of an idea that I have tried to propound for years without much success. Dr. Hoch said that he found no consistency in the pre-traumatic personality. I wish to support him in this contention. You can find every variety of pre-traumatic personality . . . (pp. 42-3).
> Dr. S. D. Vestermark: . . . It is my feeling in dealing with people that there is, as has been stated, a very definite type of underlying personality structure. I think that is related to the amount of time that we spend with these people; if we have adequate time and opportunity, we can find in most of these people some underlying pre-existing personality distortion or maladaption that would lead us to believe that eventually this individual would be a potential candidate for some type of a breakdown under various stresses and strains. (pp. 49-50)

Harry provides a referent. If his syndrome of intrusive thoughts, anxiety, insomnia, alcoholism, and irritability after the accident is due to the way he experienced the event, and would not have happened otherwise, then he has a stress response syndrome. If preexisting difficulties—for example, problems with his self-esteem and conflicts with his wife—were the main causes, then he has a mixed neurotic syndrome exacerbated by an incident which itself may have had a neurotic causation. How much is due to each of the multiple factors?

How much is "stress" and how much is "Harry" (or "marriage" or "society") ?

A Strategy of Approach to the Problem

As indicated above, a key issue concerns the existence of a set of symptoms and signs that might be considered a general stress response syndrome-general in that all persons would tend to develop such a syndrome after major external stress in adult life, although they would vary in the degree or quality of manifestations of response according to their individual predispositions.

One problem in answering such questions about generality of response with data from in-depth clinical investigations is that clinical studies rely on self-selected patients as subjects. How many persons experienced the same stress event and did not develop symptoms or come for treatment? If certain responses to stress indicate a general tendency, then many different types of persons in an exposed population should manifest similar responses.

Such questions of incidence of a syndrome in a population are best answered by field or experimental studies. If many persons exposed to such an accident had periods of intrusive experience and periods of relative denial, then it is not all Harry and his predisposition. If only a few have such syndromes, then it is not all stress but predisposition. As reviewed in the next chapter, the clinical findings are supported: there are general tendencies to both excessively intrusive and avoided experiences after stress.

BIBLIOGRAPHY

Bibring, E. (1943), The conception of the repetition compulsion. *Psychoanalytic Quarterly*, 12:486-519.

Breuer, J. & Freud, S. (1895), *Studies on hysteria. Standard Edition*, 2. London: Hogarth Press, 1955.

Brill, N. Q. (1967), Gross stress reactions II: Traumatic war neuroses. In: *Comprehensive Textbook of Psychiatry*, ed. A. M. Freedman & H. I. Kaplan. Baltimore: The Williams & Wilkins Company, pp. 1031-1035.

Fairbairn, W. R. (1954), *An Object-Relations Theory of the Personality*. New York: Basic Books.

Fenichel, O. (1945), *The Psychoanalytic Theory of Neurosis*. New York: Norton.

Freedman, A. M. (1967), *Comprehensive Textbook of Psychiatry*, ed. A. M. Freedman & H. I. Kaplan. Baltimore: Williams & Wilkins Company.

Freud, S. (1914), Remembering, repeating, and working-through. *Standard Edition*, 12:145-150. London: Hogarth Press, 1958.

Freud, S. (1920), Beyond the pleasure principle. *Standard Edition*, 18:7-64. London: Hogarth Press, 1953.

Freud, S. (1937), Constructions in analysis. *Standard Edition*, 23:255-269. London: Hogarth Press, 1964.

Furst, S. S. (1967), Psychic trauma: A survey. In: *Psychic Trauma*, ed. S. S. Furst. New York: Basic Books.

Glover, E. (1929), The screening function of traumatic memories. *International Journal of Psychoanalysis*, 10:90-93.

Greenacre, P. (1952), *Trauma, Growth, and Personality*. New York: Norton.

Hinsie, L. E. & Campbell, R. J. (1960), *Psychiatric Dictionary*, third edition. New York: Oxford University Press.

Jones, E. (1953), *The Life and Work of Sigmund Freud, Vol. I*. New York: Basic Books.

Kardiner, A. (1959), Traumatic neuroses of war. In: *American Handbook of Psychiatry*, Vol. II, ed. S. Arieti. New York: Basic Books, pp. 245-257.

Keiser, L. (1969), Accidents create opportunities. *Contemporary Psychology*, 14:434-435.

Kolb, L. C. (1968), *Noyes Modern Clinical Psychiatry*. Philadelphia: Saunders.

Luisada, P. V., Peele, R., Pittard, E. A. (1974), The hysterical personality in men. *American Journal of Psychotherapy*, 131:518-521.

Menninger, K. (1954), Regulatory devices of the ego under major stress. *International Journal of Psychoanalysis*, 35:412-420.

Moore, B. E., & Fine, B. D. (1968), *A Glossary of Psychoanalytic Terms and Concepts*. New York: The American Psychoanalytic Association.

Murphy, W. F. (1961), A note on traumatic loss. *Journal of the American Psychoanalytic Association*, 9:519-532.

Redlich, F. C. & Freedman, D. X. (1966), *The Theory and Practice of Psychiatry*. New York: Basic Books.

Ross, W. D. (1966), Neuroses following trauma and their relation to compensation. In: *American Handbook of Psychiatry*, Vol. III, ed. S. Arieti. New York: Basic Books, pp. 131-147.

Sachs, O. (1967), Distinctions between fantasy and reality elements in reconstruction. *International Journal of Psychoanalysis*, 48:416-423.

Schur, M. (1966), *The Id and the Regulatory Process of the Ego*. New York: International Universities Press.

Sears, R. R. (1936), Functional abnormalities of memory with special reference to amnesia. *Psychological Bulletin*, 33:229-274.

Solomon, G. F. et al. (1971), Three psychiatric casualties from Vietnam. *Archives of General Psychiatry*, 25:522-524.

Stern, M. M. (1961), Blank hallucinations: Remarks about trauma and perceptual disturbances. *International Journal of Psychoanalysis*, 42:205-215.

U.S. Public Health Service (1943), WW II Conference on Traumatic Neuroses. Washington, USPHS.

Veith, I. (1965), *Hysteria: History of a Disease*. Chicago: University of Chicago Press.

Weiss, R. J. & Payson, H. E. (1967), Gross stress reaction I. In: *Comprehensive Textbook of Psychiatry,* ed. A. M. Freedman & H. I. Kaplan. Baltimore: Williams & Wilkins, pp. 1027-1031.

Windholz, E. (1945), Observations on psychiatric rehabilitation of veterans. *Bulletin of The Menninger Clinic,* 9:121-133.

CHAPTER FOUR

Field Studies on the Impact of Life Events

with Nancy Wilner

FIELD STUDIES ARE NECESSARY to determine the generality of some phenomena. Clinical studies involve patients who are self-selected and present themselves spontaneously for treatment. Without field studies, one cannot know if the rich clinical observations available from careful patient study are pertinent only to rare instances of "falling ill" or indicate general response tendencies. This review is, of course, highly selective in order to demonstrate a general stress responsivity as delineated in phases of response.

MILITARY COMBAT

Field studies of stress require the natural occurrence of some kind of disaster to a more or less extensive population. Warfare, unfortunately, provides such conditions. Oddly enough, while wars are all too common throughout history, recognition of psychological stress response syndromes was not complete until World War II since it had to be forced past considerable resistance. Physical causes were preferred as a basis for theory, because psychological causation sounded too much like weakness, cowardice, or lack of patriotism.

A torrent of psychological casualties among combat soldiers, sailors, and airmen forced recognition of some type of syndrome in World War I. Earlier observations had been made, such as "soldier's heart" in the American Civil War, but lacked influence. Instead of calling them coronary symptoms due to the strains of combat, the presence of daze, fear, trembling, nightmares, and inability to function were attributed to brain disease in World War I. The cause was postulated to be cerebral concussions and ruptures of small blood vessels caused by exploding shells, hence the then common term "shell shock." The organic focus of the medical model of the day led to a concentration on "expectable symptoms" such as those known to characterize acute and chronic brain syndromes.

Multiple observations eventually revealed that physical traumas were not invariably antecedents to combat reactions. Anyone exposed to terrible sights might respond with prolonged symptoms, even if he emerged physically unharmed and even if only a single exposure occurred. Symptoms appeared frequently in persons exposed to extended combat situations, with antecedent physical traumas not necessarily the cause.

Freud (1920) was impressed with the quantity, intensity, and prolonged duration of symptoms in veterans of World War I. These observations of combat reactions, especially the symptoms of recurrent nightmares which repeated scenes of terror, forced him to revise his theory of dreams. He recognized that the recurrent nightmares of combat were not wish fulfillments, that they were "beyond the pleasure principle," and were manifestations of a "compulsion." Freud also revised his theory of psychic trauma and neuroses: sexual threats were sufficient triggers for neuroses but they were not the exclusive antecedent; threats to safety also might cause neurotic symptoms.

The vast populations presenting symptomatic responses to stress events in World War II again forced phenomenological studies of the relative frequency of symptoms. A good example is the study of combat reactions by Grinker and Spiegel (1945). Their summary of the nineteen most frequent symptoms which persisted long after removal from combat are shown by rank order in Table I. The organization of tabulation, as in most phenomenological studies, is in order of frequency of occurrence.

TABLE 1

Most Common Signs and Symptoms of Operational Fatigue
as found by Grinker, et al. (1945).
(In rank order by frequency).

1. Restlessness	11. Tremor
2. Irritability or aggression	12. Difficulty concentrating, confusion
3. Fatigue on arising, lethargy	13. Alcoholism
4. Difficulty falling asleep	14. Preoccupation with combat
5. Anxiety, subjective	15. Decreased appetite
6. Fatigue easily	16. Nightmares
7. Startle reactions	17. Psychosomatic symptoms (e.g., vomiting, diarrhea)
8. Feeling of tension	18. Irrational fears (phobias)
9. Depression	19. Suspiciousness
10. Personality change and memory loss	

These symptoms are typical of those found in other studies of soldiers, as well as studies of civilians exposed to natural disasters such as fire and shipwreck (Cobb and Lindermann, 1943; Baker and Chapman, 1962). Such symptoms are also not uncommon after the kind of disastrous auto accident experienced by Harry.

Even the categories of symptoms slated for observation and codification by Grinker and Spiegel may reflect the theory of the time. Freud had emphasized nightmares, one form of intrusive and repetitive thought, but had played down a similar phenomenon—recurrent unbidden images of frightening scenes which occur in waking thought:

> Now dreams occurring in traumatic neuroses have the characteristic of repeatedly bringing the patient back into the situation of his accident, a situation from which he wakes up in another fright . . . I am not aware, however, patients suffering from traumatic neurosis are much occupied in their waking lives with memories of their accident. Perhaps they are more concerned with *not* thinking of it. (Freud, 1920)

Freud was incorrect in part of this observation. Recurrent unbidden images while awake are a striking occurrence after stress events ranging from combat traumas, to a single "near miss" automobile accident, to bereavement after death of a spouse (Lindemann, 1944; Parkes, 1970; Yamamoto and Imahara, 1970), to the terrible and prolonged experiences of the concentration camp (Niederland, 1968; Krystal, 1968). Recurrent unbidden images were not mentioned by Grinker and Spiegel, possibly because thought experience is, in general, harder to report than physical sensation. Many persons, unless they are specifically asked, do not express such qualities of thought as intrusive entry into awareness or unusual intensity of imagery. If asked, they may avoid discussion of such experiences as part of a general defensive effort. Thus, intrusive and repetitive conscious experiences would be indicated within Grinker and Spiegel's categories of startle reactions, difficulty concentrating, preoccupation with combat, nightmares, and irrational fears or phobias. In addition, the menace of such unpleasant intrusions probably contributes to the behavioral signs of restlessness, irritability, and insomnia.

The expression "everyone has his breaking point" evolved from experience with reactions to combat. It suggests that every person exposed to enough stress may show an acute stress response syndrome. Persons with certain latent neuroses or predispositions to certain stress triggers may respond to lower levels of external stress. Persons with high stress tolerance will not "break down" until the level of stress is higher. Brill (1967) found that soldiers with pre-existing neuroses had a seven-to-eight times greater chance of psychiatric reactions.

In a lengthy review of the literature, Hocking (1970) verifies the hypothesis that "although individuals vary in their ability to adjust to differing degrees of stress, subjection to prolonged, extreme stress results in the development of neurotic symptoms in virtually every person exposed to it." He noted that in 303 individuals involved in military combat during World War II, more than half suffered from depression, insomnia, nightmares, anxiety, tension, irritability, startle reactions, impairment of memory, and obsession with thoughts of wartime experiences. Significant numbers were also observed to be denying trauma by channeling emotional difficulties into psychosomatic symptoms. (See also the comprehensive review by Lewis and Engel, 1954.)

Despite efforts to distinguish between the symptoms and signs of acute and chronic reactions (Kardiner and Spiegel, 1947), extended field studies indicate that these stress responses are not necessarily disparate. The main difference is temporal onset or maintenance of the syndrome. This does not mean an absence of phasic changes, as will be discussed later, but simply that phases of symptoms and signs may occur a short time after the stress event (acute reactions), may persist for a long period or may begin after a long latent period (chronic reactions) (Cobb and Lindemann, 1943; Friedman and Linn, 1957; Popovic and Petrovic, 1964; Parkes, 1964; Davis, 1966).

As mentioned earlier, there is general agreement on the causal relationship of stressful events and acute reactions. There is less agreement on the causal relation between stressful events and chronic reactions. The winnowing away of the patient population accounts for this disagreement among clinicians. The majority of patients with acute stress reaction apparently recover, leaving only a minority of patients whose symptoms persist or who develop symptoms after a latent period. Some clinicians claim observations indicative of personality predispositions in the group who develop chronic stress reactions. If this were so, the chronic reactions would have a relatively stronger relationship to precipitation of a latent neurosis and a relatively lesser relationship to a general stress response tendency. Correspondingly, those persons who *never* recover from chronic stress reactions are believed, by some clinicians, to have permanent personality changes primarily due to personality predispositions. Other clinicians place more emphasis on the causal import of the stress event.

CONCENTRATION CAMPS

Additional evidence arose from the most deplorable circumstances imaginable and indicates that profound and protracted stress may have chronic or permanent effects no matter what the predisposition of the pre-stress personality. This evidence is found in the decades of study of survivors of Nazi concentration camps. Study after study, as recently reviewed in two workshops (Krystal, 1968; Krystal and Niederland, 1971), confirms the occurrence of stress response syndromes, persistent for decades, in major proportions of those populations who survived protracted concentration camp experiences. As just one example, 99% of 226 Norwegian survivors of a concentration camp had some psychiatric disturbances when intensively surveyed years after return to "normal life." Of the total population studied, 87% had cognitive disturbances such as poor memory and inability to concentrate, 85% had persistent nervousness and irritability, 60% had sleep disturbances, and 52% had nightmares (Eitinger, 1969). It should be noted that as hideous as concentration camps were, they also involved severe malnutrition and physical maltreatment that could have caused brain injury.

These studies were psychosocially motivated by a need for answers to resolve a question of litigation. The German government provided compensation for physical injuries suffered by those concentration camp victims who survived the holocaust, When claims for compensation for psychoneuroses were made, they were often rejected. Ironically, Freud, a Jew who had barely escaped the Gestapo, was used as the authority for such claim rejection.

He had, indeed, made statements about the origins of neurosis in childhood traumas. If adults were stressed, and developed neuroses, then the fault was in their childhood. It was necessary to prove the extensiveness of psychological symptoms across broad proportions of survivors before psychological compensation was permitted. There seems little doubt, on the basis of field studies of concentration camp survivors, that persons with *any* personality configuration before the stress will have symptoms such as recurrent unbidden images of camp experiences years after release.

Lifton (1967) has reported similar findings of chronic and permanent stress response symptoms or stress response types of personality damage in survivors of the atomic holocausts of Hiroshima and Nagasaki. These events were single traumatic episodes, protracted by the effects of radiation sickness and the loss of loved ones. Numbing characterized these responses, possibly to a greater extent than that experienced by concentration camp victims. The latter had been so repeatedly brutalized that numbing an denial efforts were thwarted, and intrusive repetitiousness was apparently more common for them than for survivors of the atomic destruction.

These statements about concentration camp survivors are made to support the assertion that any person subjected to extraordinary stress will show stress response symptoms and signs after removal of the external stress. While many of these are similar, whatever the quality of the external stress, there are also symptoms and signs of stress response that may differ depending on the nature of the stress event or the kind of person experiencing it. Discussion of such variance is beyond the scope of this chapter, but it should be understood that the intent is not to imply that all stress events lead to similar responses. In addition to similar symptoms such as recurrent intrusive memories, concentration camp survivors may have different symptoms and signs because of the protracted duration of their stress and the intensity of the dehumanization process inflicted by the Nazis. Such signs as the synecdoche of "success," the bleaching away of childhood memories, and the alteration in schemata of self and object relationships, may distinguish the "survivor syndrome" of concentration camp victims from stress-response syndromes in general (Ostwald and Bittner, 1968; Krystal, 1968; Furst, 1967; Lifton, 1967).

To recapitulate, while not negating the powerful influence of pre-stress personality configurations, findings from large groups of persons exposed to the most severe stress indicate that stress-response syndromes are not necessarily limited to any sub-group of the exposed populations. There is no doubt, then, that *general* stress response tendencies can be delineated.

THE CONCEPT OF PHASES OF STRESS RESPONSE

War and concentration camps produce extraordinary strain, but even so there seem to be phases of response in which denial or intrusive symptoms and signs may predominate.

Shatan (1973), in a study of Vietnam veterans, notes, 24 months after combat, the presence of intrusiveness in the form of insomnia, nightmares, and restlessness that may not have surfaced during combat. He observes that the delay in the manifestation of these symptoms has caused the government to assume that the Vietnam war produced fewer psychiatric casualties than may actually be the case. Horowitz and Solomon (in press) describe the differences between soldiers under great protracted combat stress during World War II and those in Vietnam. Soldiers in combat in World War II went initially into a period of denial and numbing. They would, nonetheless, remain continuously at the front. Stress would mount. When stress exceeded the person's ability to maintain denial, then experiences characteristic of intrusive and repetitive feelings would emerge. In Vietnam, because of repeated rotation to relative safety, and the subsequent slower pace of accumulated stress, the authors presume that it was possible for many soldiers to enter and remain in the denial phase. Other elements, such as the availability of drugs, the lack of group fidelity, and the opposition to the war, contributed to a state of alienation characterized by depersonalization and isolation. Upon return to the United States a period of relief and well-being would occur, and the denial and numbing would continue for a while. Ultimately, with the relaxation of defensive and coping operations,

Horowitz and Solomon suggest that the person might then enter the painful phase of intrusive recollection.

Chodoff (1970) observed a sequence of reactions to concentration camp life in his studies of these victims. He describes this sequence in terms of stages. First there was the universal response to shock and terror upon arriving at the camps. This fright reaction was generally followed by a period of apathy and many times by a longer period of mourning and depression. The apathy was psychologically protective, in providing a kind of emotional hibernation. Lifton (1967) suggests that this kind of depression might, in part, be characterized as a delayed mourning reaction, since victims were unable to engage in a ceremonial mourning for their dead. Gorer too, (1965), emphasizes the connection between ritual and mourning and the maladaptions which may result if this distress is not worked through.

Regression, as an adaptive measure, was a stage noted in many prisoners of war. It was the result of overwhelming pressures. Docility and submissiveness were the results of dependency of the victims on their masters. In some, identification with the aggressor was observed; irritable behavior was discharged in petty fights with other prisoners.

The most important personality defenses among concentration camp inmates during the period of imprisonment were denial and isolation of affect. Chodoff describes the most distinctive, long-term consequence of Nazi persecution observable over a thirty-year period of time, as the "concentration camp syndrome." Invariably present in this syndrome is some degree of felt anxiety, along with irritability, restlessness, apprehensiveness and startle reactions. These anxiety symptoms are worse at night, accompanied by insomnia and nightmares which are simple or slightly disguised intrusive repetitions of the traumatic experience.

Lifton (1967), insists upon the significance of psychic numbing in the behavior of Jews in Nazi camps. He says that "a most central feature of anyone's encounter with death, most characteristically during a massive holocaust, is a cessation of feeling, a desensitization or psychic numbing." An element of this kind of denial is the need to "see nothing," for if it is not "seen" it isn't happening. Added to this is the severing of human bonds of identification. "I see you dying, but I'm not related to you in your death." He describes two kinds of numbing—the apathy of the "walking corpse," or the "know nothing" who acts as though death doesn't exist.

From this, a collaborative numbing emerges, an equalizer between the victim and the victimizer—in which the Jew, the victim, is non-resistive, while the Nazi, the victimizer, is omnipotent but denies the human consequence of his actions. Such numbing and denial may be followed, even years later, by a phase of intrusive repetition of ideas and feelings related to the earlier warded-off events.

NUCLEAR HOLOCAUST

As a result of interviews with seventy-five survivors, seventeen years after the dropping of the atomic bomb on Hiroshima, Lifton (1967) describes the experience as a permanent encounter with death, consisting of four phases. The first is an overwhelming immersion in death, a "death in life" feeling similar to that of concentration camp victims. This phase is dominated by elements of extreme helplessness in the face of threatened annihilation and surmounted by an extremely widespread and effective defense mechanism which Lifton calls "psychic closing off," a cessation of feeling within a very short period of time. The unconscious process is described as closing oneself off from death, the controlling fantasy is "If I feel nothing, then death is not taking place." It is thus related to the defense mechanisms of denial and isolation, as well as to the behavioral state of apathy. It is distinguished by its global quality, a screen of protection against the impact of death in the midst of death and dying. This response to an over-all exposure to death, merges with longer term feelings of depression and despair mingled with feelings of shame and guilt. The guilty fantasy "I am responsible for his death; I killed him" was interwoven with the shameful fantasy, "I should have saved him or helped him."

The second phase of the Hiroshima encounter with death is described as "invisible contamination" in which symptoms of radiation sickness appeared at unpredictable intervals of weeks or months after the bomb had been dropped. There was fear of epidemic contamination, a sense of individual powerlessness in the face of an invisible agent, and a denial of illness when symptoms did appear.

The third phase, which occurred after many years, with the experience of later radiation effects, involved an undercurrent of imagery of an endless chain of potentially lethal impairments which, if not manifested that year, or five years later, would appear in the next generation.

The fourth phase is that of lifelong identification with death and dying, which Lifton describes as the survivors' means of maintaining life. In the face of the burden of guilt he carries for having survived, his obeisance before the dead is his best means for justifying and maintaining his own existence, and is a continued preoccupation.

Lifton describes the residual problems of the survivor, especially those of psychological imagery, which manifest themselves in various ways. Among these he notes a profound impairment of the sense of invulnerability; a sense of being among the "elite" who have mastered death, and, paradoxically, a sense of vulnerability to it at any time. Many victims carry with them seventeen years later, intrusive images of the horror of "that day" and the days that followed immediately after, and talk of still seeing pictures in their minds of people walking slowly in the streets, their skin peeling off.

A profoundly ambivalent pattern of seeking help and resenting it emerged. Working through this event, Lifton feels, involves a new formulation, a way of establishing an inner ideology as a means of dealing with overwhelming feelings, of establishing a new reality within which the victim can understand and master his experiences, his feelings of shame and of existential guilt. Faced with this form of guilt, with resistance to establishing trust in the human order, the survivor of concentration camps, of atomic bombing, and of Vietnam—needs a new identity, a sense of connection with people and of meaning and significance for his life, in order to come to terms with his past disaster and the world in which he continues to live.

To recapitulate, such field studies confirm the findings of clinical investigation of the psychological response to external stress events. As in clinical observation, a phasic tendency is noted. Intrusive repetitions may coexist or alternate with periods of denial and numbness. Like repetitions, the periods of numbness and denial are relatively involuntary in terms of degree of conscious control. The manifestations of these phases are perhaps most clearly seen in bereaved persons, whether bereavement comes from the loss of another or the threat of self loss.

BEREAVEMENT

Much of the literature on bereavement has been summarized by Parkes (1964) and was later expanded through his own studies (1970, 1972).

In summarizing the literature, Parkes referred to the classical paper by Lindemann (1944) on the varieties of reaction to bereavement found in a mixed group of psychiatric and non-psychiatric patients. He noted that Lindemann did not show the relative frequency of the various syndromes which he described, nor did he indicate how long after bereavement his interviews took place. Lindemann defined acute grief as a definitive syndrome with psychological and somatic symptomology, which may appear immediately after a crisis, or may be delayed. He described it as uniform, in that it is expressed by waves of anxiety and panic which are defended against by denial of the event and by avoidance (i.e., of visits from others, of mention of the deceased or of expressions of sympathy by others). He explained the use of denial as motivated by fear of loss of control, and emphasized the importance of the possibility of under-reaction as well as overreaction of the delayed responses which may occur.

Parkes felt that while these studies gave a fair picture of the overall reaction, they failed to reveal the interrelationships between the phases described, and the variations of each phase over a period of time. They particularly did not reveal how long the various phases of grief could be expected to last, nor did they delineate what was a pathological, as opposed to a "normal," variant of grief.

To answer some of these questions, Parkes (1970) interviewed twenty-two London widows at three-month periods, for thirteen months after bereavement. These widows were felt to be showing typical grief reactions. Of the twenty-two, only six felt that they had fully accepted the news when they were told that their husbands would die; eight frankly disbelieved it. As a result of these interviews, Parkes was able to find phases of reaction.

DENIAL-NUMBING

The initial, immediate reaction is described by Parkes as a state of numbness, often preceded by an expression of great distress. While this sense of numbness was a relatively transient phenomenon, some form of denial of the full reality of what had happened often persisted. One year later, thirteen widows said there were still times when they had difficulty believing in the reality of their husbands' deaths. Bowlby, too (Bowlby and Parkes, 1970), had revised his classification of the phases of mourning to introduce numbness as the initial phase. This is reflected, in Parkes' study, in affective reports of one group which showed little or no affect in the first week, not much in the second, but moderate to severe disturbance by the third month. A second group showed a steady increase in affect over a period of time, while a third group, which showed moderate or severe affect in the first week, tended to remain disturbed during the first two months, but improved thereafter. Each widow seemed to have her own pattern for mitigation of feelings. These included blocking out or denial of affect, partial disbelief, inhibition of painful thoughts and evocation of pleasant ones, and an avoidance of reminders.

Lindemann later came to note (1960) another form of mitigation which he calls selective forgetting. "The image of the deceased disappears from consciousness." This observation is supported by Parkes and illustrated by a woman in his sample who could not recall the face of her husband during the first month after his death, although in ensuing months she had a clear visual memory.

INTRUSIVE REPETITIONS

Parkes indicated the presence of intrusive thinking, often in the form of misidentifying (seeing the deceased in a stranger), or of hypnogogic hallucinations (Marris, 1958). For example, one woman felt initially stunned and angry after the death of her husband. For the next few days she kept busy. Then, five days later, "something moved in on me, invaded me; a presence almost pushed me out of bed. It was my husband, terribly overwhelming." During this period, feelings were seldom admitted fully to consciousness, and the mind was often distracted from the loss, but there were periodic breakthroughs.

Bowlby called the second phase yearning or protest. Parkes emphasizes the control features of grief, preoccupation with thoughts of the deceased accompanied by pining. He indicates four components to this phase which include pining and preoccupation, direction of attention toward places and objects (Rees, 1970) associated with the lost person, development of a perceptual set for the deceased, and crying for him. He indicates, too, that hallucinations and illusions occur, and notes that they have always occupied a prominent place in folklore, especially in the form of ghosts, and in the concept of being haunted.

Parkes postulated that a widow who had fully accepted bereavement and made a good adjustment would be able to look back on the past with pleasure and into the future with optimism. After thirteen months, only three widows satisfied his criteria, six found it too painful to think about, nine found it more pleasant than unpleasant, seven had mixed feelings.

In Lindemann's earlier account (1944) he states that after eight to ten interviews within a period of four to six weeks, in which psychiatrists shared the grief work, it was possible to complete the working through of ordinary, uncomplicated grief reactions. He was referring to families of victims of the Coconut Grove fire, who suffered no anticipatory grief, who participated in "group mourning" and received much sympathy and support. This statement had caused Parkes to underestimate the duration of uncomplicated and oftentimes anticipatory grief; he ultimately determined that it was necessary to follow the bereaved for a two- to three-year period.

Parkes interprets his study as confirming Bowlby's belief that grief is a phasic process, although transitions from one phase to another are seldom distinct. These phases can be described as numbness, protest or yearning, and disorganization.

Grayson (1970) finds a similarity between grief reactions to the loss of real objects, and to the loss of intangibles, particularly missed experiences and relinquished hopes. The process of diminishing the force of these wishes involves the same working through to completion as the mourning process (Lewis, 1961; Rees, 1970). Abreaction and catharsis are described by him as valuable discharges of affect without which decathecting would take longer and be less complete. He emphasizes the need for persons to break through the phase of denial to face the painful reality of the missed experience.

Agreement with the theory of phases can also be found in the work of Gorer (1965), who studied thirty-five bereaved people who sought psychiatric help, who had suffered from prolonged grief, delayed reaction, vivid nightmares, or an absence of grief which signified that all was not well. He describes the most characteristic feature of grief not as prolonged depression, but as acute and episodic pangs, or episodes of severe anxiety and psychological pain which begin within a few hours or days after bereavement and reach a peak of severity within two weeks. At first they are described as frequent and spontaneous, but as time passes, they become less frequent and take place only when something occurs that brings the loss to mind. This coincides with Bowlby's phase of yearning and protest.

Gorer notes the phenomenon of searching which fills the gap between aim and object, and gives a sense of continued presence of the deceased. He describes avoidance of the full reality of the loss as a way of mitigating the pain of grieving, and as a necessary part of distancing so that implications can be slowly worked through and dealt with cognitively. He notes the presence of two opposing tendencies—an inhibitory tendency which, by repression, avoidance, and postponement, holds back or limits the perception of disturbing stimuli; and a facilitating or reality tendency which enhances perception and thought about disturbing stimuli. He believes that an individual will oscillate between the two, over time, so that periods of intense feeling will alternate with periods of conscious or unconscious avoidance. He noted, also, that there is no clear ending to grief, but rather a turning point which reflects the abandonment of old modes of thought and behavior. Appropriate treatment is described as a form of psychotherapy in which it becomes possible for the patient to begin to express his grief and to overcome blocks to realization which have prevented him from "unlearning" his attachment to the lost person.

PERSONAL ILLNESS, DYING AND THE THREAT OF DEATH

Kubler-Ross (1969) pioneered investigations into the psychological effects of the process of dying, in her study of four hundred patients in a Chicago hospital. After experiencing initial difficulty in getting these people to talk to her, she discovered denial not only on the part of the patients, but on the part of the doctors and nurses as well. The medical staff coped with the difficulty of confronting the dying patient by the defensive maneuvers of selective withdrawal and inaccessibility.

According to her report, patients go through five stages between their awareness of serious illness and their death:

(1) *Shock and denial*—when told that they have a serious illness, with some few maintaining this defense until the very end. Aldrich (1974) mentions the impact of ambivalence on anticipatory grief. The dying person grieves in anticipation of the loss of his loved ones and yet resents being the one to die. The dying person finds it difficult to cope with this ambivalence which increases the likelihood of denial. Aldrich noted that denial will prevail until the patient's disengagement and withdrawal have progressed to a point from which he can face death and loss with relative equanimity.

(2) *Anger,* directed toward family, nurses, doctors, those who epitomize health, functioning, life itself, and remind them of what they are attempting to deny. The patients are, in effect, saying "Why me?," and by expressing their rage or anger, receive some comfort.

(3) *Bargaining for time* (for example to see a son graduate from college or a grandchild born). The patient is now saying, "Yes, me, *but,*"

(4) *Depression,* of maybe two kinds: one is a reactive depression manifested by simultaneous crying and talking about the loss which lies ahead; the other is a quiet depression in which there is crying, but no talk. Encouragement of the grieving and mourning over impending loss allows for the emergence of anticipatory grief, and leads the patient to enter the last phase.

(5) *Acceptance*—a period when the patient separates himself from those people he will leave behind. The unfinished business has been finished.

Cardiac Patients

In a group of male patients recovering from myocardial infarction, Bilodeau and Hackett (1971) found that the successful adjustment achieved by most patients in the hospital seemed to be shaken when the patient faced the stresses of life following discharge. Worries included changes in physical activity and work capability, acceptance by family, sexual adequacy, modification in smoking and drinking habits, and recurrent heart attacks with the possibility of death. Attempts to master these concerns through repression, denial and other defensive measures were attempted but were seldom successful; the threatening ideas would surface again and again.

A group of such men, ranging in age from thirty-five to fifty-three, met for twelve weeks to discuss these problems. The predominant feelings expressed at these times were those of fear and anxiety. To cope with these, and other feelings of anger, sadness, and shame, members of the group were found to use various observable techniques, including outright denial, and more covert forms of that same denial, such as joking and changing the subject. It was found that as the meetings progressed, and there was increased clarification and explanation, the use of these defensive maneuvers diminished, and feelings were directly expressed and worked through.

In another study of acute myocardial infarction, Hackett and Cassem (1970) focus on the use of denial as a defense mechanism in life-threatening illnesses, and discuss the function of this initial phase of stress response. Denial is defined by them as the conscious or unconscious repudiation of all or a portion of the total available meaning of an illness in order to allay anxiety and to minimize emotional stress. Two groups of patients were studied. The first group consisted of nineteen patients who were chosen because they required monitor cardiac pacemakers. Seven years later, the second group, fifty people requiring intensive care in a coronary unit, were studied in an effort to examine the implications of a 70% psychiatric morbidity common to these units, described as an intensive care syndrome.

Eighteen of the nineteen patients in the first study denied the presence of fear, apprehension or depression. Sixty-three percent of these were described as major deniers: those patients who stated unequivocally that they experienced no anxiety as a result of their illness. Thirty-two percent were described as partial deniers: those who initially denied their fear, and ultimately admitted concern. From this study, Hackett and Cassem conclude that most people tend to deny the fear of death from a serious illness and succeed, to a great degree.

Unsatisfied with the small sample size, and provoked by these findings, they went on to the second study. Assuming that the high level of psychiatric morbidity was true, they reasoned that some aspects of intensive care must be more stressful than others. Seven components were studied: reactions to the unit itself, to being monitored, to witnessing cardiac arrest in others, to being given the last rites, the effect of surviving cardiac arrest, and the predominant affects of patients. Thirty percent of those studied were either neutral to or reassured by the presence of the monitor, and did not object to its constant beeping. Forty of the fifty patients were judged to be anxious, eight were agitated, and eleven expressed anger at fate or circumstance. Twenty-nine were depressed, none to an incapacitating degree. None received psychiatric treatment after discharge, although the investigators felt that at least twenty-five percent could have profited from it. Eleven witnessed cardiac arrest in other patients and seventy-five percent of them denied fear either during or after the episode occurred. Of those nine who themselves survived cardiac arrest, two reported nightmares immediately afterward, two others after they returned home.

Twenty of the fifty patients were classified as major deniers, twenty-six as partial deniers, and four were labeled minimal. Statistical analysis demonstrated no significant relationship between denial and affect. Anxiety, depression, hostility and agitation were equally present. There was a definite trend for deniers to respond positively to the cardiac monitor. Although the numbers are small, it was noted that an inverse relationship exists between denial and mortality. Not one major denier died during the study of hospitalized coronary patients, while minimal deniers constituted fifty percent of the mortality rate. Chi-square analysis showed this to be significant beyond the .05 level.

The denial of fear, totally or in part, seems to be one of the main coping mechanisms used in life-threatening circumstances, and is viewed, in this study of the initial stage of response, as a process aimed at minimizing fear and utilizing defenses such as rationalization, isolation of affect, or displacement, to attain its end. Depression was found to be a more serious consequence later in convalescence, when the patient returns to the outside world and finds his functioning impaired. Follow-ups after dismissal from the hospital were not included as a part of this study and so further phases in the adaptation to this event cannot be delineated.

RAPE

Rape, or attempted rape, is a different kind of event from those previously discussed, although it, too, can be life-threatening. It involves no anticipation, no long period of time to deal with its possibilities, but certainly demands a period of time to work through its effects. Its victims also indicate a phasic response to this kind of episode.

In a study of "rape trauma syndrome," Burgess and Holmstrom (1974) followed 146 women who were seen at the emergency ward of Boston City Hospital during a one-year period. Their results were essentially similar to an earlier study of 13 women by Sutherland and Sherl (1970) in which phasic responses were noted. The rape trauma syndrome is described as "an acute phase and a long-term reorganization process that occurs as a result of forcible rape, or attempted forcible rape." These behavioral, somatic, and psychological responses are an acute stress reaction to a life-threatening situation. In the acute phase, characterized by disorganization of the life style of the victim, a wide range of emotions may be experienced. Shock and disbelief are often expressed, and two emotional styles emerge in equal number. One was the expressed style, in which feelings of fear, anger and anxiety were evidenced by crying, smiling, restlessness and tension. The other was the controlled style, in which feelings were masked or hidden and the victim appeared calm.

In the second phase, which was found to begin about two or three weeks after the attack, motor activity changes, and nightmares and phobias were especially evident. Dreams and nightmares were very upsetting. They were of two types, one in which the victim was being attacked, wishing to do something, but wakened before acting. In the second type of dream, also of attack, which occurred after a longer period of time, the victim mastered the situation and fought off the assailant. There were some instances where the victim awoke crying, after being unable to cry during daytime hours. There was phobic reaction to the traumatic situation, much like the "traumatophobia" described by Rado (1948) in his paper on the treatment of war victims. The phobia develops as a defensive reaction to the stressful event. There were fears connected with the setting in which the rape occurred (outdoors, indoors, being alone). There were sexual fears, fears of crowds, fears of being followed.

The presence of a "silent rape reaction" was also noted. A number of women in the sample stated that they had been raped or molested at earlier periods of their lives; the current rape reawakened their reaction to the earlier experience. It became clear that because they had not talked about and worked through the period of the previous rape, the syndrome had continued to develop and remained unresolved. Emphasis was placed on the need of the victim for support and comfort, for a working-through from the acute phase to reorganization to completion, and a return to normal functioning as quickly as possible.

CONCLUSIONS

In the previous chapter on findings from clinical investigations, phasic repetition and denial were described and emphasized as key observations. In field studies, similar observations are noted (Hamburg and Adams, 1967; Davis, 1966). Once again there appears to be a general response tendency visible through the variations imposed by differences in personality and event. An overall pattern of phases can be abstracted from responses in a group of persons (Coelho, Hamburg, and Adams, 1974).

These phases are not discrete or separate in terms of subjective experience. Within a phase there are episodic changes, for even grief is not a continuous experience. There are waves of sadness and preoccupation with thoughts of the lost person. After each pang there is less feeling and ideation. While phases of ideational denial and/or emotional numbness are usually followed by periods of compulsive ideation and emotional pangs, this is not invariably the case.

Hamburg and Adams (1967), in their review of studies of coping with stress, note this phasic pattern and also note that *unanticipated* stress events are followed by longer and more intense phases of denial than anticipated stress events. They suggest that this longer phase of denial after relatively unanticipated stress, accomplishes the same kind of dosing of recognitions that anticipation of the stress event allows. Janis (1958) provides observations on anticipation of stress and on the interaction of personality and stress response. He investigated the degree and quality of fear in persons as they approached, experienced, and recovered from minor surgery. Patients with anticipatory fear within tolerable limits had the least distress in the period after the operation. Those persons with the most distress during this post-operative period were either overwhelmed pre-operatively by high levels of fearful preoccupation or showed massive denial and no signs of fear during the anticipation of surgery. Janis concluded that an anticipatory phase of cognitive processing was motivated by fear and that this affective and cognitive processing had adaptational effects. He summarized by calling this pre-stress event phase "the work of worrying."

The usual pattern of stress response can now be summarized as an initial response of outcry, followed by denial, then intrusion, then working through, and finally, completion. Individual

FIGURE 1

Phases of Response after a Stressful Event

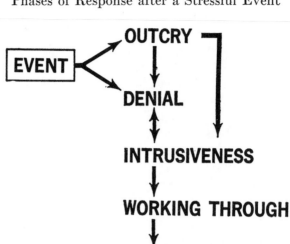

history and character patterns will effect the order of entry into phases, time in each phase, and the clinical manifestations within a phase. As shown in Figure 1, the initial outcry may enter directly into the denial period or even into the *intrusive phase.*

Outcry is an almost reflexive emotional expression upon first impact of unexpected new information. The expression may take the form of weeping, panic, moaning, screaming, or fainting. For example, a woman told that her husband has just died in a work accident may sob in anguish or cry out a denial, "No, no, it can't be true."

Denial is the term given a phase relevant to the implications of the stressful event in which there is some combination of emotional numbing, ideational avoidance, and behavioral constriction. Denial usually describes a defense mechanism in which there is avoidance of awareness of some painful aspect of reality, but in this book the concept will be used more broadly to label a phase in which there will be a gamut of defensive operations aimed at similar accomplishments. Detailed signs and symptoms of this state are grouped by cognitive systems in Table 2. The widow alluded to above might enter this phase after a day or so. For example, relatives might come to join her to both help out and participate in the funeral services. Since they are probably not as deeply affected by the loss, they may have already entered the intrusive and repetitive phase. They would have many thoughts of the deceased, cry episodically, and experience feelings of sadness and painful loss.

The widow, in contrast, might be numb, fearless, and even involved in hyperactive planning and "entertaining" of the relatives. If the relatives are charitable, but ignorant of stress response tendencies, they might say "she is very strong" and "doing very well." If they are less charitable they will say "she didn't really care for him."

Intrusion labels the period of unbidden ideas and pangs of feeling which are difficult to dispel, and of direct or symbolic behavioral reenactments of the stress event complex; a complex which is an amalgam of internal and external components of meaning. Intrusions include nightmares of the stress event, recurrent unbidden images, and startle reactions with perceptual or associational reminders. This variety of intrusive signs and symptoms is listed in Table 2 where contrasts can be drawn with roughly equivalent denial signs and symptoms.

The widow mentioned above might enter an intrusive-repetitive phase after a period of denial. But this phase might not begin until after her relatives have left. Then, six weeks or six months later, she might begin to oscillate between periods of denial and numbing and episodes in which she experienced waves of searching grief, ideas about the emptiness of her life, and even an hallucinatory sense of the "presence" of her lost husband.

TABLE 2

Tabulation of Common Stress Responses

Systems	STATES	
	Intrusive-Repetitive Phase	Denial-Numbness Phase
Perception and attention systems	Hypervigilance, startle reactions Sleep and dream disturbances	Blunting of perception and attention —daze —selective inattention —inability to appreciate significance of stimuli
Conscious representation	Intrusive-repetitive thoughts and behaviors —illusions —pseudohallucinations —nightmares —re-enactments, direct or symbolic —ruminations	Amnesia (complete or partial) Non-experience
Ideational processing systems (sequential and simultaneous organization of representations)	Over-generalization Inability to concentrate on other topics, preoccupation Confusion and disorganization	Disavowal of meanings of stimuli Loss of reality appropriacy Constriction of associational width Inflexibility of organization of thought Fantasies to counteract reality
Emotional systems	Emotional attacks or "pangs" (fear, guilt, rage, shame, sorrow)	Numbness
Somatic systems	Symptomatic sequelae of chronic fight or flight readiness (or of exhaustion of such responses) Sleep loss disturbances	Tension-inhibition type Psychosomatic symptoms
Control systems	If direct controls are insufficient, other control systems may be activated leading to such symptoms as withdrawal, substitutive or counterphobic behaviors, alteration of state of consciousness, or regression. A flight into overactivity is common in the denial phase.	

ORDER OF PHASES

Adult persons* may enter the abstract sequence of phases (as in Fig. 1) at any point and go through the sequence in any order. For instance, imagine a couple in a car that suddenly veers off a mountain road and descends a steep slope strewn with boulders and trees. The driver stays "cool," skillfully maneuvering the car past obstructions while the passenger thinks of destructive possibilities, is terribly frightened, and faints. As the car comes to a safe halt the driver relaxes, considers the same shattering possibilities, and only then feels fear or faints. When action is possible, alert perception, planning, and execution top the hierarchy of claims on cognition. Fearsome images of possible bodily damage are warded off. When passivity is possible, with relaxation of warding-off operations, then recognition of possibly disastrous outcomes and emotional flooding may occur.

Knowledge of these phases guides treatment as well as diagnosis and will be discussed in later chapters.

---

* Children and adolescents present additional complexity because of developmental differences. Both repetition and denial responses are noted as in playing-out or counterphobic behavior on the one hand and in blatant distortions of reality on the other hand. But relative differences also occur, as in children or adolescents who react to the death of a parent only with denial, do not ever grieve, or do not grieve until adulthood. The generality of patterns at any given developmental level is open to so much discussion that it is simply eliminated from further concern in the present work.

BIBLIOGRAPHY

Aldrich, C. K. (1974), Some dynamics of anticipatory grief. In: *Anticipatory Grief,* ed. B. Schoenberg et al. New York: Columbia University Press, pp. 3-9.

Baker, G. W. & Chapman, D. W. (1962), *Man and Society in Disaster.* New York: Basic Books.

Bilodeau, C. B. & Hackett, T. P. (1971), Issues raised in a group setting by patients recovering from myocardial infarction. *American Journal of Psychiatry,* 128:73-78.

Bowlby, J. & Parkes, C. M. (1970), Separation and loss. In: *International Yearbook for Child Psychiatry and Allied Disciplines,* Vol. I: *The Child in His Family,* ed. E. Anthony—C. Koupernik. New York: Wiley.

Brill, N. Q. (1967), Gross stress reactions II: Traumatic war neuroses. In: *Comprehensive Textbook of Psychiatry*, ed. A. M. Freedman & H. I. Kaplan. Baltimore: Williams & Wilkins, pp. 1031-1035.

Burgess, A. W. & Holmstrom, L. (1974), Rape trauma syndrome. *American Journal of Psychiatry*, 131:981-986.

Chodoff, P. (1970), German concentration camp as psychological stress. *Archives of General Psychiatry*, 22:78-87.

Cobb, S. & Lindemann, E. (1943), Neuropsychiatric observation after the Coconut Grove fire. *Annals of Surgery*, 117:814-824.

Coehlo, G. V., Hamburg, D. A., & Adams, J. E., ed. (1974), *Coping and Adaptation*. New York: Basic Books.

Davis, D. (1966), *An Introduction to Psychopathology*. London: Oxford University Press.

Eitinger, L. (1969), Psychosomatic problems in concentration camp survivors. *Journal of Psychosomatic Research*, 13:183-189.

Freud, S. (1920), Beyond the pleasure principle. *Standard Edition*, 18:7-64. London: Hogarth Press, 1953.

Friedman, P. & Linn, L. (1957), Some psychiatric notes on the Andrea Doria. *American Journal of Psychiatry*, 114:426-432.

Furst, S. S. (1967), Psychic trauma: A survey. In: *Psychic Trauma*, ed. S. S. Furst. New York: Basic Books.

Gorer, G. (1965), *Death, Grief, and Mourning in Contemporary Britain*. New York: Doubleday.

Grayson, H. (1970), Grief reactions to the relinquishing of unfulfilled wishes. *American Journal of Psychotherapy*, 24:287-295.

Grinker, K. & Spiegel, S. (1945), *Men Under Stress*. Philadelphia: Blakiston.

Hackett, T. & Cassem, N. (1970). Psychological reactions to life threatening illness: Acute mental illness. In: *Psychological Aspects of Stress*, ed. H. Abram. Springfield, Ill.: Charles C Thomas.

Hamburg, D. & Adams, J. E. (1967), A perspective on coping behavior, seeking, and utilizing information in major transitions. *Archives of General Psychiatry*, 17:277-284.

Hocking, F. (1970), Extreme environmental stress and its significance for psychopathology. *American Journal of Psychotherapy*, 24:4-26.

Horowitz, M. & Solomon, G. (1975), A prediction of stress response syndromes in Vietnam veterans: Observations and suggestions for treatment. *Journal of Social Issues*, in press.

Janis, I. (1958), *Psychological Stress: Psychoanalytic and Behavioral Studies of Surgical Patients*. New York: Wiley and Sons.

Kardiner, A. & Spiegel, H. (1947), *War Stress and Neurotic Illness*. New York: P. Hoeber.

Krystal, H. (1968), *Massive Psychic Trauma*. New York: International Universities Press.

Krystal, H. & Niederland, W. G. (1971), Psychic traumatization. *International Psychiatric Clinics*, 8.

Kubler-Ross, E. (1969), *On Death and Dying*. New York: Macmillan.

Lewis, C. S. (1961), *A Grief Observed*. London: Faber. (First published as by N. W. Clerk.)

Lewis, N. D. & Engel, B. (1954), *Wartime Psychiatry*. New York: Oxford University Press.

Lifton, R. (1967), *History and Human Survival*. New York: Vantage Books.

Lindemann, E. (1944), Symptomatology and management of acute grief. *American Journal of Psychiatry*, 101:141-148.
Lindemann, E. (1960), Psychosocial factors as stress agents. In: *Stress and Psychiatric Disorders*, ed. J. Tanner. Oxford: Blackwell.
Marris, P. (1958), *Widows and their Families*. London: Routledge.
Niederland, W. G. (1968), Clinical observations on the "survivors syndrome." *International Journal of Psychiatry*, 49:313-315.
Ostwald P. & Bittner, E. (1968), Life adjustment after severe persecution. *American Journal of Psychiatry*, 124:87-94.
Parkes, C. M. (1964), Recent bereavement as a cause of mental illness. *British Journal of Psychiatry*, 110:198-204.
Parkes, C. M. (1970), The first year of bereavement: A longitudinal study of reaction of London widows to the death of their husbands. *Psychiatry*, 33:444-467.
Parkes, C. M. (1972), *Bereavement*. New York: International Universities Press.
Popovic, M. & Petrovic, D. (1965), After the earthquake. *Lancet*, II:1169-1171.
Rado, S. (1948), Pathodynamics and treatment of traumatic war neurosis (traumaphobia). *Psychosomatic Medicine*, 4:362-368.
Rees, W. D. (1970), The hallucinatory and paranormal reactions of bereavement. MD thesis.
Shatan, C. (1973), The grief of soldiers: Vietnam combat veterans' self help movement. *American Journal of Orthopsychiatry*, 43:640-653.
Sutherland, S. & Scherl, P. J. (1970), Patterns of response among victims of rape. *American Journal of Orthopsychiatry*, 40:503-511.
Yamamoto, J. & Imahara, J. (1970), America and Japan—Two ways of mourning. Article prepared for the American Psychiatric Association meeting, 1970.

CHAPTER FIVE

Experimental Findings
with Stephanie Becker and
Nancy Wilner

CLINICAL AND FIELD STUDIES are concordant in findings of general human responses to stress which include a central tendency to intrusive repetion and a counteractive tendency labeled grossly as denial. The idea of a general tendency has another meaning beyond "pertaining to many people." A general tendency may occur after stress events that vary in magnitude. Clinical and field studies involve persons after major stress events; minor events do not usually motivate persons to seek help. The study of responses to stress events that are from minor to moderate in intensity can, however, be examined in the laboratory. Such experimental studies are advantageous for several reasons: the degree of generality across kind of events and kinds of persons can be examined under controlled circumstances, and the precise operational definitions necessary for experimental work may sharpen theoretical reflection.

All experiments summarized here used volunteer subjects who reported their conscious experiences before and after viewing a variety of stressful films. The findings indicated that intrusive and repetitive thought tended to follow this more moderate, non-traumatic kind of stress, and that positive-affect inducing films and depressing films produced effects equivalent to those produced by a film that threatened bodily injury. These data will be summarized in this chapter; the details have been published previously.

EXPERIMENTAL BACKGROUND

Films afford a well-studied and replicable laboratory device for providing visual stress events (Lazarus, 1966; Lazarus and Opton, 1966; Nomikos et al., 1968; Goldstein et al., 1965). Intrusive and repetitive thought can be defined in operational terms and then quantified using self report and content analysis procedures. Aside from the stress film method, the experimental literature on stress research provides few leads relevant to this paradigm, (Higbee, 1969). Fortunately, there is now a return to the measurement of conscious experience fostered by dream and hallucinogen research, and most recently by interests in altered states of consciousness (Hartmann, 1967; Barr et al., 1972; Tart, 1969). Lazarus (1966) has developed a cognitive paradigm for experimental research on the impact of stressful films. Several teams have studied the effects of stress films on subsequent dreams (Breger, Hunter and Lane, 1971; Witkin and Lewis, 1965; Witkin, 1969; Cartwright et al., 1969). In capsule form, these studies indicate that the stressful experience incurred while awake is repeated later while in dreaming sleep. The repetition often occurs in covert forms. Contrary to clinical observations of response to traumas, nightmares were not noted. This omission of observation was due perhaps, to the mildness of the experimental stress events or the heightened defensiveness of subjects in a laboratory setting. Intrusive thoughts were not measured in these studies.

A study more relevant to changes in waking thought experiences was done by Antrobus, Singer and Greenberg (1966). After exposure to a stressful radio broadcast, subjects given a signal detection task had error levels similar to those in the control situation. During the same period however, subjects reported significantly more task-irrelevant thoughts.

METHODS

A Series of Experiments

The hypothesis states that after a visually perceived stress event imposed by film, subjects from a variety of population groups, given a variety of instructional sets, would report more intrusive thoughts, more repetitions of film contents, and more visual images than after a less stressful contrast film. This hypothesis was first tested in a pilot study and, when signficant positive results were found, a series of replications with additional controls were conducted. In the series there was variation in the selection of subject populations, in the instructions and demand set given to subjects, and in the contents and order of the stress films. An outline of sequence and references is found in Figure 1. Only a general description of methods will be given here.

Design

In a prototypic experiment, groups of subjects saw a stress film and a neutral contrast film in counterbalanced order. Before and after each film, measurements were taken to obtain baseline, post-neutral film (referred to as neutral) and post-stress film (referred to as stress) scores on selected variables.

Subjects

Volunteers in different experiments were college students and enlisted men in military service.

Film Stimuli

The stress films were: (1) "Subincision," which depicts circumcision as part of a puberty rite, (2) "It Didn't Have to Happen," a film showing woodshop accidents, and (3) an auto accident film. The neutral contrast film used was "The Runner," which shows a man running through the countryside meeting people along the way. All films were silent and edited to run from six to nine minutes.

Signal Detection Task and Mental Content Reports

Periods for reporting mental contents were interspersed between segments of a signal detection task which, while boring,

FIGURE 1

An Outline of the Sequential Organization of
the Series of Experiments

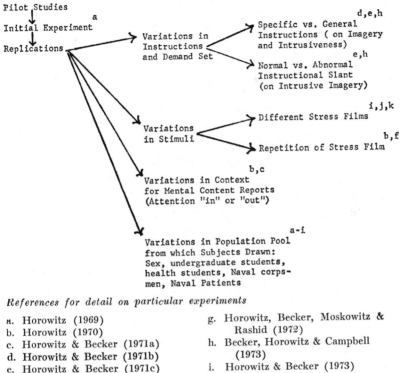

References for detail on particular experiments

a. Horowitz (1969)
b. Horowitz (1970)
c. Horowitz & Becker (1971a)
d. Horowitz & Becker (1971b)
e. Horowitz & Becker (1971c)
f. Horowitz, Becker & Moskowitz (1971)

g. Horowitz, Becker, Moskowitz & Rashid (1972)
h. Becker, Horowitz & Campbell (1973)
i. Horowitz & Becker (1973)
j. Horowitz & Wilner (in press)
k. Wilner & Horowitz (1975)

demanded continuous attention as subjects judged whether a tone was higher, lower, or the same as the preceeding tone. At the end of each segment, during a two-minute break, subjects wrote a report of their mental contents, defined as "any thoughts, feelings, visual images, other images, observations, 'flashes,' memories, or anything else that occurs in the mind" during the tone task (Horowitz, 1969, 1970; Horowitz and Becker, 1971c).

Self-ratings of Affect

Affect ratings consisted of eleven mood words that subjects rated on a nine-point scale to indicate their feelings at different points in the experiment. A composite of negative affect words included anger, contempt, disgust, fear, nervousness, pain, sadness, and surprise. Positive affect words included happiness, interest and pleasantness.

Quantification of Data on Conscious Experience

Content Analysis. The raw data from mental contents reports were content analyzed by judges for intrusive thoughts, film references, and several other variables of less relevance here. The Spearman rank difference correlations for the two or three judges used in the separate experiments ranged from .85 to .94 for intrusions and .91 to .99 for film references.

Briefly, an *intrusive thought* is any thought that implies non-volitional entry into awareness, requires suppressive effort or is hard to dispel, occurs perseveratively, or is experienced as something to be avoided. A *film reference* is any thought that refers directly to the film, film setting, or film experience, and includes anticipations of seeing the film.

Instructional Demand

The different experiments varied in terms of demand sets incorporated into instructions to subjects because in studying conscious experience, such variables have been found to exert significant effects (Rosenthal, 1966; Orne, 1962). The main instructional variances, as indicated in Figure 1, were to suggest to some subjects that intrusive images were minor equivalents of a *pathological* process such as that which leads to hallucinations, and to others that such images were an unconsciously motivated *normal* process aimed at mastery of a stress event.

Data Analysis

Recent computer implementation of the Finn Multivariate Analysis of Variance for a non-orthogonal design has made possible the cross-experimental data analysis reported here (Finn, 1972). The analysis was divided into stages, because not every variable was scored for every experiment, and not every design included baseline, neutral, and stress conditions. The main variables, scored for every experiment, were subjected to an analysis of variance for 133 subjects who had data in all three conditions. Included as potential sources of variance for this analysis were the subject groups, the demand set incorporated in instructions, the order in which films were viewed, the baseline, neutral, and stress conditions, interaction effects, and between and within-subjects variances.

RESULTS

The hypothesis that intrusive and repetitive thought would occur most frequently in the stress condition was confirmed.

Intrusions and Film References

Tables 1 and 2 report an ANOVA and adjusted means for the effects of all factors and conditions on intrusions and film references. The population consisted of 133 subjects in various experiments who each had data on the variable in all conditions (baseline, neutral and stress). At the $p < .05$ cutoff level, only the change in conditions exerts a significant effect on both intrusions (MS $= 57.5$, df $= 2$, F $= 2.07$, $p < .001$), and film references (MS $= 146.5$, df $= 2$, F $= 49.1$, $p < .001$). Population differences (health sciences students, college students, military personnel), film order (stress or neutral first), sex of subjects, and instructional demand (general, specific, abnormal, normal slants) did not exert a significant effect. Intrusions and film references correlated positively in the stress condition ($r = .51$, $p < .001$, n $= 133$).

The adjusted means in Table 2 indicate deflections of a content analysis item from a norm of zero, with zero computed as the expectable level based on word length alone. Positive scores indicate the number of intrusions per subject above expectation

TABLE 1

Analysis of Variance Data for Intrusion and Film References Considering All Factors and Conditions for 133 Subjects

INTRUSIONS

Sources of Variance	MS	df	f	p
Between Subjects				
Population of Sample	7.46	2	1.01	<.37
Instructional Demand	16.16	3	2.18	<.09
Sex	16.84	1	2.27	<.13
Order of Films	1.14	1	.15	<.70
Between-subjects Error	7.42	117		
Within Subjects				
CONDITION	57.51	2	20.69	<.001
Cond. X Pop.	6.39	2	2.30	<.10
Cond. X Instruc.	1.67	3	.60	<.50
Cond. X Sex	3.13	1	1.13	<.30
Cond. X Order	1.05	1	.38	<.50
Within-subjects Error	2.78	234		

FILM REFERENCES

	MS	df	f	p
Between Subjects				
Population	32.75	2	2.11	<.13
Instruct.	1.16	3	.07	<.97
Sex	1.73	1	.11	<.74
Order	4.52	1	.29	<.59
Between-subjects Error	15.51	117		
Within Subjects				
CONDITION (s)	146.51	2	49.08	<.001
Pop. X Cond. (s)	14.04	2	2.57	<.10
Instruc. X Cond. (s)	6.93	3	1.27	<.20
Sex X Cond. (s)	5.72	1	1.05	<.30
Order X Cond. (s)	12.01	1	2.20	<.20
Within-subjects Error	5.47	234		

Table 2

Combined Means on Intrusions and Film References as
Adjusted According to Report Length

Factor	N	INTRUSIONS			FILM REFERENCES		
		Base	Neutral	Stress	Base	Neutral	Stress
Population							
Military Inpts.	23	—.44	—.16	.41	—1.69	—.88	—.08
Civil. Students	82	—.83	—.40	1.38	—2.14	—.23	1.51
Health Students	28	—.50	—.11	.39	—1.53	.08	1.61
Sex							
Male	99	—.66	—.33	.55	—1.81	—.13	.98
Female	34	—.80	—.20	2.33	—2.29	—.69	2.05
Instructional Demand							
Normal	24	—.72	—.30	1.73	—2.26	—.53	2.44
Abnormal	25	—.63	.02	1.79	—1.96	—.25	1.65
Specific	16	—.49	.01	.93	—1.70	.07	.86
General	68	—.76	—.49	.49	—1.86	—.28	.78
Order							
Stress 1st	51	—.67	—.20	.57	—1.82	.16	.86
Neutral 1st	82	—.71	—.36	1.27	—2.00	—.55	1.50
Overall	133	—.69	—.30	1.00	—1.23	—.29	1.23

while negative scores indicate less than expectable levels. The significant condition effect for intrusions is accounted for by the stress film. Baseline film references are, of course, especially low because no film has yet been seen, and only occasional anticipatory remarks are made. The neutral and stress condition film reference levels are significantly different. Overall, 77% of subjects were scored by two or three judges as having at least one episode of intrusions in the stress condition.

*Intrusions Tend to Correlate with the Degree
of Reported Stress*

In the stress condition, persons who rate themselves high on negative emotions tend also to report high levels of intrusions. The adjusted intrusion scores, in 133 subjects who did the same affect report measure during the stress condition, correlated significantly and positively with a composite of negative affects ($r = .27$, $p < .001$), and significantly and negatively with a composite of positive effects ($r = -.16$, $p < .05$). The highest correlation with specific individual affects was with pain ($r = .38$, $p < .001$) and surprise ($r = .35$, $p < .001$). With large numbers of subjects, some low-levels of correlation (e.g. $r = -.16$) may reach statistical levels of significance but indicate only a small size of effect.

A group of 77 subjects also rated themselves after the stress film on $1 - 100$ "thermometer"-type scales for emotional and physical stress, following the method of Stevens (1966). Both scales correlated significantly and positively with intrusion levels. For emotional stress the correlation was $r = .39$, $p < .01$, for physical stress $r = .34$, $p < .01$.

MIXED AFFECT EXPERIMENT

The previous series of experiments indicated that the tendency to intrusive thought is general in that it occurs even after the mild to moderate stress of seeing a silent film and is thus not restricted to traumatization or overwhelming stress. However, the theme of each stress film used was one of bodily injury, a topic usually evocative of fear. While fear is highly relevant to the concept of stress and trauma, it is a specific and limited emotion. If intrusive repetitiousness is a general response tendency, it would be expected after the arousal of other types of emotion associated with other sets of information. This would include prediction of intrusive episodes even after arousal of positive affects.

To test this hypothesis, four stimulus conditions were used to evoke fearful, sad, pleasant, and comparatively neutral states. To maintain coherence with the previous series of studies, equivalent designs and measures were used. It was predicted that the three affect arousal states would all lead to intrusive and repetitive thought, and that these responses would be significantly greater than those resulting from the comparatively neutral stimulus.

METHODS

Design

Subjects were drawn from the same population pool. They were ranked for emotional responsivity according to pre-test data on their usual responses to horror, pornographic, and tragic films. Following ranked order they were evenly assigned to view films depicting either the separation of a small child from his parents, nude erotic interactions, or the bodily injury, or neutral film used in the previous experiments. After collection of data, as described earlier, subjects were informed about an investigator interest in qualities of thought, and taught how to rate themselves retrospectively for frequency and intensity of intrusive and repetitive thought. The data was analysed by groups, designated according to the particular film stimulus. There were eight film showings, two at each of four experimental sessions. Each of the four was shown as first film during one session and as second film during another session.

Films

All films were silent and edited to run between six and nine minutes. The woodshop film provided the bodily injury stimulus, the runner film the neutral stimulus. To provide a separation theme, *John,* a documentary (1969), was edited and depicts an eighteen-month-old boy whose mother has just died. His father places him in a foundling home and makes occasional brief visits. The film portrays John's initial gregariousness, his subsequent angry, crying and searching behavior, and finally, his lethargy, despair and withdrawal. There are poignant close-ups of his facial expressions, some as he is rejected by his father, but no such shocking scenes as characterize the other negative affect film with its depiction of bodily injury. The basic theme of this film is the sadness of separation.

Erotic Film

The erotic film depicts a loving heterosexual couple enjoying foreplay and intercourse. The film is pleasurable and erotically

arousing, with no hints of perversion. The erotic arousal, sup-
plemented by activation of voyeuristic-exhibitionistic themes,
is regarded as stressful because of the absence of immediate potential for reduction of arousal.

Subjects

The subjects were 75 health science students.

Data Analysis

Direct means per subject, derived by averaging scores of three
judges, were used for analysis of mental content data, since word
length of reports was noted to be consistent between subject
sub-groups. Analyses of variance were used to determine the
significance of film, order, and sex effects. T-tests were used to
examine the significance of differences between particular cells
of data.

RESULTS

Film Effects

As predicted by the main hypothesis, *intrusions* and *film references* were high after the erotic, separation, and bodily injury
films, and low after the neutral film. This variation in films contributed the main effect according an analyses of variance (See
Tables 3-4).

The bodily injury film, least evocative of *intrusions* of the
three stress films, differed from the neutral film significantly
($t = 3.5$, df $= 78$, $p < .001$). The greatest differences among
the three stress films was between the separation film (more intrusions) and the bodily injury film (less intrusions) but this
difference was not significant. The stress films did not differ
significantly for film references. The lowest *film reference* scores
after a stress film were also those after the bodily injury film.
This level was significantly higher than that noted after the neutral film ($t = 2.47$, df $= 78$, $p < .02$). Persons with high levels
of *intrusions* tended to have high levels of *film references* after

TABLE 3

Intrusions: Analysis of Variance and Means
by Sex and Film

Source of Variance	df	MS	F	p
Order (1st or 2nd)	1	6.01	2.24	.14
Sex	1	8.93	3.33	.07
FILM (CONTENT)	3	18.31	6.82	.0003
Sex X Film	3	3.91	1.46	.23
Film X Order	3	4.39	1.63	.18
Between Ss Error	134	2.68		

	COMBINED MEANS				
	Erotic	Neutral	Separation	Injury	
Males	1.68	.62	1.42	1.58	1.27
Females	1.98	.68	2.98	1.74	1.83
	1.81	.64	2.23	1.65	

	NUMBER OF SUBJECTS				
	Erotic	Neutral	Separation	Injury	
Males	22	27	15	20	84
Females	17	17	16	16	66
	39	44	31	36	150

the separation film (r = .61, p < .01), the bodily injury film
(r = .49, p < .01) and the neutral film (r = .36, p < .05) but
not after the erotic film (r = .16, p = NS).

These *content analysis* variables had significant and positive
correlations with the *self-ratings* completed by subjects during
the retrospective phase of the experiments, except for frequency
and intensity of film repetitions after the erotic film (See
Table 5).

Affects

The data on affects conform to what one would expect from
the themes of the films. In analyses of variance, the film effects
dominated and were highly significant for every affect (p values
< .0001). Pleasantness, interest and happiness were greatest

TABLE 4

Film References: Analysis of Variance and Means by Order and Film

Source of Variance	df	MS	F	p
Order (1st or 2nd)	1	49.54	2.74	.10
Sex	1	25.02	1.39	.24
FILM (CONTENT)	3	81.99	4.54	.0046
Sex X Film	3	14.03	.78	.51
Film X Order	3	44.02	2.44	.07
Between Ss Error	134	18.06		

COMBINED MEANS

	Erotic	Neutral	Separation	Injury	
Order 1	3.94	3.16	5.32	3.12	3.80
Order 2	5.92	1.50	6.28	6.24	5.00
	5.26	2.48	5.72	4.68	

TABLE 5

Correlation of Content Analysis and Self-report Variables

CONTENT ANALYSIS VARIABLES	SELF REPORT VARIABLES					
	Frequency of Non-deliberate Film Repetitions			Intensity of Non-deliberate Film Repetitions		
INTRUSIONS	Erotic	Separation	Bodily Injury	Erotic	Separation	Bodily Injury
Erotic	.32*			.42**		
Separation		.62***			.49**	
Bodily Injury			.71***			.68***
FILM REFERENCES						
Erotic	.25			.15		
Separation		.60***			.47**	
Bodily Injury			.54***			.36*

  * p<.05
 ** p<.01
*** p<.001

TABLE 6

Frequency and Intensity of Film Repetitions by Self-report. Group Means on a 1 (Low) to 9 (High) Scale for Frequency and Intensity

	Erotic	Neutral	Separation	Bodily Injury
Frequency of Repetition	4.23	2.06	3.77	3.75
Intensity of Repetition	4.38	2.11	4.06	4.03

after the erotic film. Sadness and anger were greatest after the separation film. Contempt was rated equally high for the bodily injury and separation films. Fear, nervousness, physical sensations, pain and disgust were greatest after the bodily injury film.

Correlations of selected individual affects with levels of instructions after the separation film show a positive correlation between intrusions and sadness, greater than that of any other affect. Intrusions after the bodily injury film correlate positively but not significantly with reports of nervousness and physical sensations during the film. Intrusions after the erotic film also correlate positively and significantly with physical sensations as well as with happiness and nervousness.

Self-report of Intrusions and Repetitions

The self-ratings of non-deliberate film repetitions during the signal detection task, and the intensity of these repetitions, were significantly affected by the kind of film seen before the task ($f = 4.15$, $df = 110$, $p < .008$ for repetitions, $F = 4.87$, $df = 110$, $p < .003$ for intensity). This difference was due to the mild effects of the neutral film as opposed to the films evocative of strong emotions, as shown in Table 6.

Conclusion

The tendency to intrusive and repetitive thought after stressful events is observed concordantly in clinical, field, and experimental modes of investigation. This concept is clear and can be submitted to operational definition and hence quantification. Both field and experimental studies supplement the rich texture of clinical understanding by indicating that the tendency is a general one, found across divergent populations. Experimental studies also reveal another aspect of the generality of this pattern. Intrusive and repetitive thoughts tend to occur after stress that varies in terms of the emotion that is aroused, and the intensity of that emotion in a range from mild to moderate to severe. The tendency can be regarded as a proven observation; explanation is the task of the next chapter.

BIBLIOGRAPHY

Antrobus, J. S., Singer, J. L. & Greenberg, S. (1966), Studies in the stream of consciousness: Experimental enhancement and suppression of spontaneous cognitive processes. *Perceptual & Motor Skills, 23*:399-417.

Barr, H. L. et al. (1972), *LSD: Personalities and Experience*. New York: John Wiley and Sons.

Becker, S. S., Horowitz, M. J. & Campbell, L. (1973), Cognitive response to stress: Effects of demand and sex. *Journal of Abnormal Psychology, 82*:519-522.

Breger, L., Hunter, I. & Lane, R. (1971), The effect of stress on dreams. *Psychological Issues, 73*:1-213.

Cartwright, R. D., Bernick, N., Borowitz, G. & Kling, A. (1969), Effect of an erotic movie on the sleep and dreams of young men. *Archives of General Psychiatry, 20*:262-271.

Finn, J. D. (1972), *Multivariance: Univariate and Multivariate Analysis of Variance, Covariance, and Repression*. Ann Arbor: Natinal Education Resources.

Goldstein, M. J., Alexander, F. G., Clemens, T. L., Flagg, G. W. & Jones, R. B. (1965), Coping style as a factor in psychophysiological response to a tension arousing film. *Journal of Personality & Social Psychology, 1*:290-302.

Hartmann, E. (1967), *The Biology of Dreaming*. Springfield, Illinois: Thomas.

Higbee, K. L. (1969), Fifteen years of fear arousal: Research on threat appeals: 1953-1969. *Psychological Bulletin, 72*:426-444.

Horowitz, M. J. (1969), Psychic trauma: Return of images after a stressful film. *Archives of General Psychiatry, 20*:552-559.

Horowitz, M. J. (1970), *Image Formation and Cognition*. New York: Appleton-Century-Crofts.

Horowitz, M. J. & Becker, S. S. (1971a), Cognitive response to stress and experimental demand. *Journal of Abnormal Psychology, 78*:86-92.

Horowitz, M. J. & Becker, S. S. (1971b), Cognitive response to stressful stimuli. *Archives of General Psychiatry, 25*:419-428.

Horowitz, M. J. & Becker, S. S. (1971c), The compulsion to repeat trauma: Experimental study of intrusive thinking after stress. *Journal of Nervous and Mental Disease,* 153:32-34.

Horowitz, M. J., Becker, S. S. & Moskowitz, M. L. (1971), Intrusive and repetitive thought after stress: A replication study. *Psychological Reports,* 29:763-767.

Horowitz, M. J., Becker, S. S., Moskowitz, M. L. & Rashid, K. (1972), Intrusive thinking in psychiatric patients after stress. *Psychological Reports,* 31:235-238.

Horowitz, M. J. & Becker, S. S. (1973), Cognitive response to erotic and stressful films. *Archives of General Psychiatry,* 29:81-84.

Horowitz, M. J. & Wilner, N. (in press), Stress films, emotions and cognitive response. *Archives of General Psychiatry.*

Lazarus, R. S. (1966), *Psychological Stress and the Coping Process.* New York: McGraw-Hill.

Lazarus, R. S. & Opton, E. M. (1966), The use of motion picture films in the study of psychological stress: A summary of experimental studies and theoretical formulations. In: *Anxiety and Behavior,* ed. C. Speilberger. New York: Academic Press.

Nomikos, M. S., Averill, J. R., Lazarus, R. S. & Opton, E. M. (1968), Surprise versus suspense in the production of stress reaction. *Journal of Personality & Social Psychology,* 8:204-208.

Orne, M. T. (1962), On the social psychology of the psychological experiment: With particular reference to demand characteristics and their implications. *American Psychologist,* 17:776-783.

Robertson, J. and J. (1969) John, Seventeen Months: Nine Days in a Residential Nursery Cafilm). London: Tavistock Institute of Human Relations, Tavistock Clinic.

Rosenthal, R. (1966), *Experimental Effects in Behavioral Research.* New York: Appleton-Century-Crofts.

Stevens, S. S. (1966), A metric for the social consensus. *Science,* 151:530.

Tart, C. T. (1969), *Altered States of Consciousness.* New York: John Wiley and Sons.

Wilner, N. & Horowitz, M. J .(1975), Intrusive and repetitive thought after a depressing film: A pilot study. *Psychological Reports,* 37:135-138.

Witkin, H. A. & Lewis, H. B. (1965), The relation of experimentally induced pre-sleep experience to dreams. *Journal of the American Psychoanalytic Association,* 13:819-849.

Witkin, H. A. (1969), Influencing dream content. In: *Dream Psychology and the New Biology of Dreaming,* ed. M. Kramer. New York: Charles C Thomas.

Part III
GENERAL THEORY

CHAPTER SIX

Explanation of Phases of Denial and Intrusion

THE BASIC EXPERIMENTAL, field, and clinical findings about stress response syndromes can be summed up as a list of observations to be accounted for by any theory. These findings are:

1. There are general response tendencies to stressful events. Although the degree of response varies with different people, those subjected to enough stress may be expected to show some stress responses.

2. The response tendencies are also general in that they may appear after a variety of stress events which differ in quantity and quality. Different kinds of stress events may result in a variety of permutations of both general and particular response.

3. General response tendencies are inclined to occur in temporal phases, at least after major stress events. Phases may overlap and persons may vary in their entry into and emergence from a phase, and in their sequence and termination of phases. A given person may functionally operate in different phases with regard to different complexes of ideational and emotional responses.

4. Many stress responses persist long after termination and resolution of the external event. Some responses to external stress begin only after an interval of extended relief.

5. In the period after termination of the external stress event, one of the main observations in clinical, field, and

experimental studies is of intrusive repetition in thought, emotion, and/or behavior. A set of related but antithetical responses, including ideational denial, emotional numbness, and behavioral listlessness, are also frequently noted.

6. Phases of response characterize the period after relative termination of the external stress event. Abstracting a general stress response tendency from a wide range of variation in individuals and kinds of stress events, one arrives at this cognitive and emotional sequence:

   a. Phase of initial realization that a stress event has occurred (labeled *Outcry* in Chapter 4, Figure 1).

   b. Phase of denial and numbness.

   c. Mixed phase of denial *and* intrusive repetition in thought, emotion, and/or behavior.

   d. Phase of further ideational and emotional processing, working through and acceptance (or stable defensive distortion) with loss of peremptory quality of either the denial or recollection of the stress event.

In what follows, the early psychoanalytic and contemporary psychological models for explaining general stress responses will be presented first. Then an integration of models will be discussed to determine their effectiveness in explaining the above observations.

CLASSICAL PSYCHOANALYTIC MODEL

Freud, in his theoretical model of psychic trauma, hypothesized that traumas occur when an excessive influx of stimulation overexcites the psychic apparatus. He accounted for variations in response to the same kind of external stress event by hypothesizing variation in the "stimulus barrier" (Freud, 1920). This barrier against stimulation was a theoretical construct to account for regulation of the perceptual entry of information and energy from external events into the psychic apparatus. Freud also conceptualized the motive for alteration in the stimulus barrier. Anxiety is activated as an external stress event is anticipated, or sampled by initial perception. As anxiety increases, the stimulus barrier is augmented. The result is reduced input.

The term "anxiety," as used here, is a theoretical construct and not necessarily a felt emotion. The term "stimulus barrier" also refers to a theoretical construct. While widely used in the early psychoanalytic literature, the term has unfortunate concrete implications. Reduction and augmentation functions would be performed by multiple processes at various levels of stimulus processing. The concept of regulation is relevant but to avoid the concrete metaphor of a "barrier" the term *modulation* of stimulus input is substituted.

Freud's simple theoretical model, because it conceptualized a feedback loop, has profound explanatory power. Suppose there is the possibility for continuous perceptual sampling of an ongoing external stress event. The degree of internalization of information is regulated by modulation. The degree of this modulation, in turn, depends on the magnitude of anxiety. Initially, as information input increases, anxiety increases. Anxiety motivates an increase in modulation, so there is reduction of input. Anxiety decreases, and as it does so, the motive for modulation decreases. With less modulation there is then more perception or stimulation, and anxiety increases again. Granted a dynamic system that is unstable at extremes, the feedback loop and transactional arrangement may lead to phases where there would be a decrease from higher levels of anxiety and an increase from lower levels. In information processing models this is called marginal instability.

Freud's clinical theory of traumatization was developed in his collaboration with Charcot, the French scholar of hypnosis, and in his subsequent work with Breuer (Breuer and Freud, 1895). Mentioned in Chapter 3, the Breuer-Freud theory of the traumatic etiology of hysterical symptoms emphasized not only the role of external stress events but the importance of repression of certain ideas and emotions triggered by the event and by contributants to the prior internal stress events. "Hysterics suffer mainly from reminiscences" because they cannot remember

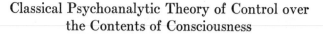

FIGURE 1

Classical Psychoanalytic Theory of Control over
the Contents of Consciousness

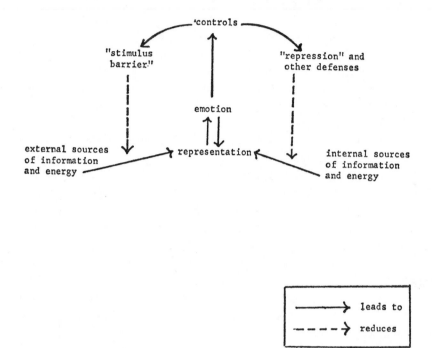

and they cannot *not* remember. When they attempt to remember, they have either partial amnesia or an overwhelming
uncontrolled recollection. When they attempt to not remember,
they have intrusive "breakthroughs" such as unbidden images.

In these early formulations, *repression* is a control concept
rather similar to modulation of external input by the stimulus
barrier. The difference is that in repression the inhibition is directed against memory rather than against perceptions. The
classical psychoanalytic theory of control over the contents of
consciousness can thus be diagrammed as a system of dual entry
of information from internal and external sources with a feed-

back loop to both (see Fig. 1). Symptoms of amnesia are explained in this model as the products of over-extensive repressive control. Intrusions are failures of repressive control. In later formulations this thesis was complicated by the need to include other unconscious defensive operations involved in the formation of symptoms which, earlier, had seemed to be due to repressive failures.

The classical psychoanalytic theory of symptomatic responses to stress has been described summarily. The numerous qualifications concerning the theory are omitted but are not denied. At this stage the model does not explain symptomatic responses to stress in sufficient detail. This will be covered in the material that follows. It does, however, emphasize the feedback loop involved in the interrelationship between thought, emotion, and control.

Thought, schematically indicated with the word "representations" in Figure 1, mediates between the external stress event and emotional response. Controls operate upon thought formation, to alter levels of emotion. Further modeling of the cognitive process will be shown as subsumed under such global labels.

CONTEMPORARY MODELS OF COGNITIVE PROCESSING

Evocation of a stress state requires that the person register and interpret incoming stimuli as cues of threat. One reason for variance in individual responses to stress events is that persons differ in registration and interpretation as well as in styles and capacities of response systems. In recent decades psychologists have worked increasingly with cognition and have attempted to model the place of cognitive mediation in the sequence from stress event to stress response. Their theoretical contributions led to expansion of the early psychoanalytic model to specify cognitive processes that were assumed but not explicitly stated.

Lazarus (1964; 1966; Lazarus, Averill and Opton, 1969), an influential experimentalist and theoretician in the psychology of

FIGURE 2

A Diagram by Lazarus of How Cognitive Processes Affect Emotion

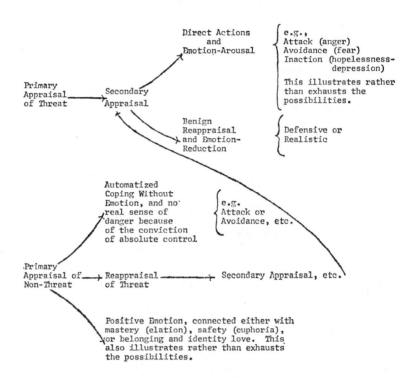

cognitive aspects of response to stress, has emphasized the importance of the cognitive processes of appraisal in coping with threat. To state his theory very simply, in a form most suitable for modeling, he considers emotions as responses to cognitive operatious, as shown in one of his diagrams (Fig. 2; Lazarus, 1968). The diagram follows the interpretation of environmental cues as threatening or non-threatening through primary and secondary appraisals. The degree of threat appraised and reappraised leads to variations in emotions such as fear, anger, depression, euphoria, and elation. The secondary appraisals involve comparison of threat with coping resources, with several reappraisals of threat to see if it exceeds coping capacity. The discrepancy between degree of threat and available coping capacities accounts for the emotion activated. An initial emotional response such as fear or anger may be reduced when a benign reappraisal of threat is made through cognitive processing.

A cognitive elaboration of the psychoanalytic model of stress response has been developed by Janis, another leading psychological theorist and investigator (Janis, 1958, 1967, 1969; Janis and Levanthal, 1968). Again a liberty is taken in forcing the richness of his theories into a starkly simple model. Janis and Lazarus agree on the importance of cognitive processing, although Janis tends to regard emotions as motives, in contrast to Lazarus, who regards them as responses to cognitive processing (Lazarus, Averill, and Opton, 1969).

Janis follows and elaborates the classical psychoanalytic model as he emphasizes the distinctive motivational properties of what he calls "reflective fear." He joins the term "reflective" to fear to obtain a term more precise than the hypothetical construct "signal anxiety." The word "reflective" emphasizes that both threat and information from cognitive processing affect the magnitude of this kind of emotional response to danger. When aroused, reflective fear can lead to three modes of adjustment of the stress state. Janis terms these adjustments as increases of needs for vigilance, for reassurance, or fusions of the two divergent tendencies into a compromise.

Vigilance needs augment cognitive processing of other cues, relevant or not, and may lead to misinterpretation of cues and unwarranted increases in reflective fear. Startle reactions from the intrusive list of symptoms are one example. Reassurance needs may motivate thought processes that lead to either appropriately or inappropriately reassuring ideas. In pathological degrees, reassurance needs lead to "blanket reassurance," a reduction in reflective fear, and hence to unwarranted and perhaps maladaptive complacency. In extreme forms then, reassurance has elements of denial and numbness.

Figure 3

A Diagram by Janis in Which the Emphasis Is on Emotion
as a Motive for Ideational and Perceptual Organization

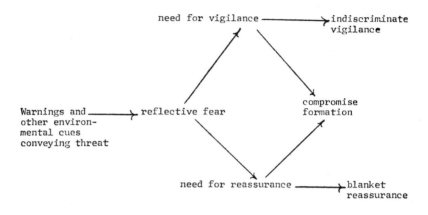

One of Janis' diagrams of his model is presented in Figure 3 (Janis, 1962).

The difference of emphasis on emotions as motives or as responses can be resolved in a manner implied in the extended written theories of Freud, Janis, and Lazarus and the model diagrammed earlier in Figure 1. That is, emotions, thoughts, and controls can be considered as they interact. Emotions are responses to thought processes and motivate controls which in turn augment or reduce thought processes, thus providing a circuit for equilibration of levels of emotional arousal.

Additional support for such transactional models, and the central importance of ideational processes, is found in Johnson, Leventhal, and Dabbs' (1971) field studies of response to surgery as related to clinically rated levels of fear before the operation. The findings by this group, and their view of the relevant literature, failed to replicate Janis' findings that anticiptory fear reduces post-operative distress. They therefore rejected his theory that fear is drive-like in its motivation of cognition such as the "the work of worrying." Instead, like Lazarus, they model emotion as a response. Saltz (1970) supported this model in his review of experimental research on anxiety and threat. He showed that data do not sustain the Taylor and Spence (1952) and Spielberger (1966) theories that anxiety functions as a drive state.

Nonetheless, emotions such as anxiety can have motivational functions when they influence the controls which in turn modify cognitive process. Low levels of emotion may act as new information, as sensation of bodily state for example, and increase associations to memories related to similar bodily-sensory states. The formulations and findings of Janis thus remain viable and useful. At high levels of emotional arousal, when inhibitory controls are activated, a reverse effect of constriction of associational width and inhibition of ideational processing may occur.

TERMINATION OF STRESS STATES BY ACTION

The role of action may be considered now because it leads to a useful elaboration of the model. Action is the prototypic terminator of stress states because action changes events. The knight who slays an attacking dragon terminates the stressful attack. He also discharges (or changes from) the rage and rage-action-plans activated by the effrontery of the dragon's attack. The knave who runs away faster than the dragon can follow, also cancels the stress of the attack and discharges (or changes) his fear and fear-action-plans. In either case, successful action terminates the stress event. Emotions such as fear of or rage at the dragon also are reduced by successful action. Such termination of states of emotions can be conceptualized in two ways. The traditional view would be that there is a discharge of aroused emotions (and drive derivatives) through action. A cognitive view is that there is a reduction of emotion due to the following sequence: action alters events, alterations of events alters representation, alteration of representations alters cognitive processing, and alteration of cognitive processing alters emotional responses.

With the addition of this concept of termination of external stress events, a model can be developed showing that termination of internalized stress states can occur by cognitive processing in the absence of actions. Such a model is relevant to understanding the symptomatic responses to stress that persist or begin *after* termination of the external stress events, a time when external action may seem relevant.

TERMINATION OF STRESS STATES
BY COGNITIVE COMPLETION

INTRODUCTION

None of the foregoing models completely explain the persistence and periodicity of responses to stress. Nor do they explain how and when compulsive repetitions may be terminated. As mentioned earlier, psychoanalysis has offered two relevant theories. One theory hypothesizes a need for mastery and predicts cessation of repetitions when mastery has occurred. The second theory states that the repetition compulsion is, in part, instinctive and will terminate upon a sufficient degree of drive discharge.

Review of the Concept of a Repetition Compulsion

Freud noted compulsive repetitions both in persons with psychoneuroses and persons exposed to external stress events. For example, the repetitions of combat experiences in nightmares occurred in veterans for years after the end of the First World War. Such an exteremely painful type of dream life could not, it seemed to Freud, be explained by the pleasure-unpleasure principle. This observation provoked him to revise his theory of instinctual drives into a duality of aggressive and libidinal drives. Freud used the compulsive repetition observations as a springboard for further speculation on the possibility of a death instinct which would contribute a component of the aggressive drive. But Freud also posited a need to master the traumatic event as a motive for compulsive repetitions (Freud, 1920).

Like Freud, Waelder (1964) divided "the repetition compulsion" into two components, one a tendency of id functions toward re-experience of painful situations, the other a tendency of ego functions toward assimilation and mastery of the experience. Milton Horowitz (1963) emphasized this latter aspect of assimilation and mastery and considers the repetition compulsion to result from one of the main regulative trends of the mind because the repetitions "bind energies and bring them from a state of 'flow' to one of 'rest' " (Gifford, 1964).

Hartmann (1939) also considered the concept of compulsive repetition to have two aspects. The "id-aspect" was the instinctual compulsion and the "ego-aspects" resulted from interaction between the impulse, and ego functions such as thinking and memory. Like Hartmann, Bibring (1943) separates the repetition compulsion into id components, the reproductive tendencies, and ego functions which are attempts to work off or work through the painful experience.

Schur (1966) clarified the matter further when he suggested that a trauma leaves the ego with "an uncompleted task" in the sense illustrated by the Zeigarnik effect (the tendency to remember uncompleted tasks better than completed tasks). The uncompleted task leads to an "ego wish," to complete the task either by primary process or secondary process thinking. Because of this "ego wish," the tendency to compulsive repetition is not "beyond the pleasure principle" and Schur suggests that the term "repetition compulsion" be dropped in favor of a simply descriptive label of an observed tendency (such as "compulsive repetitiveness" or "compulsive stereotyped repetitiveness") (For a further review see Gifford, 1964, or Schur, 1966).

The present argument will follow Schur in regarding the motives for repetition as an aspect of ego-functioning. However, his concept of an "ego-wish" will be replaced with the idea of a completion tendency as a specific property of cognitive process.

A Completion Tendency

The need to match new information with schemata based on older information, and the revision of both until new concordant schemata are achieved is called, for brevity, a completion tendency. Festinger (1957) described similar forms of cognitive processing as part of a need to reduce cognitive dissonance, just as French (1952) described in detail the condensation of divergent complexes as ideas pass through integrative fields.

Assumption of a completion tendency inherent in plans or programs is not new. Mandler (1964) has observed a completion tendency in a complex series of behavioral responses that are interrupted. Once an organized response has been interrupted, this tendency to completion persists as long as the situation remains essentially unchanged. Mandler avoids attributing energies to the tendency for completion; he follows Miller, Galanter and Pribram (1960) in attributing this effect to a built-in tendency to execute successive steps.

A similar avoidance of postulation of instincts, by use of information processing models, has been suggested by Peterfreund (1971). As an example, suppose a task plan is interrupted. The incompleted portion automatically remains stored in working memory. The problem is shifted from explaining the source of energy pressing for completion, to explaining how and when a given plan is terminated or "switched off" (Mandler, 1964; Miller, 1963).

In an earlier but parallel theory, Lewin (1935) postulated that any intention to reach a goal (an initiation of a plan) produces a tension system that is preserved until a goal is reached, then released. It was this theory that led to prediction of the Zeigarnik effect. Mandler (1964) suggests that, in addition to the completion tendency of initiated plans, interruption may lead to a state of increased arousal which is distressing and which is maintained until completion occurs. The organism then favors completion in order to terminate this distress. In his theoretical model of peremptory ideation, Klein (1967) has further developed this concept of the completion tendency and the distress-reduction tendency of plans or programs. He adds the concept of conscious and unconscious plans for processing thought and also the concept of defenses as interruption of programatic sequences. When repressive capacity (inhibition) is lessened, or when motives (which Klein calls "primary regions of imbalance") increase, the ideomotor cycle resumes operations again, follows the interrupted and repressed plan, and the result may be an episode of peremptory ideation. The concept of an ideational cycle carries with it the principles of cycle completion. Thus the tendency towards cognitive completion is emphasized in various associationistic and gestalt approaches to cognitive processing.

Model of Tendency to Repetition as a Property of Active Memory

One key assumption in the following model is that there is a type of memory with motivational properties in that this memory tends to investigate a "next step" in cognitive processing. Because of this intrinsic property it will be labeled as active memory. The assertion is that *active memory storage has an intrinsic tendency towards repetition of representation of contents until the contents held in active memory are actively terminated.* A second key assumption is that *this tendency to repetition of representation is part of a general tendency toward completion of cognitive processing, and hence that completion of cognitive processing is what actively terminates a given content in active memory storage. Granted these assumptions, one can develop a simple model to account for the intrusive, repetitive and denial-numbing responses after stress events.*

Active memory storage, with a tendency toward repeated representation in thought, is contrasted with inactive memory. "Active" and "inactive" memory could correspond to current usage of the terms "short-" and "long-" term memory, respectively. The term "active memory" is preferable, here, to "short-term memory" because intrusive stress-event recollections may occur and recur for a long time. This assumption of an active memory with special properties of recurrent representation is compatible with current experimental findings involving more neutral contents in the fields of perception, attention, and memory. For example, Broadbent (1971) has summarized this research and developed a model in which there are several forms of "short-term" memory that occur subsequent to sensory registration and prior to transformation of information into long term memory.

Broadbent includes three kinds of "short-term memory." One is a "buffer storage" which would hold images for a while after cessation of sensory registration. The second is a "rehearsal buffer" which would retain important images for longer periods than the rapid decay of information in "buffer storage." The third is "primary memory by slots" in which certain memories would remain in a kind of "active information bank." It is of greatest relevance to the present formulation that information would be retained in the primary memory slots until it was terminated by replacement with other presumably more important information. Stress-related information would, by definition, be very important and hence not terminated until it was assimilated.

Comparison of Processing of Stressful and Nonstressful Events

The recurrence of a familiar nonstressful event is likely to be quickly and automatically assimilated. Completion of cognitive processing will occur and the information in active memory storage will be rapidly terminated. The information involved in novel and stressful events, however, cannot be rapidly processed. The point of relative completion is not achieved and so termination of active memory retention does not occur. Relevant codings of information will remain in active memory storage.

Assuming a limited capacity for cognitive processing, such codings will remain stored in active memory even when other cognitive "programs" (those used for processing other sets of information) have greater priority in the hierarchy of claims for the channels involved in representation and cognitive processing. These actively stored contents, however, will tend to be repeatedly represented. Each episode of representation will trigger resumption of cognitive processing. Thus whenever this set of information gains a high enough place on a system of priorities, representation and cognitive processing will resume. If interrupted by controls that regulate priorities for use of limited channels, the various levels of representation involved will remain in coded form in active memory.

Incongruity

Completion involves the resolution of differences between new information and enduring schemata. News of the death of a loved one is incongruent with an entire world picture which includes not only wishes and hopes, but habits and schemata of self and object relationships. Even news that is not new or novel can be incongruent with existing schemata if the quality is greater than readiness for processing. A hurricane is not just "more wind than a breeze," but an overwhelming increase of a quantity that develops a qualitatively different state.

Thus, in order to complete cognitive processing, the alteration of existing internal schemata, a sometimes quite gradual procedure, is necessary. Completion occurs only when the new and the old have been changed so that they mesh, and schemata are "up to date."

The functional flow of information in this sequence can be followed in Figure 4. The stress event was represented initially and the information of that representation is stored in active memory. This information is repeatedly represented whenever access to representational processes is possible. Cognitive processing is reinitiated when representation occurs and may evoke unpleasant emotions such as fear or anxiety.

If fear or anxiety are likely to increase beyond limits of toleration, controls are activated which will modify the cognitive processes. For example, the path from active memory storage to representation and cognitive processing can be inhibited. This reduction in cognitive processing reduces anxiety and, in turn, reduces motivation for control operations. With reduction in control, the tendency of active memory towards representation reasserts itself. Other immediate cognitive programs may be interrupted with repeated representation of the stress related information. Cognitive processing of the stress related information resumes, anxiety increases, control increases, and the cycle continues.

The simple model leads to oscillatory states of high and low anxiety, high and low degrees of representation, and continuation and cessation of cognitive processing. The oscillation continues because of the intrinsic tendency of active memory towards repeated representation until the point of completion. Only stable controls or absent controls would lead to a steady state, a situation seldom encountered in human psychology.

With each "on" phase of cognitive processing, more and more is accomplished until completion occurs. This progressive integration of new information with old schemata is symbolized in the diagram by progressive shortening of lines between representations of external and internal sources of information. With relative completion of cognitive processing the cycle terminates because the relevant contents are cleared from active memory storage. The "new" information has now been integrated with "internal sources of information," that is, with inactive memory. Put in another way, schemata have been revised so that they are now congruent with new information about the self and the world.

Assimilation

This simple model can account for recurrent and phasic episodes of stress event-related thoughts and emotions long after the stress event. The term "cognitive processing" has implied many functions, however, and additional detail should be added. The inherent purpose of cognitive processing is what Piaget (1954) has defined as assimilation and accommodation.

Briefly, assimilation includes processes that translate and coordinate incoming information into various meanings and relate it to suitable categories of pre-existing schemata of the

Figure 4

Completion of Cognitive Processing as a Terminator of
Repetitive Representational Tendencies That Persist
after Termination of the Inciting Event.

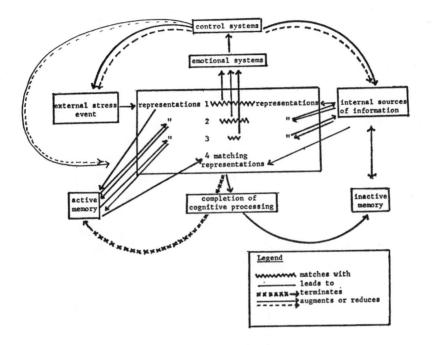

self and the world. These processes can be conceptualized as a
series of matchings. For example: New stimuli are matched
with expectancies based on current needs or fears, new information about the world is matched with schematic representations
of the world, current body sensations are related to previous
body images, images are matched with relevant labels such as
words, new demands are matched with available coping strategies, and so forth.

When there is not a good immediate fit between new information and existing schemata, further cognitive processing then
leads to progressive modifications of the meaning of recently

acquired information and/or to progressive modifications of the pre-existing schemata. This processing for fit leads to a series of approximating representations of both the stress event and the relevant schemata activated from memory or unconscious fantasy.

When there is limited channel capacity for representation and cognitive processing, and when these channels are "claimed" by problems that have greater priority, then the progressive series of representations that do not yet "fit" together would be stored in active memory. This set of information or aspects of it will be represented again when it has relatively high priority (e.g., when it is associatively triggered or primed, when more urgent business is finished, as when the driver of a car stops after a near accident and then reconsiders the possibly disastrous outcome).

Several different "complexes" or "programs" of ideation might be set in motion by a given event. The degree of fit in each of the various "programs" of cognitive processing would lead to differing affects. Threat that exceeds coping capacity might lead to fear. New self-information that matched poorly with ego-ideals might lead to shame or guilt, and so on. Excessive emotion, as stated earlier, will activate controls which will in turn interrupt representation and processing, reduce affect to tolerable limits, but also predispose the entire system to repetition of the same set of information. Some ideational programs might complete promptly, others might remain in a state of intermittent activity and inhibition. It is possible, however, to speak abstractly about phases of a given complex of ideas, emotions, and controls initiated by a stress event.

Phases of Response

Earlier, phases of clinical response to stress events were described as initial realization or outcry, denial, intrusion, working through, and completion. These separable phases can now be modeled in terms of states of the systems diagrammed in Figure 4. In Figure 5, segments of the overall organization are

FIGURE 5

Active Sectors of the Model during Different Phases of Stress Response

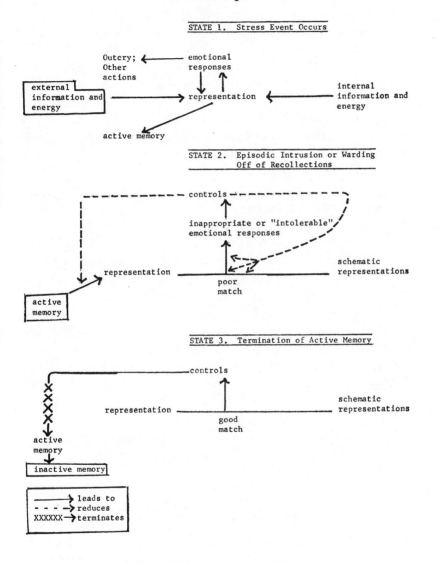

boxed to indicate that they are centers of the stress-event-related information as various states of the assimilation process.

In State 1 external events stimulate an internalized stress event compounded of both external and internal factors. Outcry may be the result. Internal factors include the current drive and motivational state of the person, his defensive and coping capacities and weaknesses, and the meaning of the external events to him personally. The persons' own responses are themselves represented in a continuing process. Representations are maintained in active memory when other problems or thoughts have priority over conscious thought representation. Such storage leads into State 2, modeled here as a time after the external events and responsive actions.

Although the external events are over, the active memory contents tend to emerge in State 2. Memories of the stress tend to return to awareness because they have not yet been fully processed. The memories are warded off because they are internally appraised as potentially provocative of "too much" emotional response (the theory of signal anxiety and other affective signals). When control capacity is high, the repetitions can be warded off, and the result is the phase of ideational denial and emotional numbing. But control capacity varies as do internal or external associative stimuli that may trigger recollection. Hence there may be episodic intrusions of active memory contents into representational systems, and this creates the phase of ideational intrusion and emotional pangs. Each recurrence may further processing, however, and this leads to State 3.

In State 3, there is a relatively good enough mesh due to sequential modifications of previously incompatible sets of information ("acceptance"). The tendency to repetition ceases (relatively) with erasure of information in active memory and coding of the event by relevant associations in inactive memory.

In real life, "perfect" completion seldom occurs. Even after mourning is "completed" waves of grief may resurface. But the "oscillations" from denial numbness to intrusion-repetition are less frequent and of less intensity. The autonomous repetition diminishes and recollections depend more and more on the presence or absence of situations that are associational triggers to memories of loss.

The theoretical explanation of intrusive repetitions, alternating at times with phases of numbness, repression, and denial, has been modeled. As with any effort at model construction, where priority is given to clarity and grasp of intersystemic relationships, drastic oversimplifications were allowed. The relationships modeled were not exclusive. The systems are open to undesignated and undiagrammed entries and exits of information. Two considerations postponed earlier can now be discussed: the first is consciousness and adaptation, the second concerns drives.

The Relationship between Consciousness and Adaptative Change

Information about events, emotions, and defenses can become a conscious experience only by translation of the information into representational form (e.g. as words, images, or enactions. See also Bruner, 1964; Horowitz, 1970, 1972a, b). While only representations can become a conscious experience, all representations do not necessarily gain this special form of attention. Even when representations become conscious, there are varieties and degrees of awareness; representations vary in intensity, quality, duration, degree of reflective awareness, memory for episodes of awareness and memory for contents of awareness (Natsoulas, 1970).

Theoreticians such as Hartmann (1939) and Kubie (1958) assume a range of thought from automatic and relatively non-conscious forms of representational processing to conscious and non-automatic processing. Roughly speaking, the more conscious the thought the greater the probability of solving problems but the slower the thought process. When information can be processed by habitual and automatic routes, then time is saved by doing so, with minimal degree of conscious awareness. This is what Lazarus means by automatized coping (in

Fig. 2). It follows that consciousness is most useful for working over representations that: a) have high relevance, and b) do not fit well into habitual organizations of information.

Suppose consciousness is the experiential product of "recognizers" of representations which have high relevance or are not matched successfully with enduring schemata. Stress events would have a greater tendency to gain conscious levels of awareness than non-stress events because stress events are, by definition, of high relevance. Representations associated with stress events that were difficult to process to completion would also be "recognized." The "recognizer function" would be a kind of conceptual enlargement perhaps, as suggested by Tomkins (1962), some way of reduplication, increased intensity, or spatial expansion of information. This "enlargement" would result in conscious experience of the representation.

The recurrent stress event representations, often reported as intrusive and unusually vivid when compared to ordinary conscious experience, would be due to the "recognition" and propulsion to consciousness by both the "important" and "stymied" recognizers. These representations, at the moment of conscious awareness, might be experienced as intrusive for several reasons: the association with emotional pain, the unusual vividness, intuitive knowledge that the representational process has been opposed by inhibitory controls, and the emergence of representations without recognized relationship to the immediately previous and consciously intended train of thought.

In spite of the conscious experience of intrusiveness, however, the end result might be adaptational. This could occur because the conceptual processes initiated by the conscious representation might lead to revision of the automatic ways of processing such information, to revision of relevant schemata, to invention of new solutions, and to resultant completion of processing of the stressful information.

In psychotherapy of stress-response syndromes, the process of using conscious awareness for change is of central importance. The interventions of the psychotherapist and the safe re-

FIGURE 6

Overriding Inhibitory Controls May Block Oscillation

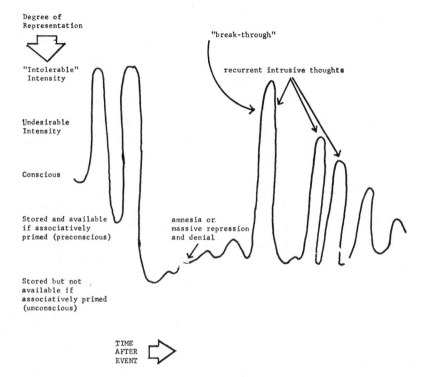

lationship established with the patient are aimed at altering the maneuvers by which the stress-related ideas are warded off, and the intolerable emotional states that threaten to emerge if the ideas are not warded off. Consciousness is not the goal, it is used as a tool for unlearning automatic associations and resolving seemingly irreconcilable conflicts between ideational complexes. Change is accomplished by the revisions, learning, and the creation of new solutions described in general form here and in detail in later sections.

To summarize, repeated episodes of intensely conscious representation occur because 1) active memory tends toward repeated representations and 2) because representations of stress-related information are recognized as important and as hard to process to completion. Such episodes of consciousness may be adaptational since the slower processes of conscious thought are capable of revising organizational patterns used in the faster, automatic, but unsuccessful routes of non-conscious information processing. As assimilation and accommodation occur, there is gradual reduction in the intensity, peremptoriness, and frequency of the repeated representations.

The oscillation phases of repetition with phases of denial are a form of "dosing." Each episode of repetition leads to a tolerable unit of ideational and affective response. If a given "dose" of information leads to emotion beyond limits of toleration, then overriding controls might prevent the oscillation altogether, as diagrammed in Figure 6. Otherwise a declining oscillatory scheme could be imagined. Information processing, which is automatic, or occurs in altered states of consciousness such as dreams, might continue during the flat "repressed period" (Breger, 1967). With increased toleration produced by such non-conscious or non-wakeful processing, conscious representation during wakefulness could be permitted by control systems.

Drives

For simplicity, the model has been based on entry of information from external stress events. There is a recurring tendency in the history of psychiatry and psychology to emphasize the effects of externals. But psychoanalytic studies emphasize the role of endogenous drives as contributors to stress states. A given external event may be more stressful if articulated with a high drive state. Derivatives of libidinal and aggressive drives, for example, may correlate with external stress events to cause stress states which might not occur if drives were not aroused. Similarly, the need for safety and human contact can function as a drive (Murray, 1938). Although modeling drive systems is beyond the present scope, the clinical importance of drives in stress reactions demands consideration of how drive-related information might enter and exit from the systems already modeled. Entry of drive-related information will be discussed first.

Drives may be considered in terms of both long-term and short-term impact on the systems of cognition, emotion, and control. Drives of long duration and effect allow the clearest initial statement. Because of endurance over time (e.g., episodic emergence of more or less the same drives), drives of long standing gain the status of "cognitive structure" as particular desires and needs are associated with particular aims toward particular objects (Rapaport, 1967). In other words, the pattern of previous drive emergence organizes the course of future emergence by providing a schemata of the self and object characteristics, and the activities between self and object that might provide gratification.

The cognitive representatives of a given drive would be an aspect of "internal sources of information." When drive tensions increased, pertinent codings would enter the representational system from inactive memory. Information based on these representations would be treated as described for representations of external stress events. Also, drive relevant information would be matched with new perceptions leading to appraisal of how current external events might relate to current desires and needs. Eventually, ideational processing may revise self-aim-object schemata, bringing them into accord with current realities and possibilities.

Drive tensions may also affect the reactivity level of emotional systems. Since this paper is mainly devoted to considering the cognitive aspects of the model, emotions have been discussed as signal affects. Arousal of the emotional system is not, however, necessarily limited to evocation of affective signals in response to ideational processes. Other triggers to emotional centers exist. In the present model, drive input could directly alter the sensitivity setting of emotional systems. For example, in states of high libidinal tendency, emotions of erotic attraction and sensuality would be triggered more easily. To summarize, the entry of drive-related information may be from (1) specific activation of self, object, and action schemata, and (2) specific alteration in emotional thresholds.

A third site of entry can be modeled by conceptualizing short-term drive effects as "surges." Such "surges" would lead to alterations in feeling sensations (Arnold and Gasson, 1968). Information about such changes in drive state would then enter the cognitive system as sensations or, in other words, as the representation of *events*. For example, a "surge of drive" might be associated with physiological changes which were sampled perceptually. These sensations would thus be represented in a manner similar to other perceptions and, as already modeled, entry into the psychic system could be modulated, the information transformed into various modes of representation, and various types of ideational processing, emotional response, and control interactions would occur.

Take for example a surge of sexuality at puberty. The relatively sudden increase in sexual strivings may constitute a stress event. It may lead to a variety of representations of wishes, a variety of matchings of new information with old self and object representations, and a progressive series of revised representations that reorganize libidinal structures and self and object representations. Through these ideational, affective, and control processes the "stress event" (surge of libido and associated sensation and representation) is accommodated to and assimilated. The state of stress then recedes.

These statements pertain to a simplified model, but even such simple models should include points where information exits and enters. Above, the entry of information from drive systems was discussed. Below, the exit of information from the ideation-emotional-control model to drive systems is considered. This is the transformation of information (and "energy") between systems that has been termed "the mysterious leap from mind to body" and is relevant to the psychophysiologic responses that may occur after stressful life events.

The site of transition from mental systems (where information is embodied in psychological meaning) to physical systems (where information is embodied in electrochemical or anatomical patterns) is often hypothesized to be at the level of emotions. Indeed the response-motive controversy mentioned earlier has an analogy in this area. Are conscious experiences of emotion only responses to physical changes (such as blushing, constriction of throat or stomach, etc.) which are "the" emotions? Or are "the" emotions the conscious experiences which, in turn, motivate physical changes?

Earlier in this discussion, physical changes were included as actions. Action may not be restricted only to physical impact on the external environment but should include impact on the internal environment, or the biological substrates of drives. This "intracranial" action would be an effect of conceptual processes on such neural processes as the activity of the reticular activating system, the limbic system, the hypothalmus, and the pituitary gland (Sperry, 1970). Control systems include systems for regulation of such effects. Suppose a mismatch occurs between current external events and internal needs. Suppose this mismatch leads to an emotion such as anger. Control systems will regulate the degree to which this "emotional" response ("anger") and its equivalent action plans are expressed as mental experiences, as external physical actions, or as internal actions such as augmentation or reduction of biological systems. Thus, the hierarchy of control systems is a point of exit of information from the present model to models of physiological systems.

Summary

The above model schematizes the transactional relationship between three systems involved in the intrapsychic processing of information relating the individual to stress events. These systems, labeled at a very gross level, are the ideational, emotional and control systems. The model of the ideational system included subordinate systems for perception, representation, organization, and cognitive processing. The prototype of cognitive processing was described as a match between the constructive representation of current events, current needs and drives, and enduring schemata of self and world.

The emotional systems were modeled in terms of the evocation of signal affect when there was lack of fit in matching operations. The level and kind of activity in emotional systems affected in turn the level and kind of activity in control systems. These control systems then acted in such a way as to modulate entry of sets of information into available channels for representation and ideational processing. This control of ideation completed a feedback loop.

Each "system" modeled is conceived as, in turn, a set of subsystems which can themselves be modeled in a presumably infinite regression. It is hoped however, that further subdivisions into component systems would not substantially change the configurations of the present model.

In this model, the earliest change in psychological systems in response to an external stress event was posited in the ideational system. Even after termination of the external stress event, an active memory of stress related information was assumed to persist. A key assumption was that active memory automatically tended toward repeated representation of contents until the point of relative completion of evaluation of the given contents was reached. The changes in emotion and control systems were seen as sequential transformations that, by feedback, changed the state of the ideational systems. These sequential transformations in the state of transactive systems were modeled simply, but the model could be extended to include changes in somatic and autonomic systems.

BIBLIOGRAPHY

Arnold, M. B. & Gasson, J. A. (1968), Feelings and emotions as dynamic factors in personality integration. In: *The Nature of Emotion,* ed. M. B. Arnold. Baltimore: Penguin Books, pp. 203-221.

Bibring, E. (1943), The conception of the repetition compulsion. *Psychoanalytic Quarterly,* 12:486-519.

Breger, L. (1967), Function of dreams. *Journal of Abnormal Psychology Monographs,* 72:No. 5. (Whole No. 641).

Breuer, J. & Freud, S. (1895), Studies on hysteria. *Standard Edition*, 2. London: Hogarth Press, 1954.

Broadbent, D. E. (1971), *Decision and Stress*. London: Academic Press.

Bruner, J. (1964), The course of cognitive growth. *American Psychologist*, 19:9-15.

Festinger, L. (1957), *A Theory of Cognitive Dissonance*. New York: Row, Peterson & Company.

French, T. (1952), *The Integration of Behavior*, Vol. I: *Basic Postulates*. Chicago: The University of Chicago Press.

Freud, S. (1920), Beyond the pleasure principle. *Standard Edition*, 18. London: Hogarth Press, 1962.

Gifford, S. (1964), Repetition compulsion. *Journal of the American Psychoanalytic Association*, 12:632-649.

Hartmann, H. (1939), *Ego Psychology and the Problem of Adaptation*. New York: International Universities Press.

Horowitz, M. J. (1970), *Image Formation and Cognition*. New York: Appleton-Century-Crofts.

Horowitz, M. J. (1972a), Image formation: Clinical observations and cognitive model. In: *The Nature and Function of Imagery*, ed. P. Sheehan. New York: Academic Press, pp. 281-309.

Horowitz, M. J. (1972b), Modes of representation of thought. *Journal of the American Psychoanalytic Association*, 20:793-819.

Horowitz, Milton (1963), A historical review of the concept of the repetition compulsion. A paper presented at the Fall meeting of the American Psychoanalytic Association, New York.

Janis, I. L. (1958), *Psychological Stress: Psychoanalytic and Behavioral Studies of Surgical Patients*. New York: Wiley & Sons.

Janis, I. L. (1962), Psychological effects of warnings. In: *Man and Society in Disaster*, ed. C. W. Baker & D. W. Chapman. New York: Basic Books, pp. 55-92.

Janis, I. L. (1967), Effects of fear arousal on attitude change: Recent development in theory and experimental research. In: *Advances in Experimental Social Psychology*, Vol. 3, ed. L. Berkowitz. New York: Academic Press, pp. 166-224.

Janis, I. L. (1969), *Stress and Frustration*. New York: Harcourt, Brace, Jovanovich.

Janis, I. L. & Levanthal, H. (1968), Human reactions to stress. In: *Handbook of Personality Theory and Research*, ed. E. F. Borgatta & W. W. Lambert. Chicago: Rand McNally & Company, pp. 1041-1085.

Johnson, J. E., Levanthal, H. & Dabbs, J. M. (1971), Contribution of emotional and instrumental response processes in adaptation to surgery. *Journal of Personality and Social Psychology*, 20:55-64.

Klein, G. S. (1967), Peremptory ideation: Structure and force in motivated ideas. In: Motives and Thought: Psychoanalytic Essays in Honor of David Rapaport, ed. R. Holt. *Psychological Issues*, 5:80-128.

Kubie, L. S. (1958), *Neurotic Distortion of the Creative Process*. Lawrence: University of Kansas Press.

Lazarus, R. S. (1964), A laboratory approach to the dynamics of psychological stress. *American Psychologist*, 19:400-411.

Lazarus, R. S. (1966), *Psychological Stress and the Coping Process*. New York: McGraw-Hill.

Lazarus, R. S. (1968), Emotions and adaptation. *Nebraska Symposium on Motivation,* 16:175-266. Lincoln: University of Nebraska Press.

Lazarus, R. S., Averill, J. R. & Opton, E. M. (1969), The psychology of coping: Issues of research and assessment. Paper given at a conference entitled "Coping and Adaptation" at Stanford University.

Lewin, K. (1935), *A Dynamic Theory of Personality.* New York: McGraw-Hill.

Mandler, G. (1964), The interruption of behavior. *Nebraska Symposium on Motivation,* 12:163-220. Lincoln: University of Nebraska Press.

Miller, G. A., Galanter, E. & Pribram, K. H. (1960), *Plans and the Structure of Behavior.* New York: Holt.

Miller, N. E. (1963), Some reflections on the law of effect to produce a new alternative to drive reduction. *Nebraska Symposium on Motivation,* 11: 65-112. Lincoln: University of Nebraska Press.

Murray, H. (1938), *Explorations in Personality.* New York: Oxford University Press.

Natsoulas, T. (1970), Concerning introspective knowledge. *Psychological Bulletin,* 73:89-111.

Peterfreund, E. (1971), Information systems and psychoanalysis: An evolutionary biological approach to psychoanalytic theory. *Psychological Issues,* 7: Monograph 25/26.

Piaget, J. (1954), *The Construction of Reality in the Child.* New York: Basic Books.

Rapaport, D. (1967), *The Collected Papers of David Rapaport,* ed. Merton Gill. New York: Basic Books.

Saltz, E. (1970), Manifest anxiety: Have we misread the data? *Psychological Review,* 77:568-573.

Schur, M. (1966), *The Id and the Regulatory Process of the Ego.* New York: International Universities Press.

Sperry, R. W. (1970), An objective approach to subjective experience: Further explanation of a hypothesis. *Psychological Review,* 77:585-590.

Spielberger, C. D. (1966), Theory and research on anxiety. In: *Anxiety and Behavior,* ed. C. D. Spielberger. New York: Academic Press, pp. 3-20.

Taylor, J. & Spence, K. (1952), The relationship of anxiety level of performance in serial learning. *Journal of Experimental Psychology,* 44:61-64.

Tomkins, S. S. (1962), *Affect, Imagery, Consciousness, Vol. I: The Positive Affects.* New York: Springer Publishing Company.

Waelder, L. (1964), Statements as reported by Gifford, S. in "Repetition Compulsion." *Journal of the American Psychoanalytic Association,* 12: 632-649.

CHAPTER SEVEN

General Treatment Principles

IN THIS CHAPTER, general principles of treatment will be based upon the phases of stress response and the theoretical understanding of these phases. To ease the burden of abstraction imposed by the latter chapter, Harry (of chapter two) is once again considered as a concrete referent.

HARRY IN PSYCHOTHERAPY

As you will recall from the earlier vignette, four weeks after the truck accident Harry had a nightmare in which mangled bodies appeared.

A section of the story is repeated here to freshen memory. He awoke with an anxiety attack. Throughout the following days he had recurrent, intense, and intrusive images of the dead girl's body. These images, together with ruminations about the girl, were accompanied by anxiety attacks of growing severity. He developed a phobia about driving to and from work. His regular habits of weekend drinking increased to nightly use of growing quantities of alcohol. He had temper outbursts over minor frustrations, and experienced difficulty concentrating at work and even while watching television.

Harry tried unsuccessfully to dispel his ruminations about feeling guilty for the accident. Worried over Harry's complaints of insomnia, irritability, and increased alcohol consumption, his doctor referred him for psychiatric treatment.

111

Harry was initially resistant, in psychiatric evaluation, to reporting details of the accident. This resistance subsided relatively quickly and he reported recurrent intrusive images of the girl's body.

During the subsequent course of psychotherapy, Harry worked through several complexes of ideas and feelings linked associatively to the accident and his intrusive images. The emergent conflictual themese included guilt over causing the girl's death, guilt over the sexual ideas he fantasied about her before the accident, guilt that he felt glad to be alive when she had died, guilt for having broken company rules, and fear and anger that he had been involved in an accident and her death. To a mild extent, there was also a magical or primary process belief that the girl "caused" the accident by her hitchhiking, and associated anger with her, which then fed back into his various guilt feelings.

Before continuing with those conflicts triggered by the accident, it is helpful to consider, at a theoretical level, the ideal route of conceptualization which Harry "should" follow. To reach a point of adaptation to this disaster, he should perceive the event correctly, translate these perceptions into clear meanings, relate these meanings to his enduring attitudes, decide on appropriate actions, and revise his memory, attitude, and belief systems to fit this new development in his life. This would lead to a point of relative completion. During this information processing Harry should not ward off implications of the event or relevant associations to the event. To do so would impair his capacity to understand and adapt to new realities.

Human thought does not follow this ideal course. The accident has many meanings sharply incongruent with Harry's previous world picture and his personal constructs (Kelly, 1955). The threat to himself, the possibility that he has done harm, the horrors of death and injury, and the fear of accusation by others seriously differ from his wishes for personal integrity, his current self-images, and his view of his life role. This dichotomy between new and old concepts arouses strong painful emotions which threaten to flood his awareness. To avoid such unbearable feelings, Harry limited the processes of elaborating both "real" and "fantasy" meanings of the stressful event. The general task of psychotherapy is to work through these various meanings in the context of Harry's tolerance for emotional responses.

The six problematic themes of Harry's psychotherapy can now be reconsidered as ideational-emotional structures in schematic form. These themes will also provide a concrete referent during the later discussion of character style variations in Chapters 8, 9, and 10. In Table 1 each theme is represented as a match between a current concept and enduring concepts, following the theoretical form of the preceding chapter. Since there is an incongruity between the new and the old, the elicited emotion is also listed.

Three themes cluster under the general idea that Harry sees himself as an aggressor and the girl as a victim. For example, he felt relief that he was alive when someone "had to die." The recollection of this idea elicited survivor guilt because it is discrepant with social morality. He also felt as if he had caused the girl to die. This idea was based on his wish to live, combined with a primitive concept that someone has to fill the role of dying, plus a belief in his magical power to choose who fills that role. Similarly, his sexual ideas about the girl before the crash were recalled and were incongruent with his sense of sexual morality and marital fidelity. All three themes are associated with guilty feelings. The first two, survivor guilt and guilt over aggressivity, are common post-stress themes, as discussed in Chapter 3. The third is a more idiosyncratic response to the particular situation.

Three other themes center around an opposite conceptualization of himself, this time as a victim. Harry is appalled by the damage to the girl's body, for by extension his body could also be damaged. This forceful idea interferes with his usual denial of personal vulnerability, and is inconsistent with wishes for invulnerability. The result is fear.

Harry also conceives of himself as a victim when he recalls

that he broke company rules by picking up a passenger. Since the breach resulted in a disaster, and is discrepant with his sense of what the company wants, he believes accusations would be justified and is frightened. "Harrys" with varying character pathology would experience this same theme in different ways. A Harry with a paranoid style might project the accusation theme and suspect that others are now accusing him. He might use such externalizations to make himself feel enraged rather than guilty. If Harry had an hysterical style he might have uncontrolled experiences of dread or anxiety without clear representation of the instigating ideas. Were he obsessional, Harry might ruminate about the rules; about whether they were right or wrong, whether he had or had not done his duty, about what he ought to do next, and on and on.

The last theme cited in Table 1 places Harry as a victim of the girl's imagined aggression. His fantasy, here, is that she made the disaster happen by appearing on the highway. This matches with his enduring concept of personal innocence in a way that evokes anger. These angry feelings are then represented as a current concept and responses occur to these concepts which again transform Harry's state. His felt experience of anger and his concept of the girl as aggressor do not mesh with his sense of reality. The accident was not her fault and so, as the state of ideas changes, his emotional experience (or potential emotional experience) changes. He feels guilty for having irrational and hostile thoughts about her. With this switch from the feelings of victim to the feelings of aggressor, there has been a change in emotions from anger to guilt and, as diagrammed in Table 1, in state, from B3 to A2. Two of these three themes; fear of identification or merger with victims, and aggression at the source are also common ones after stress events. The third theme, fear of accusation from the company, is partially idiosyncratic to this specific situation.

All six themes might be activated by the accident. In "Harrys" of different neurotic character styles, some themes might be more important or conflictual than others. In an hysterical

TABLE 1

Themes Activated by the Accident

Current Concept — Incongruent with —	"Enduring" Concept →	Emotion
A. Self as "Aggressor"		
a1. Relief that she and not he was the victim	Social morality	Guilt
a2. Aggressive ideas about the girl	Social morality	Guilt
a3. Sexual ideas about the girl	Social morality	Guilt
B. Self as "Victim"		
b1. Damage to her body could have happened to him	Invulnerable self	Fear
b2. He broke rules	Responsibility to the company	Fear (of accusations)
b3. She instigated the situation by hitchhiking	He is innocent of any badness; the fault is outside	Anger

Harry, sexual guilt themes (A3) might predominate and influence his bad dreams, intrusive images, and pangs of emotion. In an obsessional Harry, aggression-guilt (A2) and concern for duty (B2) might predominate in recurrent thoughts, ruminations, and spasms of self-doubt and anxiety. In a narcissistic Harry, "self as an innocent victim" themes (B3), and fears of body vulnerability might be central. Guilt over being a survivor (A1) and fear of repetition (not tabulated) seem to occur universally (Furst, 1967; Lifton, 1967).

The important point is that even speaking in simple generalizations, there will be a multiplicity of themes connected with the stress event during the course of processing associated information to a point of completion. Any given self-image, as a victim or as an aggressor, and any emotional experience such as guilt, fear, or anxiety, will be overdetermined in that not one but several themes may link together to form the image or affect. No stress response syndrome is ever a matter of a single conflicted train of ideational and affective response. There are always multiple factors resulting from the mind's tendency to seek similarities and integrations.

Harry experienced a period in which there was relative denial and numbness for all of these themes. Later, at various times after the accident, some themes were repressed, others emerged; eventually some were worked through so that they no longer aroused intense emotion or motivated defensive efforts. The first emergent themes were triggered by the nightmare of mangled bodies and the daytime recurrent unbidden images of the girl's body. The themes of bodily injury and survivor guilt (A1 and B1) were no longer completely warded off but rather occurred in an oscillatory fashion with periods of both intrusion and relatively successful inhibition. In psychotherapy these intrusive themes required early attention. The other themes, such as sexual guilt, emerged later.

Psychotherapy was aimed as conflict-resolution in terms of all relevant themes, in approximate order of their emergence. That is, an effort was made to bring each theme to a point of completion. This task used all the usual techniques of psychotherapy, but it is necessary to re-contemplate techniques here in terms of their timing, in this chapter, and in terms of Harry's predisposition, in the next three chapters.

There have been general strategies suggested for working through the various meanings and the complex interplay of impulsive and avoidance aims in stress response syndromes. As it happens, inspection of a phenomenology of the main treatments advocated in the past shows that they correspond to the main phases of stress response. Some treatments aim at reliving, analyzing, and working through the stress event. Others aim at suppressing and moving away from the stress event. The former set of treatments are analogous to intrusive repetitions although the techniques may be aimed at counteracting the *opposite* phase of signs and symptoms, that is, denial numbing. The latter "rest" treatments are analogous to denial numbing although usually prescribed to end intrusive symptoms. This will be clarified in a review of relevant literature.

Historical Review of Treatment Strategies

Combat neuroses presented a massive treatment problem in World Wars I and II, as already mentioned. In World War I, the medical corps of the German army recognized the psychological nature of the many cases of "shattered nerves" and "shell shock." Some military physicians reasoned that these cases were due to fear of bodily damage or death in the trenches. They decided to counteract that rational fear with a greater threat of real pain. The "nerve cases," or stress-response syndromes as they would now be termed, were given excruciatingly painful electric shock treatment.

As these military doctors hoped, many soldiers returned to the front to escape the "treatment." Others committed suicide to avoid either disaster. After the war, Freud was part of a commission to study complaints of such "treatment." This experience probably contributed to his writing "Beyond the Pleasure Principle" (1920), his key work on trauma and the repetition compulsion. His theories about compulsive repetitiousness have already been discussed. One of them is quite pertinent to therapy: the repetitions as an automatic effort toward mastery. In more technical approaches to the psychoanalytic treatment of psychological trauma, Freud (1914) consistently emphasized the importance of remembering, repeating, understanding, and working through.

The aim was to overcome resistance to emotional expressions and repression, and assimilate the experience. In this treatment approach the task of the patient is to remember both external events and the internal events of subjective experiences. One of the first tasks of the therapist is reconstructive. By basing inferences on historical information and observations of the current associations and behavior of the patient, the therapist fills gaps in the memory of the patient (Freud, 1937). The next task is interpretation based on the reconstructions. This is followed by working through conflicts until they are resolved.

Memories of traumas are, in the reconstructive process, regarded as having some psychological, but not necessarily historical, reality. The process of change in memories is an important clinical observation in that early versions are often found to be organizers as well as "screens" that both filter out and filter in elements of the objective event (Freud, 1899; Greenacre, 1949; Fenichel, 1954; Reider, 1953; Sachs, 1967; Glover, 1929).

ABREACTION AND CATHARSIS

In World War II, among the Allies, abreactive and cathartic treatment using hypnosis and narcohypnosis was based on Freud's ideas. Because of time pressures, and possibly ignorance of some of Freud's later writings, the dramatic aspects of abreaction received more emphasis than the lengthier, harder process of working through. The hypnotic state was induced in order to skirt the defensive avoidances, re-enact the inciting trauma in full detail of external events and internal reaction, and to work through emergent conflicts. Post-hypnotic sessions were used to complete the working-through process.

The purpose of treatment was to resolve incomplete reactions and conflicts activated by the stressful events of warfare, as soon as possible after they occurred (Zabriskie and Brush, 1941). Hypnosis, with or without the aid of amytal or pentothal, was seen as a very rapid treatment. The drugs were so effective in reducing defenses and getting at the event that they gained the mystery-magic title of "truth serum." The reliving of these events was believed to instigate two main therapeutic processes:

1. *Abreaction:* The events were recalled with florid detail and hence made known to the treatment team. Communication, in and of itself, was therapeutic because it was a social process. It worked through fears of personal alienation, especially if "selfish" thoughts had occurred on seeing a comrade killed or if the patient had wished to escape from danger and these wishes seemed to him unfair to other members of his unit. In addition, the therapist could respond in a way that facilitated a sense of social acceptance of the warded-off memories.

2. *Catharsis:* The emotions, ideas and motoric associations triggered by the events could be discharged, thus completing a cycle, much as an orgasm completes the cycle of erotic arousal.

During wakeful consciousness following the amytal or hypnotic state, therapy sessions were held to further process the information that had been elicited (Kubie, 1943). The resocialization of persons who accused themselves of "bad" and "selfish" thoughts was empirically found to be an important therapeutic factor. Group therapy became an important approach during World War II not only because it expended professional man hours in a parsimonious fashion, but because it filled an observed need to restore group ties (Bartheimer, et al, 1946).

While resocialization appeared effective, it was determined that narcohypnosis, regarded as revelatory, or a "dramatic trick," was not as therapeutic as had been originally hoped. For example, no statistically significant difference was found in 200 cases of combat exhaustion treated with narcoanalysis and 200 treated with other methods including slower, wakeful, and associatife approaches to abreaction (Bartheimer et al., 1946).

Even without "truth serums," abreaction was not a cure-all for traumatic symptoms. As Lidz (1946) put it, "the pit seemed fathomless." Abreaction led to more abreaction, to seemingly endless accounts, all related to the traumatic neurosis, but with little apparent improvement. Abreaction may relieve anxiety, but this effect can be non-specific and transient. To obtain durable improvement it seems necessary to understand the individual patient, the meaning of the experience in relation to the continuum of his life, and to revise discrepancies in self-object representations and other organizing constructs. Rest, recreation, and resocialization were found to be necessary additions, probably as techniques for reducing intrusive and repetitive syndromes and associated psychosomatic symptoms, and for reassuring the person that he was not ostracized by his peers. Support of coping and defensive processes appeared to be important in acute phases (Hoch, 1943; Bion, 1940; Rioch, 1955).

Abreaction and catharsis, in retrospect, seemed useful for re-initiating the processing of incompletely integrated stress events. It must be remembered, however, that the goals of treatment in combat medicine were often social rather than individual. That is, cohesiveness of combat groups and return to duty were as important or more important than individual adaptation. In the Korean and Vietnam wars, for example, a brief period of support, rest and sedation was considered the optimum treatment for most stress response syndromes since more men were returned to action as a result of these tactics (Glass, 1953, 1954; Bourne, 1970). Exploration of fears of bodily injury or personal guilt might not lead to motivation to return to combat, although it might be necessary at a later time for maximum individual recovery. The long term effects of suppressive treatment are still debated (Lifton, 1973; Shatan, 1973; Horowitz and Solomon, in press; Bourne, 1970).

EARLY TREATMENT

If treatment were not instituted early the recent traumas had a greater likelihood of producing pathological reactions. For example, persons act to end any state of crisis, even if this means use of the "universal defense" of general inhibition. The results range from a healthy temporary denial such as that which may actually help heart attack victims to survive, to a dazed and frozen state with reduced capacity to adapt in general (Kardiner and Spiegel, 1947; Maskin, 1941). In addition, a morbid blend of responses to the recent stress and pretraumatic neurotic conflicts might become fixated as character attitudes, rather than as ideas and feelings in current flux.

Hypnosis

Even with rapid treatment, the hypnotic approach to abreaction and catharsis proved complicated. The experiences relived so vividly were sometimes inaccurate. As Freud had found using equivalent methods to "cure" traumatic hysteria, additions were derived from earlier memories and fantasies, and elaboration continued in waking memories (Kubie, 1943; Solomon et al., 1971). Dreamlike states often do produce experiences that, because of hallucinatory vividness, are then taken by the subject to be authentic memories of external events (Horowitz, Adams, and Rutkin, 1968; Horowitz, 1974).

Further limitations on the effectiveness of treatment by abreaction, however conscious and extended in time, were noted in the treatment of survivors of the German concentration camps of World War II. For some the damage appears irreversible; the horror was too great, and treatment can become only a reliving but not a dispelling of nightmares (Straker, 1971; Koranyi, 1969; Ostwald and Bittner, 1968). It is tragic to say that true and full mourning of such a prolonged and total holocaust may be impossible.

Chemical Sleep and Stupor

Before continuing, one additional aspect of rest, support, and resocialization treatment should be mentioned. Drug induced prolonged sleep was also used in World War II to provide time for healing in automatic, dream-like processes (Breger, Hunter, and Lane, 1971) and also to reduce fatigue and anxiety attacks (Hoch, 1943; Kubie, 1943). Sometimes, with patients unresponsive to initial treatment efforts, insulin was given to reduce blood sugar and induce a semisomnulent state. During the stupor, regression and re-development were encouraged by nurses performing such acts as feeding men from baby bottles and reciting nursery rhymes to them (Bartheimer et al., 1946). Such re-parenting is periodically "rediscovered" in psychiatry and psychology. If it were an empirically useful technique, in contrast to a "speculative" and "*it sounds nice*" technique, one would expect more durability.

Brief Treatment

Treatment of combat neurosis was necessarily brief. The immediacy of the crisis, the "simple" goal of symptom relief, and the relative "ego strength" of the patients were thought to be the factors contributing to the success of brief approaches to dynamic conflict. Brief psychoanalytic psychotherapy, again with a focus on resolution of sectors of conflicts, had also been found successful in a variety of civilian crisis situations before World War II (Knight, 1971; Berliner, 1941; Deutsch, 1949; Lindemann, 1944; Sterba, 1951).

In the various dynamic approaches to brief therapy, it is important to arrive at an early formulation of a working hypothesis of the most important current conflict and a very quick appraisal of the personality patterns, especially the defensive habits of the patient (Stone, 1951; Socarides, 1954). Other sectors of function, however conflicted, may have to be omitted from attention (Pumpian-Mindlin, 1953; DeLaTorre, 1972) or even given only incomplete or inexact interpretation (Glover, 1931). Very disturbed patients seem less appropriate to such brief approach strategies (Kernberg, et al., 1972).

Brief treatment can also be conceptualized as helping a patient work through a circumscribed process such as mourning. Lindemann's (1944) important paper on the management of loss has been a major influence on all brief treatment approaches. He alerted clinicians to delayed or frozen grief and described techniques for reinstigating the "work of grieving." Caplan (1961) was also of great importance in the development of crisis-oriented brief therapy. He viewed a crisis as a period of special fluidity, one in which psychic change might even be easier or faster than during times of stability.

Crisis Intervention

The work of Lindemann and Caplan, spurred by the development of community mental health centers and the need for detailed rationales for brief and inexpensive treatment, led to the concept of *crisis intervention*. The stress model of crisis intervention views the onset of the crisis as a precipitatory event (or series of events) that is enough to exceed a person's ordinary coping capacity. In this model, crises are time limited. Although there may be turbulent societies, times or persons, a particular crisis will evoke reaction by a person, possibly in a pathological way. As in military psychiatry, there is a need to treat the person before fixed response sets are solidified. Otherwise the treatment task may be more difficult and take longer.

Jacobson (1974) has extended the crisis model into a formula for treatment. The patient comes, it is believed, because of a "cognitive impasse" in response to "a hazard." The therapist's goal is to find the hazard and solve the impasse. The hazard is to be located in changes in the person's life space, and a chronological outline helps the therapist find, in an investigative fashion, the stressful external events that the patient might avoid mentioning in a less directive interview.

This is an important point. Just as a surgical patient "guards" his abdomen to avoid pain from the hands of an examining physician, patients under stress may ward off pain by skirting around consideration of decisive events. The technique suggested by Jacobson is not only diagnostic but therapeutic because it helps the patient understand the determination of his current state. In addition to locating critical events in time, the therapist uses the usual methods of requesting details, fantasies, and associations in order to find the psychological meaning of the event, usually in terms of loss or threat of loss of some life need. A time period of six visits is set by Jacobson for dealing with these meanings. Sifneos (1972) and Mann (1973) use defined limits of ten to twelve interviews. The brevity aims to prevent dependency, diffuse exploration, and to suggest early change. The definite end point encourages both the therapist and the patient to begin to deal with the important issue of separation from each other during the middle phase of the contact.

At the end of that time period, the patient is not necessarily terminated, but may be referred to another therapist in order to adhere to the original contract. This latter aspect of his approach has the advantages cited above, but the disadvantages of external caveat and of fitting patients to a mold that may not meet their needs. The safety of an extended relationship may be a necessary condition for some types of psychological change.

Phase-oriented Treatment

While the various treatment techniques suggested in the past have their efficacy they also have their hazards. Too often the techniques are applied by therapists in a stereotyped rather than patient-specific manner. Psychoanalytically oriented psychiatrists tended, in World War II, to use abreactive hypnosis while "directive organic" types of psychiatrists, as they were then called, tended to use rest and sedation We now understand the importance of orientation to treatment not by schools but by the phase of response and the character of the patient.

Phases are determined, to a large extent, by the current degree of control over a tendency to repetition. In general, the rest and support type of treatments are efforts to supplement relatively weak controls. The treatment staff takes over some aspects of control operations and they reduce the likelihood of emotional and ideational triggers to repeated representations. In contrast, the abreactive-cathartic methods reduce controls through suggestion, social pressure, hypnosis, or hypnotic drugs. The long-range goal of the abreactive-cathartic treatment is not to reduce controls, however, but to reduce the need for controls by helping the patient to complete the cycle of ideational and emotional responses to a stress event.

Such generalities orient understanding but do not help in the prescription of person-specific treatments. Any individual treatment is constructed by selection of many specific maneuvers from the repertoire of available techniques. This selection is based upon clinical inference about the patient's immediate state and guided by theory. Unfortunately the repertoire of available techniques and theories have never been well classified. A rudimentary attempt at phase specific technique classification is presented in Table 2. The goal there is to convey a general idea, not to recommend particular treatment forms. Thus I have included chemical, social, gestalt, biofeedback, and behavior therapy techniques, along with those of psychoanalytically oriented focal psychotherapy.

Completion of integration of the meanings of an event and development of adaptational responses are the goals of treatment of a stress-response syndrome. One knows this end point is near when the person is freely able to think about, or *not* think about the event. These goals can be broken down according to immediate aims that depend upon the patient's current state. When the stress event is on-going, aims may center on fairly direct support. When the external aspects of the event are over, but the person swings between *paralyzing* denial and *intolerable* attacks of ideas and feelings, then the immediate aim is to reduce the amplitude of these swings. Similarly, if the patient is frozen in a state of inhibition of cognitive-emotional processing then the therapist must both induce further thought *and* help package responses into tolerable doses. These injunctions to "be careful" can also be tabulated as in Table 3.

Individual Variation

Any person has characteristic modes for solving problems or warding off threatening ideas and feelings. These character styles will affect both response to general stress tendencies and response to therapeutic intervention. Also, any stress event will activate many lines of associational response, some more conflicted or harder to accept than others. At any given time, one complex of ideational and affective responses may be functionally intrusive, another complex may be latent and warded off, and functionally in a "denial" phase At that time the therapist would probably deal with the active complex and remain alert to evidence that other lines of response are inhibited from aware-

TABLE 2

A Classification of Treatments for
Stress-response Syndromes

SYSTEMS	STATES	
	Denial — Numbing Phase	Intrusive — Repetitive Phase
To Change Controlling Processes	Reduce controls —interpretation of defenses —hypnosis & narcohypnosis —suggestion —social pressure and evocative situations: e.g., psychodrama Change attitudes that make controls necessary Uncovering interpretations	Supply controls externally —structure time and events for patient —take over ego functions; e.g., organize information Reduce external demands & stimulus levels Rest Provide identification models, group membership, good leadership, orienting values Behavior modification with reward or withholding Permit idealization, dependency
To Change Information Processing	Encourage abreaction Encourage description —association —speech —use of images rather than just words in recollection and fantasy —conceptual enactments possibly with addition of role playing, psychodramas, art therapy Reconstructions (to prime memory and associations)	Work through and reorganize by clarifying and educative type interpretive work Differentiate —reality from fantasy —past self-object images from current ones —self attributes from object attributes Reinforce contrasting ideas; e.g., simple occupational therapy, moral persuasion Remove environmental reminders and triggers; interpret their meaning and effect Suppress or dissociate thinking; e.g. sedation, minor tranquilizers Teach "dosing," e.g., attention on and away from stress related information
To Change Emotional Processing	Encourage catharsis Explore emotional aspects of relationships and experiences of self Supply objects and encourage emotional relationships (to counteract numbness)	Support Evoke other emotions; e.g., benevolent environment Suppress emotion; e.g., sedation or anti-anxiety agents Desensitization procedures Relaxation and biofeedback

TABLE 3

Priorities of Treatment

Priority Patient's Current State	Treatment Goal
1. Under continuing impact of external stress event	—Terminate external event or remove patient from continuity with it —Provide temporary relationship —Help with decisions, plans, or working through
2. Swings to intolerable levels: —Ideational-emotional attacks —Paralyzing denial and numbness	—Reduce amplitude of oscillations down to swings of tolerable intensity of ideation and emotion —Continue emotional and ideational support —Selection of techniques cited for states of intrusion in Table 2
3. Frozen in overcontrol state of denial and numbness with or without intrusive repetitions	—Help patient "dose" re-experience of event and implications; that is, help to remember for a time, put out of mind for a time, remember for a time, and so on. Selection of denial techniques from Table 2. —During periods of recollection, help patient organize as well as express experience. Increase sense of safety in therapeutic relationship so patient can allow resumption of processing the event.
4. Able to experience and tolerate episodes of ideation and waves of emotion	—Help patient work through associations: the conceptual, emotional, object-relations, and self-image implications of the stress event —Help patient relate this stress event with prior threats, and relationship models, and self-concepts as well as future plans
5. Able to work through ideas and emotions on his own	—Work through loss of therapeutic relationship —Terminate treatment

ness. Thus the individual therapy would be a far more complex situation than suggested by the foregoing generalizations.

Decision Points

Each transition between phases becomes a decision point within the treatment contract. Not infrequently, the act of establishing a therapeutic relationship may reduce pressure enough so that the patient can enter or regain a state of denial and numbing. If he was upset prior to this phase, he will seem and feel much better.

As the patient feels less upset he may be motivated to avoid discussing the stress event and its implications, and want to withdraw from the therapeutic relationship. This change is often manifested first in a feeling reaction of the therapist: the patient is boring, the curiosity of the therapist diminishes and his enthusiasm wanes. The first therapy hours during "upset" only begin to disclose information. The therapist wants to know much more, the patient, feeling less, discloses less. At this point, there is a danger of either premature termination or overzealous pursuit of "material" or emotionality.

Warding-off maneuvers are not unhealthy defenses to be removed, cracked, or even interpreted. Entry into a denial phase, for example, is an adaptive movement that allows the patient to resume control and will later allow him to dose the amount of reaction within tolerable limits. An appropriate therapeutic tactic is to simply continue or to make another appointment later on, in order to see when the patient enters a repetitive phase, and resume work then. Eventually the therapist can counteract denial even when it seems "frozen" or resistant to adaptation. Although both denial and completion are characterized by low upset, the difference between them can be noted clearly. During denial, the implications of the event are not conscious and the person does not have sufficient control over the stress event, memories, and responses, to discuss them freely.

Decision Points in the Middle Phase of Therapy of Stress Response Syndromes

Recent stress events bring character traits and pathology into sharp relief. They activate latent conflicts, childhood fantasies, magical thinking, and memories of past stress events. These observations have led to various positions on what direction therapy should take To sharpen the issue, two divergent extremes can be stated:

1. States of stress are ideal times to work on character pathology, neurotic conflicts, and previous unintegrated stress events because change is necessary, static positions are disrupted, and the issues are unusually clear (Sifneos, 1972).

2. In spite of activation of traits, conflicts, and past memories, the main aim in treatment of stress response syndromes should be to work through *that* syndrome to a point of relative completion. At that point the traits and conflicts will subside to latent status, and earlier traumas will be less emergent.

This divergence of views indicates a decision point rather than a controversy. This decision point can be located during the repetitive phase when the patient is bringing up the event and associative contents and reactions. One route is toward character or "core neurotic conflict" analysis, the other toward working through the stress event to completion. There are, of course, many intervening choices:

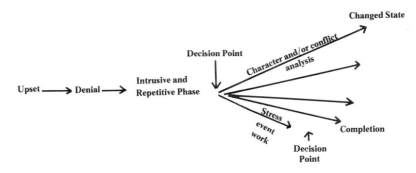

Note that the route that focuses on completion of the stress event is diagrammed as shorter in time and is followed by a decision point at which character or conflict analysis can be recommended. On the basis of multiple factors, the direction at either decision point is followed by the informed patient working with the therapist's recommendations. Of course the stress-event work cannot proceed without some work on relevant character traits, activated conflicts and memories. The decision of how far to go in this direction includes consideration of the degree to which traits, conflicts, and compulsive repetion of past traumas contribute to:

1. the occurrence of the recent stress event
2. present reactions to the recent stress event
3. difficulties in working-through the recent events or difficulties in the therapeutic relationship.

Other concerns in this decision include:

4. the general maladaption of the patient
5. the readiness and capacity of the patient to change
6. a kind of ratio consideration between the "objective" magnitude of the stress event and the degree of reaction of the patient
7. cost and sufficiency factors.

In what follows, we presume the decision is made on aiming to work through the stress response syndrome. Interpretations of defenses, resistances, and transferences will still be necessary. But generally, as illustrated in what follows, these interpretations also maintain a focus on the meanings of the stress event.

Interpretation of Defenses and Transference in Terms of a Particular Event

All patients will have a combination of reactions to stress events and their pre-stress problems. It is desirable that therapists attend to the manifestations of characteristic defensive styles and the emergence of transference even during the comparatively brief treatment of a stress response syndrome. What does the therapist do with this information? Does he interpret defenses, interpret and try to work through transference? Or does he work around defense and transference to bring the stress event reactions to a point of completion? Each patient-therapist pair can arrive at a satisfactory end point by different routes. Nonetheless, "using the gestalt of the stress event" can be one of the guiding principles.

This means that defensive modifications and self-object dyad interpretations can be made, and they can be centered on the specific contents of the stress-event memories. An example of such connection-forming interventions follows.

A young woman had attacks of incapacitating anxiety for months after she was raped. She had flirted with the man and encouraged his advances but when she wished to go no further in the steps of sexual encounter, he forced her to have intercourse with threats of violence. She decided not to report the matter to either the police or a physician. She came for help later because of increased anxiety.

The first work involved her telling the story of how she was traumatized by the vicious behavior of this man. This, plus the establishment of a therapeutic relationship, helped reduce anxiety, but a sense of her own participation, in an unclear way, remained and required further therapeutic attention.

During psychotherapy she was generally vague in her verbal communication. Non-verbally, there were gestures in her bodily movements which the therapist did not respond to but found somewhat erotically stimulating. When the therapist failed to show interest in her physical attributes and movements, the patient seemed to feel hurt, looked dejected, withdrew, and talked in a self-depreciating manner. In spite of this reactivity, the patient did not appear to be conceptually aware of either her bodily "gambits," the lack of attention to them on the part of the therapist, or her "hurt" responses.

Through many such observations of process, the ther-

apist made two inferences. One was that she had a repres-
sive-denying and dissociative style. The other concerned a
pattern for interpersonal relationships in which she offered
an erotic surrender to a domineering other person, and expected attention and care in return.

These inferences were not interpreted directly, or in
terms of the transference manifestations. Instead, they were
used as information to help in reconstruction of the rape
and preceding events. The rape was seen as a pattern contributed to by the real but unrecognized assaultative nature of the man involved, her general pattern of relating
to men, and her method of avoiding appraisal of this particular man.

In this way, some aspects of the fear, anger, guilt, and
shame evoking ideas about the event were worked through.
In addition, the therapeutic process allowed some progressive change in her self and object attitudes. For example,
one unconscious attitude present before the stress event
was that an erotic approach was the only way to get attention because she herself was so undeserving. She must give
her body in order to get attention. In work on the meaning
of the rape she became aware of this defective self-image
and related rescue fantasies. She was able to revise her attitudes, including her automatic and unrealistic expectations that dominant others will feel *guilty* about exploiting
her and *then* be motivated by guilt to be concerned and
tender.

The relatively clear contents of the stress event memories provided a concrete context for this work. The focus
of discussion was outside of the therapeutic relationship
although there was a tendency to compulsive repetition of
the "raper-rapee" relationship in the transference situation.
The therapeutic alliance was maintained but might have
been disrupted by the anxiety that would occur if interpretation of the same self-object transactions were directed to
the transference situation.

At some point, *if advisable*, it would be possible to extend
recognition of the same patterns to the transference, to childhood relationships, and to current interpersonal relationships.
That is, this focus on the stress events does not mean that interpretation of transference is omitted from stress-focused

treatment. Malan (1963) has shown that such interpretations may be crucial to good outcome in brief therapy. But there is no intent to allow a transference neurosis to evolve, and transference interpretations will tend to focus on negative responses which are likely to impede therapy. Another example illustrates a blend of transference recognition with a focus maintained on the recent stressful event.

A young woman patient broke her leg in a fall from a ladder while helping her father paint his house. A partial paralysis complicated matters and disrupted her plans to take an available teaching position on graduation from college. She came for therapy because of a reactive depression. One of the dormant psychological complexes activated by her injury was hostility towards her father for not taking good enough care of her. The relevant theme of the stress event was anger that her father had given her a rickety, second-class ladder while he used a good one. She had, in the past, been unable to recognize her own ambivalence towards her father, even when he gave her good cause to be hostile. Awareness of her anger was warded off at the time of treatment onset.

During one treatment hour, the emotion closest to the surface was anger at the therapist because he would not prescribe sleeping pills for her insomnia. While the therapist was able to infer this emotion, it was not recognized or expressed *clearly* by the patient.

We will now artificially dichotomize the immediate issue in the question of whether the therapist should interpret the anger in terms of the transference, or in terms of the stress event. In general, a therapeutic rule of thumb is to focus on negative transference reactions, such as her surfacing anger at the therapist [Wolberg, 1967]. The reason for this "rule" is that negative reactions interfere with other therapy processes, and the patient might even quit or withdraw. The problem is how to deal not only with negative transference feelings, so that they are reduced enough for the therapy to progress, but to use the information gained to work through the stress event. One determinant of whether or not to focus on the emergent anger is the therapist's diagnostic impression of the strength of the patient. If the patient is capable of tolerating it, the therapist will tend to interpret what is going on. If the patient is in danger of fragmentation, as in severe narcissistic and borderline characters, the therapist may not interpret the anger directly. Instead he may deal with it in a counteractive way or give it a peripheral interpretation in relation to characters outside the treatment situation.

If the therapist decides to interpret the anger in a fairly direct manner, he still has to decide which line of interpretation would be most therapeutic. For example, he could choose among four lines of approach such as:

1. You are angry with me because you feel that I am not taking care of you, just as your father did not take care of you (interpretation of the transference link to father).
2. You are angry at me and are afraid to express it or even know it. (interpretation of the fear of being angry)
3. You are angry at me and so you withdraw (interpretation of the defensive maneuver).
4. You get angry when your dependency needs are not met (interaction of underlying wishes).

These are of course not the wordings of the interpretations, but a shorthand illustration of the various possible directions. In a full segment of work, each aspect of the interpretation might be made.

Whichever type of interpretation is made first, it might be possible to link the exploration of the anger to the recent stress event, even though the focus remains on working through the immediate negative sentiments toward the therapist. For example, the interpretation might be worded as follows, except it would be given in short phrases rather than all at once:

"You are angry at me right now because I am not meeting your need for a sleeping pill, just as you are still angry with your father because you feel he took poor care of you by giving you a lousy stepladder."

The principal advantage of this type of wording, which links current transference to the model of the stressful event, is that it maintains a conceptual clarity about the goals and priorities of the treatment. If the focus is only on the transference meanings of a patient-therapist transaction, the transference is accentuated as a topic of interest to the therapist. Some transference work makes for more transference work because the interest of the therapist in the transference aspects of treatment has an intrinsic transference evoking effect, a paradoxical cycle. The tendency would be toward a character analysis [Oremland, 1972] rather than working through the life event and then terminating or establishing some other therapeutic contract.

Another example is provided by a young male patient who came for treatment because of depression following the death of his mother.

During the first three interviews the work focused on his attitude that his mother had left him alone by dying. As a result of this work, feelings of intense loneliness decreased. The pain and threat of the loss had been reduced to a level where his available defensive and coping strategies could inhibit further emotional responsivity. During ensuing interviews, feelings of sadness and ideas of being left were not present.

In spite of the symptomatic relief, the therapist inferred that the stressful event had not been completely worked through but rather had only been worked on to the point where denial and numbness had become possible. At this point in treatment, as is common, the patient searched for topics to discuss because he did not want to lose the therapist through treatment termination. That is why in one hour he brought up a current problem, an argument the night before with his girlfriend.

There was no doubt that the emotion nearest the surface was anxiety about the argument, and the therapist gave his attention to this situation. But in his interventions he chose not to explore the relationship between the patient and his girlfriend in detail because he felt it would be a deflection of the therapeutic path to interpersonal relationships in general, and from there into a long term therapy. Instead he linked the fears of losing the girlfriend to the recent loss of the mother by saying, "Another loss might be very hard for you to contemplate right now."

This remark was enough to link the current emotional state to the incompletely processed stress event. Through such maneuvers it was possible to avoid diffusion of the therapy to many topics. With this patient, a decision to go for general characterological revision might be made after more work on the loss.

These examples do not mean that the work of relating the meaning of subsequent occurrences to the stress event can be forced. In some patients, especially adolescents or young adults, loss of a parent or sibling may be worked on only to a point where denial can set in. Then the implications of the loss are vigorously inhibited and attempts at connection, such as illustrated here, will not succeed. In such instances the therapeutic goal must be reconsidered, the defenses accepted, and the patient either seen over a considerable period of time with a therapeutic strategy, or terminated until any later work is indicated.

To recapitulate, the treatment of stress-response syndromes is centered on the goal of completion of information processing cycles initiated by the stress event. The phase of stress response is recognized by an informed interview for signs and symptoms, and treatment techniques are used according to the current phase, in order to accomplish progressive movement. At times this includes facilitation of warding-off maneuvers just as at other times the patient will be helped to set aside unconscious defensive operations. Transference and core neurotic conflicts will be a part of the therapeutic work but will tend to be interpreted in terms of their real relationship to the current stress. This will permit a clear focus for brief therapy. The nuances of the therapy technique, beyond the general strategies, will depend on the patient's character style (and that of the therapist). Ensuing chapters examine approaches when the patient tends to inhibit, slide, or shift away from meanings associated with a stressful event.

BIBLIOGRAPHY

Bartheimer, C., et al. (1946), Combat exhaustion. *Journal of Nervous and Mental Disease,* 104:359-525.

Berliner, B. (1941), Short psychoanalytic psychotherapy: Its possibilities and its limitations. *Bulletin of the Menninger Clinic,* 5:204-213.
Bion, W. (1940), The "war of nerves": Civilian reaction, morale and prophylaxis. In: *The Neuroses in War,* ed. E. Miller. New York: Macmillan, pp. 180-200.
Bourne, P. (1970), *Men, Stress and Vietnam.* Boston: Little, Brown.
Breger, L., Hunter, I. & Lane, R. (1971), Effect of stress on dreams. *Psychological Issues,* 73:1-213.
Caplan, G. (1961), *An Approach to Community Mental Health.* New York: Grune & Stratton.
De La Torre, J. (1972), The therapist tells a story: A technique in brief psychotherapy. *Bulletin of the Menninger Clinic,* 36:609-616.
Deutsch, F. (1949), *Applied Psychoanalysis.* New York: Grune & Stratton.
Fenichel, O. (1954), The concept of trauma. In: *The Collected Papers of Otto Fenichel,* 2:49-69. New York: Norton.
Freud, S. (1899), Screen memories. *Standard Edition,* 3:303-322. London: Hogarth Press, 1962.
Freud, S. (1914), Remembering, repeating and working through. *Standard Edition,* 12:145-150. London: Hogarth Press, 1958.
Freud, S. (1937), Constructions in analysis. *Standard Edition,* 25:255-269. London: Hogarth Press, 1964.
Furst, S. S. (1967), Psychic trauma: A survey. In: *Psychic Trauma,* ed. S. S. Furst. New York: Basic Books.
Glass, A. (1953), Problem of stress in the combat zone. *Symposium on Stress.* Washington: National Research Council and Walter Reed Army Medical Center, pp. 90-102.
Glass, A. (1954), Psychotherapy in the combat zone. *American Journal of Psychiatry,* 110:725-731.
Glover, E. (1929), The 'screening' function of traumatic memories. *International Journal of Psychoanalysis,* 10:90-93.
Glover, E. (1931), The therapeutic effect of inexact interpretation: A contribution to the theory of suggestion. *International Journal of Psycho-Analysis,* 19:457-459.
Greenacre, P. (1949), A contribution to the study of screen memories. *Psychoanalytic Study of the Child,* 3-4:78-84.
Hoch, P. (1943), Etiology and pathology of traumatic war neuroses. Paper presented to USPHS conference on war neurosis.
Horowitz, M. J. (1974), Microanalysis of working through in psychotherapy. *American Journal of Psychiatry,* 131:1208-1212.
Horowitz, M. J., Adams, J. E. & Rutkin, R. (1968), Visual imagery in brain stimulation. *Archives of General Psychiatry,* 19:469-486.
Horowitz, M. J. & Solomon, G. F. (1975), A prediction of stress response syndromes in Vietnam veterans: Observations and suggestions for treatment. *Journal of Social Issues,* in press.
Jacobson, G. F. (1974), "The Crisis Interview," presented to symposium on "Comparative Psychotherapies," presented by University of Southern California School of Medicine, Department of Psychiatry, Division of Continuing Education, San Diego, Ca., June 24-28, 1974.
Kardiner, A. & Spiegel, H. (1947), *War, Stress and Neurotic Illness.* New York: P. Hoeber.
Kelly, G. (1955), *The Psychology of Personal Constructs,* Vol. 2. New York: W. W. Norton & Company.

138 / STRESS RESPONSE SYNDROMES

Kernberg, O., et al. (1972), Psychotherapy and psychoanalysis. *Bulletin of the Menninger Clinic,* 36:3-275.
Knight, R. (1971), Evaluation of research of psychoanalytic therapy. *American Journal of Psychiatry,* 98:434-446.
Koranyi, E. A. (1969), Psychodynamic theories of the "survivor" syndrome." *Canadian Psychiatric Association Journal,* 14:165-174.
Kubie, L. S. (1943), Manual of emergency treatment for acute war neuroses. *War Medicine,* 4:582-599.
Lidz, T. (1946), Psychiatric casualties from Guadalcanal. *Psychiatry,* 9:143-213.
Lifton, R. J. (1967), *History and Human Survival.* New York: Vantage Books.
Lifton, R. J. (1973), *Home from the War.* New York: Simon & Schuster.
Lindemann, E. (1944), Symptomatology and management of acute grief. *American Journal of Psychiatry,* 101:141-148.
Malan, D. H. (1963), *A Study of Brief Psychotherapy.* London: Tavistock.
Mann, J. (1973), *Time Limited Psychotherapy.* Cambridge: Harvard University Press.
Maskin, M. (1941), Psychodynamic aspects of the war neuroses. *Psychiatry,* 4:97-115.
Oremland, J. D. (1972), Transference cure and flight into health. *International Journal of Psychoanalytic Psychotherapy,* 1:61-75.
Ostwald, P. & Bittner, E. (1968), Life adjustment after severe persecution. *American Journal of Psychiatry,* 124:87-94.
Pumpian-Mindlin, E. (1953), Conspirations in the selection of patients for short-term psychotherapy. *American Journal of Psychotherapy,* 7:641-652.
Reider, N. (1953), Reconstruction and screen function. *Journal of the American Psychoanalytic Association,* 8:82-99.
Rioch, D. (1955), Problems of preventive psychiatry in war. In: *Psychopathology of Childhood,* ed. P. Hoch & D. Zubin. New York: Grune & Stratton.
Sachs, O. (1967), Distinctions between fantasy and reality elements in memory and reconstructions. *International Journal of Psychoanalysis,* 48:416-423.
Shatan, C. (1973), The grief of soldiers: Vietnam combat veterans' self-help movement. *American Journal of Orthopsychiatry,* 43:640-653.
Sifneos, P. (1972), *Short-Term Psychotherapy and Emotional Crisis.* Cambridge: Harvard University Press.
Socarides, C. W. (1954), On the use of extremely brief psychoanalytic contacts. *Psychoanalytic Review,* 41:340-346.
Solomon, G. F., et al. (1971), Three psychiatric casualties from Vietnam. *Archives of General Psychiatry,* 25:522-524.
Sterba, R. (1951), A case of brief psychotherapy by Sigmund Freud. *Psychoanalytic Review,* 38:75-80.
Stone, L. (1951), Psychoanalysis and brief psychotherapy. *Psychoanalytic Quarterly,* 20:215-236.
Straker, M. (1971), The survivor syndrome: Theoretical and therapeutic dilemmas. *Laval Médical,* 42:37-41.
Wolberg, L. (1967), *The Technique of Psychotherapy,* 2nd ed. New York: Grune & Stratton.
Zabriskie, E. & Brush, A. (1941), Psychoneuroses in wartime. *Psychosomatic Medicine,* 3:295-329.

Part IV
INDIVIDUAL VARIATIONS

CHAPTER EIGHT

Inhibitory Operations: Reaction to Stress and Psychotherapy with Hysterical Personalities

THE NEXT THREE CHAPTERS model methods for countering the tendency to intrusion and painful emotional response by three maneuvers: inhibition, switching, and altered valuation. Since the former has been frequently associated with "hysterical styles," the second with "obsessional styles," and the third with "narcissistic styles," appropriate historical backgrounds about these neurotic character patterns begin the discussion of each maneuver.

HISTORICAL BACKGROUND: HYSTERICAL STYLE

The concept of hysterical character was developed in the context of psychoanalytic studies of hysterical neuroses even though these neuroses may occur in persons without hysterical character and persons with hysterical styles do not necessarily develop hysterical neurotic symptoms. The discussion will develop the "ideal" typology of hysterical style with the assumption that most persons will have only some of the traits and no person will fit the stereotype perfectly.

The main symptoms of hysterical neuroses are either conversion reactions or dissociative episodes (Janet, 1907). Both symptoms sets have been related to dynamically powerful but repressed ideas and emotions that would be intolerable if they gained conscious expression (Breuer and Freud, 1895; Freud,

1893). In classical analytic theory, the intolerable ideas are a wish for a symbolically incestuous love object. The desire is discrepant with moral standards and so elicits guilt and fear. To avoid these emotions, the ideational and emotional cluster is warded off from awareness by repression and denial. Because the forbidden ideas and feelings press for expression, there are continuous threats, occasional symbolic or direct breakthroughs, and a propensity for traumatization by relevant external situations. While later theorists have added the importance of strivings for dependency and attention ("oral" needs), rage over the frustration of these desires, and the fusion of these strivings with erotic meanings, the correlation of hysterical symptoms with efforts at repression has been unquestioned (Easser and Lesser, 1965; Marmor, 1953; Ludwig, 1972).

Psychoanalysts view hysterical character as a configuration that either *predisposes* towards the development of conversion reactions, anxiety-attacks, and dissociative episodes or exists as a *separate entity* with similar impulse-defense configurations but different behavioral manifestations. The hysterical character is viewed as typically histrionic, exhibitionistic, labile in mood, and prone to act out unconscious fantasies without awareness.

Because of a proclivity for acting out oedipal fantasies, clinical studies suggest that hysterical persons are more than usually susceptible to stress response syndromes after seductions, especially those which are sadomasochistic, after a loss of persons or of positions which provided direct or symbolic attention or love, after a loss or disfigurement of body parts or attributes used to attract others, and after events associated with guilt about personal activity. In addition, any event that activates strong emotions such as erotic excitement, anger, anxiety, guilt, or shame would be more than usually stressful even though an hysteric might precipitate such experiences by his behavior patterns.

Clinical studies also indicate the kinds of responses that may be more frequent in the hysteric during and after the external stress event. Under stress the prototypical hysteric becomes emotional, impulsive, unstable, histrionic, and possibly disturbed in motor, perceptual and evaluative functions.

Styles of thought, felt emotion, and subjective experience are of central relevance to the present theses and have been described by Shapiro (1965). He emphasized the importance of impressionism and repression as part of the hysterical style of cognition. That is, the prototypical hysteric lacks a sharp focus of attention and arrives quickly at a global but superficial assumption of the meaning of perceptions, memories, fantasies, and felt emotions. There is a corresponding lack of factual detail and definition in perception plus distractability and incapacity for persistent or intense concentration. The historical continuity of such perceptual and ideational styles leads to a relatively non-factual world in which guiding schemata of self, objects, and environment have a flat, depthless quality.

Dwelling conceptually in this non-factual world promotes the behavioral traits of hysterical romance, emphasis on fantasy meanings, and *la belle indifference*. For example, the prototypic hysteric may react swiftly with an emotional outburst and yet remain unable to conceptualize what is happening and why such feelings occur. After the episode he may remember his own emotional experiences unclearly and will regard them as if visited upon him rather than self-instigated.

This general style of representation of perception, thought, and emotion leads to patterns observable in interpersonal relations, traits, and communicative styles. A tabular summary of what is meant by these components of hysterical style is presented under these headings in Table 1.

Shapiro's formulations differ from clinical psychoanalytic opinion in terms of the stability of such patterns. Shapiro regards the patterns as relatively fixed, perhaps the result of constitutional predisposition and childhood experiences. Other analysts regard these patterns as more likely to occur during conflict. The following discussion will not contradict either position since both allow us to assume a fixed baseline of cognitive-

TABLE 1

Summary of Patterns in the Hysterical Typology

INFORMATION PROCESSING STYLE
Short-order patterns—observe in flow of thought and emotion on a topic

—global deployment of attention
—unclear or incomplete representations of ideas and feelings, possibly with lack of details or clear labels in communication, non-verbal communications not translated into words or conscious meanings
—only partial or unidirectional associational lines
—short circuit to apparent completion of problematic thoughts.

TRAITS
Medium-order patterns—observe in interviews

—attention seeking behaviors, possibly including demands for attention, and/or the use of charm, vivacity, sex appeal, childlikeness
—fluid change in mood and emotion, possibly including breakthroughs of feeling
—inconsistency of apparent attitudes

INTERPERSONAL RELATIONS
Long-order patterns—observe in a patient's history

—repetitive, impulsive, stereotyped inter-personal relationships often characterized by victim-aggressor, child-parent, and rescue or rape themes
—"cardboard" fantasies and self-object attitudes
—drifting but possibly dramatic lives with an existential sense that reality is not really real.

emotional style and an intensification of such patterns during stress.

Controlling Thought and Emotion: Harry as "Hysteric"

Harry will now be considered as if he responded to stress and treatment in a typically hysterical manner. One of his six conflictual themes, as described earlier, will be used to clarify the hysterical mode of controlling thought and emotion. This theme concerns Harry's relief that he is alive when someone had to die (see Chapter 7, Table 1, A1).

Considered in microgenetic form, Harry's perceptions of the dead girl's body and his own bodily sensations of being alive are matched with his fear of finding himself dead. The discrepancy between his perceptions and his fears leads to feelings of relief. The sense of relief is then experienced.

In the context of the girl's death, relief is incongruent with moral strictures. Harry believes that he should share the fate of others rather than have others absorb bad fate. This discrepancy between current and enduring concepts leads to guilt. Harry has low toleration for strong emotions and the danger of experiencing guilt motivates efforts at controlling the representations that generate the emotions (see Fig. 1).

While controlling helps Harry escape unpleasant ideas and emotions, it impedes information processing. Were it not for controlling efforts, Harry might think again of the girl's death, his relief, his attitudes toward survival at her expense. He might realize that he was following unrealistic principles of thought and forgive himself for feeling relief. If thinking itself was not enough, he could undertake some act of penance and remorse. Repression prevents the thought or act that would change his attitude and reduce the discrepancy between his feelings and his sense of morality.

If repression is *what* Harry accomplishes, one can go further in microanalysis to indicate *how* it is accomplished in terms of cognitive operations. These operations can be abstracted as if they were in a hierarchy. The maneuver to try first in the hierarchy is inhibition of conscious representation. The initial perceptual images of the girl's body are too powerful to ward off and immediately after the accident Harry might have behaved in an "uncontrolled" hysterical style. Later, when defensive capacity was relatively stronger, the active memory images can be inhibited, counteracting the tendency towards repeated representation. Similarly, the initial ideas and feelings of relief might be too powerful to avoid, but later, as components of active memory, their reproductive tendency can be inhibited.

Suppose this inhibition fails or is only partly successful.

FIGURE 1

Harry as Utilizing Hysterical Modes of Control
by Inhibition of Representation

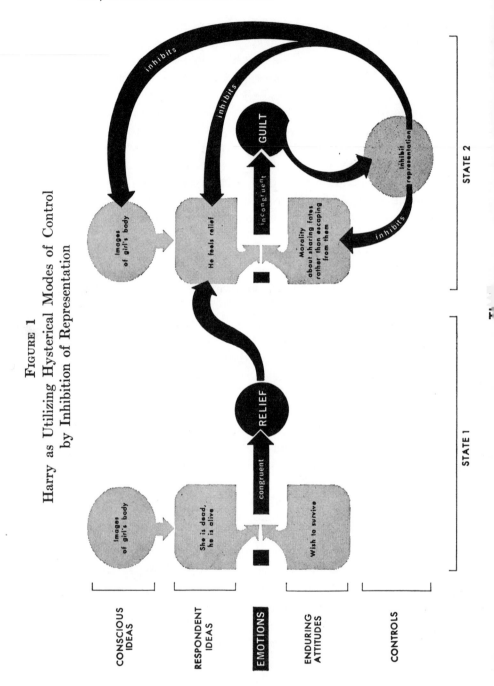

Warded-off ideas are expressed in some modality of representation. In a secondary maneuver, the extended meanings of the ideas can still be avoided by inhibition of translation from initial modes to other forms of representation. Harry could have only his visual images and avoid verbal concepts concerning death, relief, and causation.

A third maneuver is to prevent association to meanings that have been represented. This is again, hypothetically, an interruption of an automatic response tendency. Harry might conceptualize events in image and word forms but not continue in development of obvious associational connections. The purpose would be avoidance of full conscious awareness of threatening meanings.

These controlling efforts are three typically hysterical forms of inhibition: avoidance of representation, avoidance of translation of threatening information from one mode of representation to another, and avoidance of automatic associational connections. If these efforts fail to ward off threatening concepts, there are additional methods. A fourth maneuver is the reversal of role from active to passive. Harry could avoid thinking about his own active thoughts by deploying attention to how other factors (fate, the girl, the listener to his story) are involved. He could then change the attitude that he was alive because he *actively* wished to be alive even if another person died, by thinking of one's *passivity* with regard to fate, of the girl's activity in hitchhiking, and of how she got herself into the accident.

The fifth and last "hysterical" maneuver is alteration of state of consciousness. Metaphorically, if the hysteric cannot prevent an idea from gaining consciousness, he removes consciousness from the idea by changing the organization of thought and the sense of self. Harry used alcohol for this purpose, but no outside agents are necessary to enter a hypnoid state, with loss of reflective self awareness. These five cognitive maneuvers can be listed as if they were hierarchy of "rules" in the hysterical style for avoidance of unwanted ideas (Horowitz, in press).

1. Avoid representation
2. Avoid intermodal translation
3. Avoid automatic associational connections (and avoid conscious problem solving thought)
4. Change self attitude from active to passive (and vice versa)
5. Alter state of consciousness in order to (1) alter hierarchies of wishes and fears, (2) blur realities and fantasies, (3) dissociate conflicting attitudes, (4) alter the sense of self as instigator of thought and action.

The hysteric has further maneuvers, but these extend into longer time periods. Harry could manipulate situations so that some external person could be held responsible for his survival. This reduces the danger of a sense of guilty personal activity. In terms of very long-range maneuvers, Harry could characterologically avoid experiencing himself as ever fully real, aware, and responsible. He could identify himself with others, real or fantasied, which would make any act, or thought of crime, their responsibility and not his.

Clarity in Therapeutic Interventions: An Important Nuance with Persons Who Have Hysterical Style

If the person of hysterical style enters psychotherapy because of stress-response symptoms, the therapist will try to terminate the state of stress by helping him to complete the processing of the stress related ideas and feelings. This activity will include thinking through ideas, including latent conflicts activated by the event, experiencing emotions, and revising concepts to reduce discrepancies. The interpretation of defense may be useful to remove impediments to processing, but the main goal in the present model is to end or reduce a state of stress rather than to alter the character style. Even with such limited goals, character style must be understood and the usual therapy techniques used with appropriate nuances.

These nuances are versions, variations, or accentuations of major techniques such as clarification. One example is simple repetition of what the patient has said. The therapist may, by repeating a phrase, exert a marked effect on the hysteric who may respond with a startle reaction, surprise, laughter, or other emotional expressions. The same words uttered by the therapist mean something different from those thought or spoken by the hysteric himself; they are to be taken more seriously.

Additional meanings accrue and some meanings are also stripped away. For example, a guilty statement by Harry, repeated by the therapist in a neutral or kind voice, may seem less heinous. More explicitly, to call this "repetition" is to be correct only in a phonemic sense. Actually, the patient hears meanings more clearly, hears new meanings as well, and the previously warded-off contents and meanings may seem less dangerous when repeated by the therapist.

Simple repetition is, of course, not so "simple." The therapist selects particular phrases and may recombine phrases to clarify by connection of causal sequences. At first, when Harry was vague about survivorship, but said "I guess I am lucky to still be around," the therapist might just say "yes" to accentuate the thought. A fuller repetition, in other words such as "you feel fortunate to have survived," may also have progressive effects; it "forces" Harry closer to the potential next thought . . . "and she did not, so I feel badly about feeling relief."

Left to his own processes, Harry might have verbalized the various "ingredients" in the theme, might even have painfully experienced pangs of guilt and anxiety, and yet might still not have really "listened" to his ideas. In response to this vague style, the therapist may pull together scattered phrases: "You had the thought, 'Gee I'm glad to still be around, but isn't it awful to be glad when she's dead'?" Harry might listen to his own ideas through the vehicle of the therapist and work out his own reassurance or acceptance. This seems preferable to giving him permission by saying "You feel guilty over a thought that anyone would have in such a situation;" although this is, of course, sometimes necessary.

TABLE 2

Some of the "Defects" of the Hysterical Style and Their Counteractants in Therapy

Function	Style as "Defect"	Therapeutic Counter
Perception	Global or selective inattention	Ask for details
Representation	Impressionistic rather than accurate	"Abreaction" and reconstruction
Translation of images and enactions to words	Limited	Encourage talk Provide verbal labels
Associations	Limited by inhibitions Misinterpretations based on schematic stereotypes, deflected from reality to wishes and fears	Encourage production Repetition Clarification
Problem solving	Short circuit to rapid but often erroneous conclusions	Keep subject open Interpretations
	Avoidance of topic when emotions are unbearable	Support

As will be seen, these simple everyday maneuvers are not as effective with persons of obsessional style.

Other therapeutic maneuvers oriented toward helping the hysteric complete the processing of stressful events are equally commonplace. To avoid dwelling further on well known aspects of psychotherapy, some maneuvers are listed in tabular form as applicable to specific facets of hysterical style (Table 2). Each maneuver listed has additional nuances. For example, with some hysterics, interpretations or clarifications should be very short and simple, delivered in a matter of fact tone which would serve to counter their vagueness, emotionality, and tendency to elaborate any therapist activity into a fantasy relationship.

Nuances of Relationship with the Hysterical Patient in a State of Stress

Hysterical persons have a low toleration for emotion although they are associated with emotionality. One emotion is often used as a defense against some other emotion but even the substitute experience may get out of control. Because motivations are experienced as inexorable and potentially intolerable, the ideas that evoke emotion are inhibited. If toleration for the unpleasant emotions associated with a stressful event can be increased, then cognitive processing of that event can be resumed. The therapeutic relationship protects the patient from the dangers of internal conflict and potential loss of control and so operates to increase tolerance for warded-off ideas and feelings. The therapist effects the patient's sense of this relationship by his activities or restraint. How this is typically done is also a nuance of technique.

After a stress event, the hysterical patient often manifests swings from rigid over-control to uncontrolled intrusions and emotional repetition. During these swings, especially at the beginning and with a desperate patient, the therapist may oscillate between closeness and distance, staying always within the boundaries that characterize a therapeutic relationship.

The hysteric may consider it imperative to have care and attention. This imperative need has been called, at times, the "oral," "sick," or "bad" component of some hysterical styles (Easser and Lesser, 1965; Marmor, 1953; Lazare, 1971). During the period of imperative need, especially after a devastating stress event, the hysteric may need to experience sympathetic concern and support from the therapist. Without it, the therapeutic relationship will fall apart, the patient may regress or develop further psychopathology (Myerson, 1969). During this phase the therapist moves, in effect, closer to the patient: just close enough to provide necessary support and not so "close" as the patient *appears* to wish. This is not an endorsement of transference gratification, countertransference, or any advocacy of what has been called a "corrective emotional experience." It is simply a matter of the degree of support extended.

As the patient becomes more comfortable he may begin to feel anxiety at the degree of intimacy in the therapeutic relationship because there may be a fear of being seduced or enthralled by their own dependency wishes aimed at the therapist. The therapist then moves back to a "cooler," more "distant," or less "supportive" stance.

The therapist thus oscillates to keep the patient within a zone of safety by sensitive modification of his manner of relating to the patient. Safety allows the patient to move in the direction of greater conceptual clarity (Sandler, 1960; Weiss, 1971). Naturally, the therapist's manner includes his nonverbal and verbal cues. This is what the therapist allows himself to do in the context of his own real responses and qualities of being. This is not role playing. The therapist allows or inhibits his own response tendencies as elicited by the patient.

If the therapist does not oscillate in from a relatively distant position, and if the patient has urgent needs for stabilizing his self-concept through relational support, then the discrepancy between need and supply will be so painful that the patient will find it unendurable to expose problematic lines of thought. Inhibition would continue. If the therapist does not oscillate from a relatively close position to a more distant one, then conceptual processing will begin but transference issues will cloud working through the stress response syndrome. Neither clarity nor oscillation by the therapist may be a suitable nuance of technique with the obsessional.

BIBLIOGRAPHY

Breuer, J. & Freud, S. (1895), Studies on hysteria. *Standard Edition, 2.* London: Hogarth Press.

Easser, R. R. & Lesser, S. R. (1965), Hysterical personality: A re-evaluation. *Psychoanalytic Quarterly,* 34:390-405.

Freud, S. (1893), On the psychical mechanism of hysterical phenomena. *Standard Edition, 3.* London: Hogarth Press, 1962.

Horowitz, M. Hysterical personality: Cognitive structure and the process of change. *International Journal of Psycho-Analysis,* in press.

Janet, P. (1907), *The Major Symptoms of Hysteria.* New York: Hafner Publishing Company, 1965.

Lazare, A. (1971), The hysterical character in psychoanalytic theory. *Archives of General Psychiatry,* 25:131-137.

Ludwig, A. M. (1972), Hysteria: A neurobiological theory. *Archives of General Psychiatry,* 27:771-777.

Marmor, J. (1953), Orality in the hysterical personality. *Journal of the American Psychoanalytic Association,* 1:656-675.

Myerson, P. G. (1969), The hysteric's experience in psychoanalysis. *International Journal of Psycho-Analysis,* 50:373-384.

Sandler, J. (1960), The background of safety. *International Journal of Psycho-Analysis,* 41:352-356.

Shapiro, D. (1965), *Neurotic Styles.* New York: Basic Books.

Weiss, J. (1971), The emergence of new themes: A contribution to the psychoanalytic theory of therapy. *International Journal of Psycho-Analysis,* 53: 429-467.

CHAPTER NINE

Switching Maneuvers: Reaction to Stress and Psychotherapy with Obsessional Personalities

INHIBITORY CONTROLS ARE, after all, a capacity. Some persons may have different predispositions or learning opportunities and therefore vary in their ability to inhibit emergent information. Even with a strong inhibitory capacity, other avoidance operations may be necessary to ward off a powerful theme. Another common maneuver of defense is switching to alternate themes. These alternative mental contents jam representational systems and prevent painful recognition of the warded-off contents. This type of operation is commonly linked to obsessional style.

Historical Background: The Concept of Obsessional Style

Contemporary theory of obsessional style evolved from analysis of neurotic obsessions, compulsions, doubts, and irrational fears. Abraham (1942), Freud (1909), and Fenichel (1945) believed the obsessional neuroses to be secondary to regressions to or fixations at the anal-sadistic phase of psychosexual development. The manifestations of the neurosis were seen as compromises between aggressive or sexual impulsive aims and defenses such as isolation, reaction formation, intellectualization, and undoing. Underneath a rational consciousness, ambivalent and magical thinking were prominent. Common conflicts were formed in the interaction of aggressive impulses and predispositions to rage, fears of assault and rigid and harsh attitudes of morality and duty. These conflicts lead to the coexistence and fluctuation of dominance and submission themes in interpersonal relationships and fantasies.

Salzman (1968) emphasized the obsessional's sense of being driven, his strivings for omniscience and control, and his concerns for the magical effects of hostile thoughts. Homosexual thoughts may also intrude, although often without homosexual behavior.

Vagueness seems less possible for the obsessional than the hysteric. Since they tend more toward acute awareness of ideas, staying with one position threatens to lead to unpleasant emotions. Seeing the self as dominant is associated with sadism to others and leads to guilt. Seeing the self as submissive is associated with weakness and fears of assaults; hence, this position evokes anxiety. Alternation between opposing poles, as in alternation between sadistic-dominance themes and homosexual-submissive themes, serves to undo the danger of remaining at either pole (Sampson and Weiss, 1972; Weiss, 1967).

To avoid stabilization at a single position, and to accomplish the defense of undoing, obsessionals often use the cognitive operation of shifting from one aspect of a theme to an oppositional aspect and back again. The result is continuous change. At the expense of decision and decisiveness, the obsessional maintains a sense of control and avoids emotional threats (Barnett, 1972; Schwartz, 1972; Silverman, 1972).

While the obsessional moves so rapidly that emotions do not gain full awareness, he or she cannot totally eliminate feelings. Some obsessionals have intrusions of feelings either in minor quasi-ideational form, as expressed in slips of the tongue or intrusive images, or in major forms as expressed in attacks of rage. Even when this occurs, however, the event can be undone by what Saltzman calls "verbal juggling." This process includes alterations of meaning, the use of formulas to arrive at attitudes or plans, shifts in valuation from over- to underestimation, and, sometimes, the attribution of magical properties to word labels.

Shapiro (1965) has described how the narrowed focus of the mode of attention of the obsessional person misses certain aspects of the world while it engages others in detail. Ideal flexibility of attention involves smooth shifts between sharply directed attention and more impressionistic forms of cognition. The obsessional lacks such fluidity.

He also describes how the obsessional is driven in the course of his thought, emotion, and behavior by "shoulds" and "oughts" dictated by a sense of duty, by his fears of loss of control, and by his need to inhibit recognition of his "wants." In spite of his usual capacity for hard work, productivity, and "will power," the obsessional person may experience difficulty and discomfort when a decision is to be made. Instead of deciding on the basis of wishes and fears, the obsessional must maintain a sense of omnipotence and therefore must avoid the dangerous mistakes inherent in a trial-and-error world. The decision among possible choices is likely to rest either on a rule evoked to guarantee a "right" decision or else is made on impulse, to end the anxiety. The result of these cognitive styles is an experiential distance from felt emotion. The exception is feelings of anxious self-doubt, a mood instigated by the absence of true cognitive closure.

This brief discussion has focused on aspects of cognitive style. These are summarized with common traits and patterns of behavior in Table 1.

Obsessional Tendencies of Response to Stress

Stressful events may so compel interest that there may be little difference in the initial registration and experience of persons with hysterical or obsessional style. But, short of extreme disasters, the obsessional person may remain behaviorally calm and emotionless in contrast to the emotional explosions of the hysteric. There are exceptions, of course, to such generalizations. It should be noted that during some events, obsessionals may become quite emotional and hysterics may remain calm. The difference remains in the quality of the person's conscious

Table 1

Summary of Patterns in Obsessional Typology

INFORMATION PROCESSING STYLE

Short-order patterns—observe in flow of thought and emotion on a topic

—detailed; sharp focus of attention on details

—clear representation of ideas, meager representation of emotions

—may shift organization and implications of ideas rather than follow an associational line to conclusion as directed by original intent or intrinsic meanings

—avoid completion on decision or a given problem, instead switch back and forth between attitudes

TRAITS

Medium-order patterns—observe in interviews

—doubt, worry, productivity and/or procrastination

—single-minded, unperturable, intellectualizer

—tense, deliberate, unenthusiastic

—rigid, ritualistic

INTERPRERSONAL RELATIONS

Long-order patterns—observe in a patient's history

—develop regimented, routine and continuous interpersonal relationships low in "life," vividness, or pleasure. Often frustrating to "be" with

—prone to dominance-submission themes

—duty-filler, hard worker, seeks or makes strain and pressure, do what he "should" do rather than what he decides to do

—experiences himself as remote from emotional connection with others although feels committed to operating with others because of role or principles

experience. The hysterical person can have a "hysterical calm" because it is based on an inhibition of some aspects of potential knowledge, no emotion occurs because the implications of the stressful event are not known. If and when the obsessional behaves emotionally, it may be experienced by him as a loss of control, one to be "undone" by retrospective shifts of meaning, rituals, apologies, or self-recriminations.

After a stressful event, the obsessional and the hysteric may both exhibit similar general stress response tendencies, including phases of denial and intrusion. But they may differ in their stability in any given phase. The obsessional may be able to maintain the period of emotional numbing with greater stability, the hysteric may be able to tolerate phases of episodic intrusions with more apparent stability and less narcissistic injury.

During the oscillatory phase, when the uncompleted images and ideas of the current stressful concepts tend to repeated and intrusive representation, the hysteric is likely to inhibit representation to ward off these unwelcome mental contents. The obsessional may be precise and clear in describing the intrusive images, but may focus on details related to "duty," for example, and away from the simple emotion evoking meanings of the gestalt of the image.

It is during the oscillatory phase of both intrusions and warding-off maneuvers that styles stand out in starkest form. Instead of, or in addition to, repressive maneuvers as listed earlier, the obsessional responds to threatened repetitions with cognitive maneuvers such as shifting. By a shift to "something else," the obsessional is able to jam cognitive channels and prevent emergence or endurance of warded-off contents, or to so shift meanings as to stifle emotional arousal. That is, by shifting from topic to topic, or from one meaning to another meaning of the same topic, the emotion arousing properties of one set of implications are averted.

Controlling Thought and Emotion: Harry as an Obsessive

To model Harry as using switching operations to avoid the hazard of strong emotions, a time in psychotherapy is considered when Harry begins to talk of the unbidden images of the girl's body. At this period in therapy he begins to associate to his memory of feeling relieved to be alive. The next conceptualization, following the idealized line of working through outlined earlier, *would be* association of his relieved feelings with ideas of survival at her expense. This cluster *would be* matched against moral strictures counter to such personal gain through damage to others, and Harry *would* go on to conceptualize his emotional experience of guilt or shame (Chapter 7, Table 1, A1). Once this was clear, he could revise his schematic belief that someone had to die, accept his relief, feel remorse, even plan a penance, and reduce incongruity through one or more of these changes.

Harry does not follow this idealized route because the potential of these emotional experiences is appraised as intolerable at a not fully conscious level of information processing. A switch is made to another ideational cycle in order to avoid the first one. The second cycle is also associatively related to the images of the girl's body.

A common element in both ideational cycles allows a pivotal change and reduces awareness that the subtopic has changed. The pivot for the switch is the idea of bodily damage. In the second ideational cluster the concept is that bodily damage could happen to him, perhaps at any future time, since it has now happened to her. Through the comparison between his wishes for invulnerability and his dread of vulnerability, fear is aroused (Chapter 7, Table 1, B1 and Figure 1 of this Chapter).

While fear is unpleasant and threatening as a potential experience, the switch allows movement away from the potential feelings of guilt (theme A1). When the second theme (B1) becomes too clear, fear might be consciously experienced. The procedure can be reversed with return to A1. Harry can oscillate in terms of conscious and communicative meanings between A1 and B1 without either set of dangerous ideas and emotions being fully experienced.

Harry need not limit switching operations to the two contexts for ideas about bodily damage. He can switch between any permutations of any themes. He can transform, reverse, or undo guilt with fear or anger (Jones, 1929). He can see himself as victim, then aggressor, then victim and so forth. These shifts dampen emotional responsivity but reduce cognitive processing of themes.

This does not imply that inhibition of representation will not be found in an obsessional version of Harry or shifts of theme

FIGURE 1

Harry as Utilizing Obsessional Modes of Control by Switching Ideational Themes

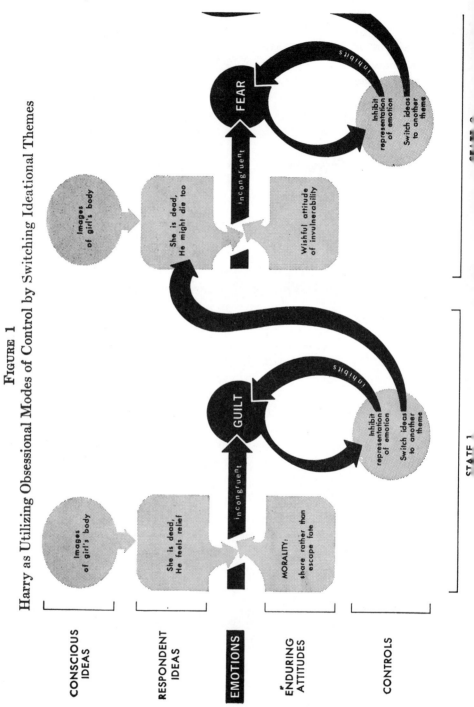

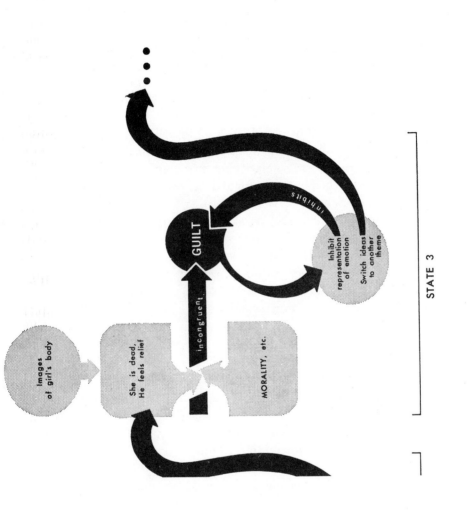

will be absent in hysterical versions of Harry. An obsessional Harry might attempt inhibitions and use his shifts when inhibitory efforts fail. A hysterical Harry might shift from active to passive, as noted earlier, but timing and quality of the shifts would differ. Obsessional Harry would tend to shift more rapidly, with less vagueness at either pole. The shift could occur in mid-phrase, between an utterance of his and a response from the therapist, or even as virtually simultaneous trains of thought.

It is because of rapid shifts that therapists who attempt clarity with obsessionals may be thwarted in their task. Suppose the therapist makes a clarifying intervention about A1, the survivor guilt theme. Obsessional Harry may have already shifted to B1, his fear of body injury, and thus hear the remarks in a non-congruent state. The clarification procedure may not work well because Harry was not unclear or vague in the first place, is not listening from the earlier position, and will undo the therapist's intervention by further shifts. An interpretation to the effect that Harry fears bodily damage as a retribution for his survivor relief and guilt would be premature since, at this point, he has not fully experienced either the fear or the guilt.

Holding to Context: An Important Nuance with Persons Who Habitually Use Switching Maneuvers

Holding a person who shifts to a topic or to a given context within a topic is equivalent to clarifying for the person who typically inhibits ideas. Metaphorically, the switcher avoids conceptual time where the inhibitor avoids conceptual space. The goal of holding is reduction of shifting so that the patient can progress further along a given conceptual process. The patient must also be helped to tolerate the emotions that will be experienced when he cannot quickly divert ideas into and out of conscious awareness.

Holding to context is more complicated than clarification. One begins with at least two current problems, such as the dual themes of A1 and B1 in Harry. When the patient is not shifting with extreme rapidity, the therapist may simply hold the patient to either one or the other theme.

The patient will not comply with this maneuver and the therapist must not confuse "holding" with "forcing." Ferenczi (1926), in an effort to speed up analysis, experimented with various ways to make the obsessional stay on topic until intensely felt emotions occurred. For example, he insisted that his patient develop and maintain visual fantasies relevant to a specific theme. During this technical maneuver his obsessional patients did experience emotions, they even had affective explosions, but the transference complications impeded rather than enhanced the therapy.

The therapist has to shift, even though he attempts to hold the patient to a topic. That is, the therapist shifts at a slower rate than the patient, like a dragging anchor that slows the process. This operation increases the progress of the patient in both directions. That is, with each shift, he is able to go a bit further along the conceptual route of either theme, even though he soon becomes frightened and crowds the theme out of mind with an alternative.

The therapist may use repetitions, as with the hysteric, in order to hold or slow the shift of an obsessional patient. But this use of the same maneuver is done with a different nuance. With the inhibitor, the repetition heightens the meaning of what the patient is *now* saying. With the switcher, the repetition goes back to what the patient was saying *before* the shift away from the context occurred. With the hysteric, the repetition may be short phrases. With the obsessional, greater length may be necessary, in order to state the specific context that is being warded off. For example, if Harry is talking about bodily damage and shifts from a survivor guilt context to his fears of injury, then a repetition by the therapist has to link bodily damage specifically to the survivor guilt theme. With the hysteric, such wordy interventions might only diminish clarity.

At times, this more extensive repetition in the obsessional may include the technique of going back to the very beginning of an exchange, retracing the flow carefully, and indicating where extraneous or only vaguely relevant details were introduced by the patient. Reconstruction may add warded off details. This technique has been suggested for long-term character analysis (Weiss, 1971; Salzman, 1968), during which defensive operations are interpreted so that the patient increases conscious control and diminishes unconscious restrictions on ideas and feelings. In shorter therapy, aimed at working through a stress, this extensive repetition is still useful, because during the review by the therapist, the patient attends to the uncomforable aspects of the topic.

Increased time on the topic allows more opportunity for processing and hence moves the patient towards completion. Emotions aroused by the flow of ideas are more tolerable within the therapeutic relationship than for the patient alone. Also, time on the topic and with the therapist allows continued processing in a communicative state, emphasizing reality and problem solving rather than fantasy and magical belief systems. Identification with and externalization onto the relatively neutral therapist also allows temporary reduction in rigid and harsh introjects which might otherwise deflect thought.

Focusing on details is sometimes a partial deterrent to shifting in the obsessional just as it may aid clarity with the hysteric. The nuances of focusing on details differ because the purposes differ. In general, the aim with the hysteric is to move from concrete, experiential information, such as images, toward more abstract or more extended meanings such as word labels for activities and things. The aim with the obsessional is to move from abstract levels, where shifts are facile, to a concrete context. Details act as pegs of meaning in concrete contexts, and make shifts of attitude more difficult. This maneuver utilizes the obsessionals predisposition to details but allows the therapist to specifically select them. Again, the nuance of asking for concrete details is part of the general aim of increasing conceptualization time.

In states where shifts are so rapid as to preclude simple repetition or questioning, the therapist may use a more complex form of repetition. The therapist repeats the event, for example, Harry's intrusive image of the girl's body, and then repeats the disparate attitudes that the patient oscillates between in a single package. For example, the therapist might tell Harry that the image of the girl's body led to two themes. One was the idea of relief at being spared from death that made him feel frightened and guilty. The other was the idea of bodily harm to himself. Were the rate of oscillation less rapid, this form of "packaged" intervention would not be as necessary, since simpler holding operations may be sufficient and the therapist can focus on a single theme.

These efforts by the therapist encroach on the habitual style of the patient. The patient may respond by minimizing or exaggerating the meaning of the intervention. The obsessional is especially vulnerable to threats to his sense of omniscience, especially after traumatic events. If the therapist holds him on a topic, the obsessional senses warded-off ideas and feelings and develops uncertainties which cause his self-esteem to fall.

To protect the patient's self-esteem, the therapist uses another technical nuance. He uses questioning to accomplish clarification and topic deepening, even when he has an interpretation in mind. The questions aim the patient toward answers that contain the important, warded off, but now emerging ideas. The obsessional patient can then credit himself with expressing these ideas and experiencing these feelings. The therapist with the hysterical person might, in contrast, interpret at such a moment, using a firm, short delivery, since a question might be followed by vagueness.

To the obsessional, incisive interpretations often mean that the therapist knows something he does not know. A transference bind over dominance and submission arises as the patient either rebels against the interpretation with stubborn denial, accepts it meekly without thinking about it, or both.

Timing is also important with obsessionals working through stress-activated themes. After experience with a given patient,

TABLE 2

Some of the "Defects" of Obsessional Style and Their Counteractant in Therapy

Function	Style as "Defect"	Therapeutic Counter
Perception	Detailed and Factual	Ask for overall impressions and statements about emotional experiences
Representation	Isolation of ideas from emotions	Link emotional meanings to ideational meanings
Translation of images to words	Misses emotional meaning in a rapid transition to partial word meanings	Focus attention on images and felt reactions to them
Associations	Shifts sets of meanings back and forth	Holding operations Interpretation of defense and of warded off meanings
Problem solving	Endless rumination without reaching decisions	Interpretation of reasons for warding off clear decisions

the therapist intuitively knows when a shift is about to take place. At just that moment, or a trifle before, the therapist asks his question. This interrupts the shift and increases conceptual "time and space" on the topic about to be warded off. These technical nuances are put in a crude, broad context in Table 2.

Nuances of Relationship with Obsessional Patients in a State of Stress

The oscillation in degree of support described as sometimes necessary with the hysterical style in extreme stress is not as advisable with the obsessional style. Instead, the therapist creates a safe situation for the patient by remaining stable within his own clear boundaries (e.g., objectivity, compassion, understanding, concern for the truth, or whatever are his own personal and professional traits).

The patient learns the limits of the therapist within this frame. It gives him faith that the therapist will react neither harshly nor seductively. This trust increases *the patient's* breadth of oscillation. He can express more aggressive ideas if he knows the therapist will neither submit, be injured, compete for dominance, or accuse him of evil. Harry could express more of his bodily worries when he knew the therapist would not himself feel guilty or overresponsible.

If the therapist changes with the obsessional's tests or needs, then the obsessional worries that he may be too powerful, too weak, or too "sick" for the therapist to handle. Also, the obsessional may use the situation to externalize warded-off ideas or even defensive maneuvers. The therapist shifts, not he. This is not to say the obsessional does not, at times, need kindly support after disastrous external events. But his propensity for shifting makes changes in the degree of support more hazardous than a consistent attitude, whether kindly supportive, neutral-tough, or otherwise.

Suppose the therapist becomes more kindly as Harry goes through a turbulent period of emotional expression of guilt over survival. Harry may experience this as an increase in the therapist's concern or worry over him. He might shift from the "little" suffering position that elicited the therapist's reaction, to a "big" position from which he looks down with contempt at the "worried" therapist.

Similarly, if the therapist is not consistently tough-minded, in the ordinary sense of insisting on information and truth-telling, but shifts to this stance only in response to the patient's stubborn evasiveness, then the patient can shift from strong stubbornness to weak, vulnerable self concepts. Within the context of this shift, the therapist comes to be experienced as hostile, demeaning and demanding.

Unlike the hysteric, then, the obsessional's shifts in role and attitude within the therapeutic situation are likely to be out of phase with changes in demeanor of the therapist. The obsessional can chance further and more lucid swings in state when he senses the stability of the therapist.

Transference resistance will occur despite the therapist's efforts to maintain a therapeutic relationship. The "stability of the therapist" will be exaggerated by the patient into an omniscience that he will continually test. When negative transference reactions occur, the therapist will act to resolve those that interfere with the goals of therapy. But some transference reactions will not be negative even though they act as resistances. The hysteric may demand attention and halt progress to get it. The obsessional may take an oppositional stance not so much out of hostility or stubborness, although such factors will be present, as out of a need to avoid the dangerous intimacy of agreement and cooperation. Since the therapist is not aiming at analysis of transference to effect character change, he need not interpret this process. Instead, with an obsessional patient in an oppositional stance, he may word his interventions to take advantage of the situation.

That is, interventions can be worded, when necessary, in an oppositional manner. Suppose Harry was talking about picking up the girl and the therapist knew he was predisposed to feeling guilty but was warding it off. With an hysterical Harry the therapist might say, "You feel badly about picking up the girl." With an obsessional and cooperative Harry he might say, "Could you be blaming yourself for picking up the girl?" With an oppositional obsessional stance, the therapist might say, "So you don't feel at all badly about picking up the girl." This kind of Harry may disagree and talk of his guilt feelings.

To summarize, holding to a topic or subtopic is a nuance of technique used to help persons disposed to switching types of warding-off maneuvers to complete the processing of stress related ideas. Clarity, while useful with those who inhibit, is not as directly helpful with the switcher who may require both clarity and holding to a topic. Distortion of meanings, a third type of control maneuver, is used frequently to avoid conflictual ideas triggered by stress events, and requires other nuances of technique, illustrated in the next chapter.

BIBLIOGRAPHY

Abraham, K (1942), A short study of the development of the libido, viewed in the light of mental disorders. In: *Selected Papers*. London: Hogarth Press.

Barnett, J. (1972), Therapeutic intervention in the dysfunctional thought processes of the obsessional. *American Journal of Psychotherapy*, 26:338-351.

Fenichel, O. (1945), *The Psychoanalytic Theory of Neurosis*. New York: Norton.

Ferenczi, S. (1926), *Further Contributions to the Theory and Technique of Psychoanalysis*. London: The Hogarth Press and the Institute of Psychoanalysis, 1950.

Freud, S. (1909), Notes upon a case of obsessional neurosis. *Standard Edition*, 10:155-318. London: Hogarth Press, 1955.

Jones, E. (1929), Fear, guilt, and hate. *International Journal of Psycho-Analysis*, 10:383-397.

Salzman, L. (1968), *The Obsessive Personality*. New York: Science House.

Sampson, H. & Weiss, J. (1972), Defense analysis and the emergence of warded off mental conflicts: An empirical study. *Archives of General Psychiatry*, 26:524-532.

Schwartz, E. K. (1972), The treatment of the obsessive patient in the group therapy setting. *American Journal of Psychohrapy*, 26:352-361.

Shapiro, D. (1965), *Neurotic Styles*. New York: Basic Books, Inc.

Silverman, J. S. (1972), Obsessional disorders in childhood and adolescence. *American Journal of Psychotherapy*, 26:362-377.

Weiss, J. (1967), The integration of defenses. *International Journal of Psycho-Analysis*, 48:520-524.

Weiss, J. (1971), The emergence of new themes: A contribution to the psychoanalytic theory of therapy. *International Journal of Psycho-Analysis*, 52:549-567.

CHAPTER TEN

Sliding Meanings: Reaction to Stress and Psychotherapy with Narcissistic Personalities

NARCISSISM HAS BEEN REGARDED as an important aspect of human character throughout recorded history. It is summarized in Ecclesiastes, "Vanity of vanities, all is vanity." Freud's (1914) explorations of the unconscious led him to emphasize the compensatory nature of such vanity, and Adler (1916) centered a psychology on inferiority and narcissistic compensations for deflated self concepts. Recently, there has been a major resurgence of interest in the psychodynamics of the narcissistic character (Kohut, 1966, 1968, 1971, 1972; Kernberg, 1970, 1974). Pertinent to such interest is the question of how persons of narcissistic character respond to the inevitable stresses of life such as injury or loss. The typical narcissistic response of sliding meanings is contrasted with the classical typologies of the hysteric and obsessional, as well as the nuances of therapy that help to alter this defensive avoidance.

BACKGROUND

Freud (1914) used the concept of narcissism as a polarity between self-centeredness and relationships with others. He characterized some syndromes as "narcissistic neuroses." This now defunct term meant syndromes characterized by a withdrawal of interest in others. The contrasting set of syndromes were called "transference neuroses" in which interest, however distorted, remained centered on other persons. This duality was based on a theoretical position that psychic energy, in the form of libido, was distributed either towards the self or toward objects, that libido was in limited supply so that increased self-concern would mean decreased concern with others (Hartmann, 1964).

This theory has since been rejected because it does not conform well enough with clinical observations. Instead, the development of self-interest and self-concepts is now seen in two simultaneously, interrelated, but partially independent series. In one series the self-representation and self-regard is gradually evolved as an independent function. In the other series there is interdependence of one person and another, that is, self-representation and self-regard are gradually evolved in relationship to the development of object representations, object interests, and patterns of self and object transaction (Kohut, 1971). Increased narcissism can be motivated by either a need to compensate for a deflated self-concept, without associated withdrawal of interest from objects, or by a problem in relationships with others that must be handled by increased self-interest (Kernberg, 1970).

In the narcissistic character, an exquisite vulnerability of the self-concept is hypothesized to underlie a more superficial self-love, grandiosity, or idealization of others regarded as appendages to the self (self-objects). In psychoanalytic reconstructions, vulnerability of the self, the tendency to discohesive self-images under stress, has been traced to difficulties during the period of differentiating the self from the mother or other early parenting figure (Mahler, 1968). Dominance of narcissistic traits in either or both parents may predispose a child to difficulties in developing a flexible, accurate, and independent self-presentation because the parents may treat the child as if he were a function of themselves rather than a separate entity.

Being an only child or having a real or "special endowment" projected by a parent may build a sense of unusual importance into the child, one that is doomed to a rude awakening when he moves socially beyond the nuclear family. That is, any atmosphere that encourages and gratifies inflated self-representations will also predispose a child to traumas when realistic limitations, inability to perform, or depreciating types of interpersonal treatment are encountered. Such encounters will also occur in the family when the child develops enough will and ability to contest parental superiority and power, and to feel betrayed and let down when his own power is insufficient to achieve his own goals.

Narcissistic Responses to Stress

When the habitual narcissistic gratifications that come from being adored, given special treatment, and admiring the self are threatened, the results may be depression, hypochondriasis, anxiety, shame, self-destructiveness, or rage directed toward any other person who can be blamed for the troubled situation. The child can learn to avoid these painful emotional states by acquiring a narcissistic mode of information processing. Such learning may be by trial and error methods, or it may be internalized by identification with parental modes of dealing with stressful information. The central pillar of this narcissistic style is polarization of good and bad, with externalization of bad attributes and internalization of good attributes in order to stabilize the self-concept. These operations demand distortion of reality and imply either a willingness to corrupt fidelity to reality, a low capacity to appraise and reappraise reality and fantasy, or a high capacity to disguise the distortions. The disguises are accomplished by shifting meanings and using exaggeration and minimization of bits of reality as a nidus for fantasy elaboration.

Distortions in the self-concept, achieved by selective externalizations often lead to various clusters of self-related information. That is, the narcissistic mode of information processing predisposes the child to several sets of self-representations as well as incompletely developed and unrealistic sets of object representations.

Three co-existent but split part self-concepts that are common in narcissistic personalities have been described by Kohut (1971). They are (1) the grandiose self in which there is an inflated, exaggerated, exhibitionistic self-image, (2) the low esteem, shamed, and vulnerable self-image, and (3) the dangerously chaotic, shattered, discohesive self image. Complimentary images for parental figures are maintained and include the idealized figure who, by caring or attending, will bolster low self-esteem and inflate it by reflections of "glory," as well as the mirroring figure who will support the grandiose self-image by serving as admirer, source of praise, and evidence of personal power.

These prototypical distorted self and object representations are heavily balanced towards self-concern, and interpersonal relations will be more characterized by "I-it" than "I-Thou" relationships as described by Buber (1923). Issues of power and control, also common in obsessional personalities, will be prominent in interpersonal relations, but with important differences. The obsessional is involved in an intrapsychic and perhaps interpersonal struggle over the distribution of power between himself and a significant other. The goal is gratification of certain interpersonal desires or avoidance of certain interpersonal threats. The narcissistic personality is concerned with possessing the power to enhance his *own* sense of competence and control, or with self-enhancement through affiliation with a powerful person. Similarly, the obsessional and the hysteric may wish to be admired by another person as part of a core wish for closeness; this may even include homosexual closeness. The narcissistic personality also desires admiration from the other person, but the core of this desire is the use of admiration or closeness for maintenance of self-esteem.

The narcissistic personality is especially vulnerable to personal deflations or losses of those who support his self-concept. When faced with such stress events as criticism, loss of self-objects, withdrawal of praise, or humiliation, the information involved may be denied, disavowed, negated, or shifted in meaning to prevent a reactive state of rage, depression, or shame. If such measures should fail, in addition to externalization of bad attributes and internalization of good qualities, there may be a shift not only in affect but in global "being." This change in state includes changes in self-imagery, demeanor, and style. If the stress event, for example, criticism of the person, leads to a mild level of threat, then the behavioral response may be an increased effort toward obtaining external "narcissistic supplies." That is, there may be a search for other persons to erase criticism, supply praise, or provide, by idealized power, a useful umbrella that can be extended over the self. Much like the hysterical personality, there will be efforts to woo or win attention from sources which enhance self-esteem.

If the stress event is of greater magnitude, or if restorative efforts as outlined above should fail, then narcissistic types of deviation from realistic information processing occur more prominently. The goal of these deflections from knowing reality, is to prevent a potentially catastrophic state in which a cohesive sense of self is lost. The hazard is not simply guilt because ideals have not been met. The loss of a good and coherent self feeling, if it occurs, is associated with intensely experienced emotions such as shame and depression, plus an anguished sense of helplessness and disorientation. *To prevent this state, the narcissistic personality slides the meanings of events in order to place the self in a better light.* That which is good is labeled as of the self (internalization). Those qualities that are undesirable, are excluded from the self by denial of their existence, disavowal of related attitudes, externalization, and negation of recent self-expressions. Persons who function as accessories to the self may also be idealized by exaggeration of their attributes. Those who counter the self are depreciated.

Such fluid shifts in meanings permit the narcissistic personality to maintain apparent logical consistency while minimizing "evil" or weakness and exaggerating innocence or control. As part of these maneuvers, the narcissistic personality may assume attitudes of contemptuous superiority towards others, emotional coldness, or even desperately charming approaches to idealized figures.

Reality testing and reality-fantasy differentiation are not as readily lost in the narcissistic personality as in borderline or psychotic personalities. But the distorted meanings force further distortions as cover-ups. The resulting complications lend a subjectively experienced shakiness or uncertainty to ideational structures. Lapses in these defensive arrangements of ideas may occur during states of stress. Rages or paranoid states may occur as may episodes of panic, shame, or depersonalization. Self-destructive acts may be motivated by wishes to end such pain, to achieve a "rebirth," to harm the offending self, to feel something, and for achievement of secondary gains such as obtaining sympathy or enacting a "wounded hero" role.

These and other attributes of the narcissistic personality are summarized in Table 1.

Controlling Thought and Emotion: Harry as a Narcissist

To recapitulate, during Harry's psychotherapy, several conflictual themes activated by the accident became apparent. Prominent among these were feelings of fear that he might have been killed, guilt over his own sexual ideas, guilt for "causing" the death of the hitchhiker, remose for feeling relieved upon realizing he was alive and she was dead, and anger at her and the other driver for causing the accident.

Let us consider one of these various themes, worked through in different phases of therapy. The presumed context, now, is the time in psychotherapy when Harry is talking about the intrusive images of the girl's body and the association between these images and ideas about his own vulnerability to death. Conceiving his possible death is highly incongruous with Harry's wishful attitude of invulnerability. The hazard of the incompatibility of these ideas is especially great for a narcissistic per-

Table 1

Summary of Patterns in the Narcissistic Typology

INFORMATION PROCESSING STYLE
Short-order patterns—observe in thought and emotions on a topic

—Slides meanings of information that might damage self-concept. Also uses denial, disavowal, and negation for this purpose.
—Attention to sources of praise and criticism.
—Shifts subject-object focus of meanings, externalizes bad attributes, internalizes good attributes.
—Occasionally maintains incompatible psychological attitudes in separate clusters.

TRAITS
Medium-order patterns—observe in interviews

—Self-centered.
—Overestimates or understimates self and others.
—Self-enhancement (or pseudohumility): in accomplishments real or fantasied, in garb or demeanor.
—Avoids self-deflating situations.
—Variability in demeanor, depending on state of self-esteem and context, common demeanors include:
  —charm, "wooing-winning" quality, controlling efforts, charisma
  —superiority, contemptuousness, coldness or withdrawal
  —shame, panic, helplessness, hypochondriasis, depersonalization or self-destructiveness
  —envy, rage, paranoia, or demands

INTERPERSONAL RELATIONS
Long-order patterns—observe in patient's history

—Often impoverished interpersonally *or* oriented to power over others *or* controlling use of others as accessories (self-objects).
—Absence of "I-Thou" feelings.
—Social climbing or using others for positive reflection.
—Avoidance of self-criticism by goading others to *unfair* criticism.
—Discarding or even depreciating persons no longer of use to them.

sonality since he has to maintain a brittle, but inviolately ideal, self image.

Conceptually experienced, the incongruity tends to evoke fear beyond a level of toleration. Controls are instituted to prevent continuation or enlargement of such felt emotion. There is a double reason for such controls: to prevent the threatening levels of fear, and to avoid representation of fear because it would also be a "narcissistic injury" for Harry to admit that he is scared. This "double jeopardy" of the narcissistic personality makes insight treatment difficult, as will be discussed shortly.

A microanalysis of the ideational-emotional structure begins, in State 1 of Figure 1, with a repetition of an image of the girl's dead body. This is the intrusive symptom Harry developed after the accident as part of a general compulsive repetition syndrome. The associated and responsive idea is that, since she is dead, he too might die. The concept of personal death vulnerability is grossly incongruous with an enduring concept of personal invulnerability and this discrepancy evokes anxiety.

Defensive maneuvers are motivated by such signal anxiety. Subject designation is inhibited, leading to a more abstract idea, "someone dies," a less frightening concept than that the self may perish. By externalization and disavowal of the death construct, he slides the meaning of personal mortality into personal immortality, a version of undoing. Instead of anxiety, the shifts of meaning allow a sense of triumphant excitement by State 2. The very image that evoked anxiety now leads by a slight irrationality into a more positive emotional experience. State 2, because of its defensive nature, is essentially unstable, and Harry tends to repeat Step 1.

Meanwhile there is disavowal of any similarity between himself and the girl. Narcissistic Harry exempts himself from this group membership by thinking, in effect, "She is the kind who dies, I am not." To use an exaggerated version of this prototypical narcissistic defense, Harry classifies himself as an exception, perhaps with an extension of the idea that someone has to die. If someone has to die then someone has been *chosen* to die, and it was she and not he. This then means he has been *saved* by this selection, presumably because he is special. This membership in the chosen group is like a sign of immortality, it is incongruent with the enduring concept of humans as vulnerable to death. This is a positive affect kind of incongruity: things are better than anticipated. As diagrammed, Harry feels a kind of triumphant excitement in response to this set of ideas. Thus a complete reversal of emotions has been accomplished by

FIGURE 1
Microanalysis of the Ideational-Emotional Structure
Utilizing Narcissistic Modes

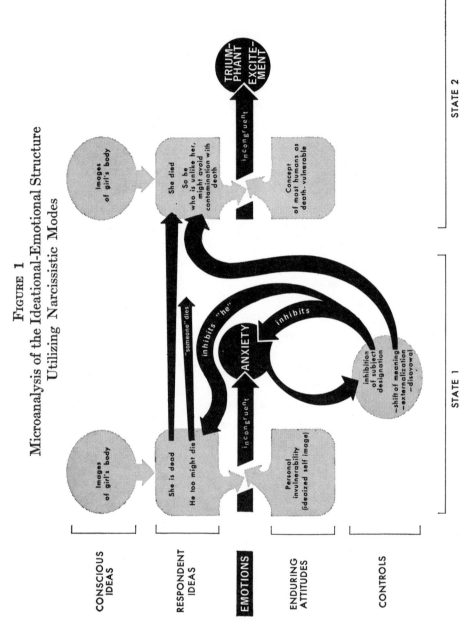

shifting and undoing meanings and externalizing mortal contaminants such as death and vulnerability.

This sliding meaning maneuver is similar to an obsessional device that uses one train of thought to block out another. But unlike a prototypical obsessional, a narcissistic Harry experiences emotions, perhaps both fear and triumph. Also, the narcissistic Harry will not as readily go back and forth in endless undoing operations. In pure narcissistic form he will not have to undo the triumph by feeling scared even though he remains vulnerable to fear and may repeat the sliding of meanings whenever fear related ideas are re-emergent.

Tactful Reconstruction of Experience: An Important Nuance with Persons Who Have Narcissistic Character Style

In terms of cognitive-emotional processing, a useful counteractant in therapy is *reconstruction*. In terms of the nuance of relationship in therapy, tact is of great importance (Kohut, 1971). The narcissistic personality presents a double problem, as mentioned before. There is *both* the threat of warded-off ideas and experiences *and* the realization that he has been warding something off. Interpretations of defense and of latent content are intolerable for narcissistic personalities unless they are tempered by proper dosage, timing, nuance of delivery, and the right kind of context in the therapeutic relationship. Otherwise the patient recognizes that he has distorted information in unrealistic ways and can have three traumas: (1) recognition of the self-threatening information previously avoided by distortions, (2) shame that he needed to be told and was "caught" distorting something, and (3) experiencing a reactive need to relinquish the unrealistic but sustaining gratification of seeing himself as a person chosen by destiny for immortality.

Tact is also vital because, like the hysteric, the narcissistic personality may be more attentive to the therapist than to topical meanings. The therapist is an important current source of praise or criticism; the real or fantasied observations of the degree of interest or disinterest of the therapist will affect the general equilibrium of the patient.

In the psychotherapy of a narcissistic Harry, during his expression and avoidance of the death themes just discussed, it would be helpful to recover and reconstruct the sequence of his fear of dying, including his memories of conceptual experiences during the accident. This procedure should be done as slowly as necessary to help Harry avoid a threat sufficient to throw him into a state of self-fragmentation.

During the reconstruction the therapist should also be unusually careful to obtain agreement with Harry's self-experiences as an instigator and as an object. This is similar to the importance of scrutinizing activity and passivity in hysterical styles. Both therapist and patient would sort out ideas about how involved Harry was in every aspect of action in terms of what was really his deed, and what happened for external reasons. This sorting out would include discriminations between realities, real probabilities, and fantasies about his personal vulnerability. In the sorting out and reconstruction some particular externalizations would be reversed although the general tendency to externalization might not necessarily be interpreted.

For example, suppose a narcissistic Harry expresses rage at the other driver who forced him off the road. This externalizing of blame is an effort to symbolize to "all" that the fault lies with the other driver, not with Harry. Underlying this are not only threatening ideas of his realistic faults but unrealistic potential accusations about his full culpability. The reconstruction involves every possible element of "blame": how responsible is he for picking her up, for the cars in near collision, for pulling off the road in the way that he did, for actions after the crash. Some end point of realistic decision, reached for each topic, relieves Harry of the unrealistic components of blame. In the narcissistic personality these blame components are *not* necessarily an unconscious or conscious sense of guilt but rather criticisms that may come from any source and demolish self-esteem. The therapeutic action of review and reconstruction allows Harry to come to a conscious decision about his degree of culpability and allows him the experience of not being assaulted with criticism by the therapist (even when the therapist is goaded to make such assaults by the patient's flagrant externalizations).

Reconstructions and reviews will include the fear evoking theme used for illustration. Working through this vulnerability theme will be especially difficult for narcissistic Harry. Realistic threats to the self-integrity are his Achilles' heel, probably already lacerated by earlier traumas which may be revived and reopened in this context. These recollections, when seen, will also require reconstruction in the light of the present. These reconstructions with narcissistic patients need special extended efforts clarifying self- and object-distinctions about motives, beliefs, actions and sensations.

During this process there will be shifts in topical meaning so that holding to a given aspect of a topic, as with obsessional patients, may be indicated. The nuance common with the narcissistic personality is to arrive at more stable meanings by encouraging the one meaning which has implications of current importance. For example, the "someone dies" idea has multiple meanings such as "each may die" or salvation of one through the "sacrificial death" of another. The grandiose idea of the sacrificial absolution is deflated by holding and discussing the more important fear themes around "each may die." If necessary, interpretation of the corruption in reality adherence, as implied by the sacrifice-exemption theme, may be necessary but can only be possible if the therapeutic situation in some way provides adequate support for the patient's self-esteem.

Nuances of Relationships with Narcissistic Patients
in a State of Stress

Treatment of narcissistic personalities is often difficult for the therapist because the relationship with the patient is less infused by the real therapeutic alliance and the transference-countertransference colorations than with hysterical and obsessional patients. The narcissistic patient uses rather than relates to the therapist.

In spite of feeling unimportant as a real person, or distant, or bored, the therapist must understand what is going on and provide a closer relationship with the patient. The therapist may have to be supportive for a period, as with the hysterical patient in great stress. With the narcissistic patient, support and closeness may not be so much a matter of warmth as a matter of accepting externalizations without interpretations. This will not be done without consequence, however, because later in therapy it may be necessary to interpret and discourage such externalizations.

The sense of safety necessary to experience and express usually warded-off ideas and feelings is achieved by the narcissistic personality through two types of quasi-relationships. One form is characterized by personal grandiosity with the expectation of admiration, the other by idealizing the therapist with the expectations of being all right because he is related to by an ideal figure (Kohut, 1971).

The grandiose quasi-relationship will tend to occur either at the beginning of treatment or during recovery from an initially defeated state of mind precipitated by the stress event. Bragging and self-endorsements will occur in subtle or gross forms and function to take conceptual time away from stress relevant topics. Tact, as emphasized earlier, will take the form of allowing these efforts to restore self-esteem, rather than insisting upon staying with core conflicts or interpreting the grandiose effort as compensatory.

This tact and forbearance may be unusually difficult for therapists who are used to relying on the therapeutic alliance or positive transference to tide the patient over periods of hard work on threatening ideas. It is difficult to remember that the relationship with narcissistic patients is not stable and that their need is imperative but not coordinated with the usual concerns, however ambivalent, for the person toward whom they direct their needs.

TABLE 2

Some of the "Defects" of Narcissistic Style and Their
Counteractants in Therapy

Function	Style as "Defect"	Therapeutic Counter
Perception	Focused on praise and blame Denial of "wounding" information	Avoid being provoked into either praising or blaming. Tactful timing and wording to counteract denials.
Representation	Dislocates attributes as to whether of the self or another person	Clarify who is who in terms of acts, motives, beliefs, and sensations.
Translation of images into words	Slides meanings	Consistently define meanings, encourage decisions as to most relevant meanings or weightings.
Associations	Overbalanced in terms of finding routes to self-enhancement.	Hold to other meanings; cautious deflation of grandiose meanings.
Problem solving	Distortion of reality to maintain self esteem, obtain illusory gratifications, forgive selves too easily.	Point out corruptions (tactfully), encourage and reward reality-fidelity. Support of self-esteem during period of surrender of illusory gratification (real interest of therapist, and identification with therapist as non-corrupt person, helps). Help develop appropriate sense of responsibility. Find out and discourage unrealistic gratification from therapy.

In idealizing the therapist, the second most common form of quasi-relationship, the repair of damage is effected as the patient imagines that he is once again protected and given value by a powerful or attractive parent. The stress response syndrome becomes a ticket of admission for this kind of self-supplementation. Again, tactful tolerance is necessary, early in the treatment, when the person is still partially overwhelmed by the stress response syndrome. It would be an error to see behavior, such as giving exaggerated testimonials about the therapist's unique ability, as equivalent to the transference motivated seduction gambits of some hysterical patients or the undoing of negative feelings on the part of obsessional patients. The testimonials simply indicate idealization which provides a momentary repair of damage to the self, a safer time during which some work on processing and integrating stress events may occur.

Even externalizations can help a patient gain sufficient emotional distance from loaded topics so that he can tolerate thinking about them. For example, if a feeling of disgust about death is projected onto the therapist, the relevant nuance would be to ask the patient to talk further about how the therapist feels. This allows the patient to work along the ideational route as if it were the therapist's route. A direct interpretation, such as "you are disgusted by death," should only come later.

Narcissistic considerations are present in every character type, not just narcissistic personality, and some of these nuances of treatment might be pertinent at any time. The "defects" commonly found in the typical narcissistic personality and comparable therapeutic counters are roughly summarized in Table 2.

BIBLIOGRAPHY

Adler, A. (1916), *The Neurotic Constitution: Outline of a Comparative Individualistic Psychology and Psychotherapy.* Translated by B. Gluck and J. Lind. New York: Moffat Yard.

Buber, M. (1923), *I and Thou.* Translated by Ronald Gregor Smith, 2nd Edition. New York: Charles Scribner & Sons, 1958.

Freud, S. (1914), On narcissism: An introduction. *Standard Edition,* 14:69-102. London: Hogarth Press, 1957.

Hartmann, H. (1964), *Essays on Ego Psychology.* New York: International Universities Press.

Kernberg, O. (1970), Factors in the psychoanalytic treatment of narcissistic personalities. *Journal of the American Psychoanalytic Association,* 18: 51-85.

Kernberg, O. (1974), Further contributions to the treatment of narcissistic personalities. *International Journal of Psycho-Analysis,* 55:215-240.

Kohut, H. (1966), Forms and transformations of narcissism. *Journal of the American Psychoanalytic Association,* 14:243-272.

Kohut, H. (1968), The psychoanalytic treatment of narcissistic personality disturbances. *Psychoanalytic Study of the Child,* 23:86-113.
Kohut, H. (1971), *The Analysis of the Self.* New York: International Universities Press.
Kohut, H. (1972), Thoughts on narcissism and narcissistic rage. *Psychoanalytic Study of the Child,* 27:360-400.
Mahler, M. (1968), *On Human Symbiosis and the Vicissitudes of Individuation.* New York: International Universities Press.

CHAPTER ELEVEN

Treatment Variations: Behavior Therapy*

THE PREVIOUS CHAPTERS discussed the therapy of stress-response syndromes using a psychodynamic approach. The theory of stress response should also provide a basis for discussing the rationale and effects of therapeutic techniques developed within other points of view such as learning theory. Thus the behavior therapy techniques of systematic desensitization and implosion will be examined. Once again, Harry is used as a pliable model for the trial of ideas.

BEHAVIOR THERAPY OF HARRY

Behavioral therapy is problem oriented. In initial discussions with Harry the most important problems would be crystalized in terms of behavior to be modified. Choosing those behaviors to be shaped would rest, finally, with Harry, but would evolve through discussion with the therapist. The relevant problem list might be as follows:

Problems to be solved that relate to the acute episode are:

1. The recurrent unbidden images of the girl's body and the associated anxiety.

---

* The author is indebted to the work of Stewart Agras, M.D., Professor of Psychiatry at Stanford University, who discussed behavioral treatment of "Harry" in a conference on multiple therapeutic approaches to this same case (University of California, June 1974).

2. The secondary reactions such as irritability and alcoholism.
3. The fear of driving.
4. Avoidance of thinking about the accident would be designated as a possible problem, since Harry had a period of denial. Even during the period of intrusive images, he tried to ward off other memories or reactions to the accident.

Problems that existed prior to the acute episode and continue, include:

1. Communication difficulties with his wife, probably including sexual impairments.
2. Drinking as a problem.

In typical behavior therapy, one problem would be selected for the first work. In Harry's case, the central issue might well be recurrent images of the girl's body. One hope would be that if this symptom is relieved, other problems such as his driving phobia might also dissipate.

The recurrent unbidden images would be regarded, in behavior therapy, as a failure of extinction. That is, under normal circumstances, the natural and automatic processes of the mind would lead to a gradual reduction in the power of the images to arouse fear. The purpose of the therapy is to aid these natural processes leading to extinction of the conditioned association between a given stimulus idea and the unpleasantly strong emotional responses.

Two kinds of behavioral technique, both using images, would be the main choices for first work on the problem. These would be implosion (Stampfl and Lewis, 1967) and systematic desensitization (Wolpe, 1958). Both techniques aim to sever the association between stimulus idea and emotional response, although the operations are quite different.

In systematic desensitization, the therapist and patient construct a hierarchy of images from a mild to a maximal fear stimulus. The patient is then taught systematic relaxation of the body, on the grounds that fear or anxiety cannot be as readily experienced in a state of relaxation. The mildest stimulus is suggested first to the patient. He silently images this content and tries to maintain bodily relaxation. If he feels anxious, he may signal the therapist by raising a finger. The therapist at once tells him to stop the image, then deepens relaxation by suggestion, and tries again. Later, the therapist may discuss the patient's subjective experiences and accessory ideas with him.

The patient is praised as he progresses successfully through the hierarchy. Gradually it becomes possible to deliberately form the most feared images without emotional arousal. In addition to the deconditioning of the idea-emotion associational bond, the patient has learned two others kinds of control. Through practice he has learned to invoke images volitionally, and he has also learned to terminate them at the therapist's suggestion. Hopefully he can generalize this effect to dispel images at his own volition (Horowitz, 1970, Chapter 14; Singer, 1974).

While the aim with implosive technique is similar, the approach is strikingly different in terms of emotion. Instead of starting with a mild stimulus and a relaxed state, the therapist suggests the most lurid and frightening forms of the feared stimuli. The goal is to evoke so much anxiety that the idea-emotional system will "implode" inwards upon itself. Less metaphorically, the technique operates on the assumption that fantasy and reality can be differentiated. Hence comparisons between imagination and actuality will reduce the patient's anxiety. In implosive therapy, the patient would be asked to visualize not only the girl's mangled body, but perhaps to enlarge upon this in "dynamically oriented" ways, such as imagining being covered with blood, killing the girl, being blamed by her, having intercourse with her, and so on (Stampfl and Lewis, 1967). Every phase of the story would be used as a stimulus, elaborated into highly charged and conflictual forms.

A behavioral therapist would evaluate the problem in the light of Harry's character and the nature of the initial relationship between Harry and the therapist. With an hysterical Harry the first choice might be systematic desensitization; with an obsessional Harry the first choice might be implosive therapy (Agras, 1974).

Systematic Desensitization of an Hysterical Harry

Systematic desensitization can use either a realistic or imaginary approach. That is, slides of accidents and bodies could be shown in mild to severe order, or else a hierarchy of suggested visual images could be used. Suppose the latter in what follows. An hysterical Harry would be encouraged by this technique to represent that which he has attempted to inhibit. Since the image period is usually one minute long, there is opportunity for many associations, as recently demonstrated by Brown (1969) and suggested by others (Breger and McGaugh, 1965).

Associations would be extended, and images would be translated into words in the discussion with the therapist that would follow the period of silent relaxation and directed imagery. Thus the first three defenses on the hysterical list of Chapter 8, page 148, would be counteracted, indirectly, though the suggested technique. Representations would be encouraged, translation of images into words would be fostered, and associations extended.

The patient would also be encouraged to maintain a steady state in relation to passivity and activity. He would be instructed and practiced in controlled alteration of level of relaxation and even in state of consciousness. Initially, the therapist describes a sequence of procedures to the patient and obtains consent to undertake these procedures. The patient is reassured that the sequence of procedures will be gradual, that the therapist is in charge, that he will announce each small increment as it is about to happen, and especially initially, appears to be the source of ideas.

The therapist suggests the images to form, when to form them, and when to stop them. The partial passivity required of the patient reassures an hysterical Harry, who feels responsibility lies with the therapist. Free of responsibility, Harry can change his state of consciousness, as in entering a relaxed state and allowing the images to come to mind. The patient can make the therapist "order" him out of that state by signaling his anxiety with a finger movement. Although the patient causes the cessation by signalling the therapist, he experiences the situation within a role model in which it is the external authority figure who tells him to start and stop mental contents which are fearsome and "out of control." There is a permitted passivity and a moratorium on responsibility which fits well with the typical hysterical maneuver of externalizing the source of activity in guilt arousing situations.

Similarly, systematic desensitization has a "good fit" with hysterical styles of selective inattention and impressionistic reporting of perception, in that the procedures tend to counteract such styles. The instructions point attention in a specific direction. The construction of a hierarchy demands detailed reports and considerations.

The various conformities of patient style to the desensitization procedure explain why this technique, rather than the implosive technique might be used for persons with hysterical defensive styles. Of course, the fit is not perfect. Other aspects of the hysterical personality, such as the tendency to misinterpretations based on schematic stereotypes and the short circuits to rapid but erroneous conclusions are not particularly well handled by the desensitization technique. But a clinically experienced and well trained behavior therapist would probably use the methods of psychoanalytically oriented brief treatment to supplement the desensitization procedure (Feather and Rhoads, 1972).

Systematic desensitization would not fit as well with the defensive styles of Harry as an obsessional character. Obsessionals can often image without emotional reaction because they can focus on emotionally irrelevant or counter-relevant details of the conscious experience. The images suggested in the hierarchies might not be unusual conscious experiences, but images already reviewed in dozens of ruminations. Warded-off stimulus ideas might not be revealed to the therapist in the first place and not included in the procedure.

Relationship Issues in the Behavior Therapy of an Hysterical Harry

In the conduct of the systematic desensitization, the therapist shows a kindly concern for the anxiety experienced by the patient. He encourages comfort through the instructions in muscle relaxation and he terminates images that arouse too much tension. After each period of image contemplation, he asks about subjective experiences. The therapy contract is very clearly demarcated, and has been explained in detail to the patient. Each person has defined roles. Within this safe context, the hysterical patient can experience the warmth, attention, and personalized support he usually craves with some desperation, in moments of stress.

The role relationship, with an obsessional, might have less favorable aspects. Relaxing by orders of the therapist, or imaging on instructions, may seem too much like submission. Resistance to such threats might interfere with the treatment. There might, however, be a balance: the orderliness of the procedures, and the clear details of what to expect might be appealing and add a sense of safety. With an obsessional Harry, the therapist might emphasize these aspects of the technique. Thus nuances of techniques of treatment in behavior therapy might evolve with hysterical and obsessional character differences, just as was discussed earlier with psychodynamic therapy.

An analagous nurturative, supportive, and directive role would be preserved in another behavioral technique that might be used to treat an hysterical Harry. Suppose the driving phobia continued and the therapist elected the technique of flooding. Flooding is practice of the feared activity as guided by the therapist. Harry would be encouraged to drive a graded distance each day, to keep track of his performance, and to report to the therapist. The therapist would react in a neutral manner to disappointing performances and praise Harry for good performances. Harry would be in a state where he anticipates bad relationships in the form of accusations from an introject of the dead girl, from his wife attacking him for picking up a girl, or from his superiors. The responsible, supportive, and praise-giving therapist counteracts the importance of these punitive introjects.

Implosive Therapy of an Obsessional Harry

A behavior therapist might select implosive treatment with an obsessive Harry on the grounds that the treatment will both counteract the defense of isolation and control the patient's tendency to shift away from emotionally evocative aspects of memory and fantasy. The therapist would learn of Harry's anxiety provoking images of the girl and elaborate upon them. The elaboration would be based on general theory, intuition about Harry, and observation of Harry's on-going responses (Stampfl and Lewis, 1967). He would infer Harry had wanted to have sex with the girl, felt guilty over his own survival, and feared his own bodily damage. He would tell Harry, in detail, how to image himself vividly completing the scenario of sex with the girl, the expected reactions of his wife, his own dismemberment, and the girl's damaged body.

To my knowledge, implosive therapy has not been tried on real stress response syndromes of this sort. A behavior therapist would probably restrict the use of lurid imagery to the more fantastic expectations of the patient. For example, if Harry were encouraged to imagine the girl accusing him of causing her death, and were to become excruciatingly anxious during this procedure, then he would also become aware of the discrepancy between the fantasy of such an accusation and the reality that no accusation is justified or possible. He did not deliberately do anything to harm her, he attempted to help her with a ride, he tried to avoid the collision, and he would really have helped her were she injured and not dead. The girl will not return to accuse him, except in his fantasies.

Harry may not yet have faced such fantasies as his own, but

the story lines may have been initiated in his associations. In implosive therapy, the therapist puts these fantasies into words. This may allow Harry to confront them and also react against them as if they were the therapist's ideas. Harry may thus reach a point of relative, if partially disavowed, completion.

The therapist is quite forceful in his direction of imagery in the implosive technique. Harry, provided he follows the main instructions, cannot shift from fearsome ideas to guilty ideas. When the therapist is talking about Harry being impaled by the pipes, breathing and vomiting his own blood, it restricts Harry to imagining his own potential harm. He must become frightened. Because the therapist in implosive therapy goes right on talking, because Harry is expected only to imagine as instructed, not to reveal his thoughts, he can tolerate the fear. He is supposed to be afraid, it is his "duty" in the therapy, and he also does not expose himself by doing it wrong, as the obsessional usually fears. Similarly, when the therapist imposes imagery about guilt, Harry cannot shift back to the fear images because he is not given conceptual space for such a maneuver. In this manner, the therapy counteracts the prototypic defensive maneuvers of the obsessional as discussed in Chapter 9.

Relationship Issues in the Behavioral Therapy of an Obsessional Harry

In implosive therapy, the therapist seems sadistic; he is deliberately and forcefully making the patient anxious. Of course the effect is paradoxical. He is cruel to be kind. This seeming cruelty may have two effects. It may counteract the guilt of the obsessional patient. It may evoke a counterreactive aggression on the part of the patient. For example, the therapist may be telling Harry to visualize the guilt activating imagery. Harry may do this in imagery but in word representations he may defy the therapist by saying mentally "I am not guilty," "It was not my fault," "It was an accident."

The activity of the therapist, pushing aside defenses and bringing ideas into the open, also modifies the self and object schemata situation. Instead of internalized aggressive presences (introjects) telling Harry he is bad, here is a real person describing bad images and making him feel uncomfortable. Harry can stubbornly resist. In a sense, he gets up to date as he both aggressively resists, submissively cooperates, is punished, and is cared for in a tough way. Oddly enough, the obsessional may feel comfortable in this interpersonal situation. The increased safety may help him work through many of the conflicts triggered by the stress event. In contrast, the hysterical patient may feel punished, seduced, and overwhelmed by implosive therapy.

Guided practice was mentioned and might also be used with the obsessional. Following the principles outlined here, the appeal to the obsessional would not be so much the praise as the feedback and documentation that also accompany the procedure. That is, he can see how he is doing, do a little better, and feel very much in control.

In conclusion, then, the approach outlined during the main discussion of nuances of technique in psychodynamic psychotherapy is also applicable to behavioral psychotherapy. This illustrates that both the general principles of phasic response and completion, and the individual variations based on predisposition, are concepts valuable to the analysis of the rationale of any technical approach to psychotherapy

BIBLIOGRAPHY

Agras, S. (1974), Behavior therapy of stress response syndromes. Talk given at a symposium on *Stress: Psychotherapy of Stress Response Syndromes.* June 1, 1974, University of California, San Francisco.

Breger, L. & McGaugh, J. C. (1965), Critique of reformulation of "learning theory" approaches to psychotherapy and neurosis. *Psychological Bulletin,* 63:338-358.

Brown, B. M. (1969), Cognitive aspects of Wolpe's behavior therapy. *American Journal of Psychotherapy,* 124:854-859.

Feather, B. W. & Rhoads, J. M. (1972), Psychodynamic Behavior Therapy: I)Theory and rationale, II) Clinical aspects. *Archives of General Psychiatry,* 26:496-511.

Horowitz, M. (1970), *Image Formation and Cognition.* New York: Appleton-Century-Crofts.

Singer, J. (1974), *Imagery and Daydream Methods in Psychotherapy and Behavior Modification.* New York: Academic Press.

Stampfl, T. G. & Lewis, D. J. (1967), Essentials of implosive therapy: A learning-theory-based psychodynamic behavioral therapy. *Journal of Abnormal Psychology,* 72:496-503.

Wolpe, J. (1958), *Psychotherapy by Reciprocal Inhibition.* Palo Alto: Stanford University Press.

Part V

CLINICAL EXAMPLES

An Antidote to Abstraction

Clinical material follows. Instead of Harry in three imaginative character structures, real (albeit disguised) clinical instances will be presented to provide concrete illustrations. The purpose is not just clarification of patterns already described. Some demolition of the simplicity of these patterns is necessary, since actual cases never reveal a stress response syndrome in pure form. There is invariably an admixture of prior conflicts, identifications, and attitudes, in addition to the defensive styles described in the sections on hysterical, obsessional, and narcissistic typologies.

In real work there is, in short, no "stress model" separate from the fundamental psychodynamic models. Unlike physiological or chemical experiments, it is not possible to purify a psychological field of variables operationally defined as "fortuitous" (Lewin, 1935). Neither predisposing variables nor stress response variables can be examined in isolation. Instead, it is the stress itself that reveals predispositions in the active form of responses and it is predispositions that supply the meaning to events and render them stressful. The recognition of such complexities will, in what follows, supply the antidote for the generalizations presented in previous chapters.

Lewin, K. (1935), The conflict between Aristotelian and Galilean modes of thought in contemporary psychology. In: *A Dynamic Theory of Personality.* New York: McGraw-Hill.

197

CHAPTER TWELVE

Loss of a Limb

With the assistance of Robert Nadol, M.D.*

A SINGLE EXTERNAL EVENT triggers divergent reactions. These separable yet interconnected responses may be in different phases at any given moment in time. One set of ideas and feelings may be warded off, resulting in a period of relative denial; another set may be intrusive in terms of conscious experience. Xalia's story is presented here as an illustration of such phasic differences and of how these differences orient a therapist in his intervention strategy.

Xalia is a 19-year-old woman. Her left leg and knee joint were mangled in a car accident. The injury was severe but doctors at her local hospital attempted immediate restorative surgery. Gangrene set in after the emergency operation. Consultation with specialists led to a hospital transfer and an amputation. She was then discharged to recuperate at home.

Six weeks later, Xalia re-entered the hospital so that the stump could be fitted with an artificial leg. She received intensive physical therapy to strengthen the stump and learn how to use a prosthesis. During this hospitalization, she asked for a psychiatric consultation. Initially, the surgical staff resisted her request because she seemed to be doing well. They decided to comply with it when her earnestness became apparent.

---

* Dr. Nadol is presently Assistant Clinical Professor of Psychiatry at Brown University.

Xalia was seen by a resident psychiatrist. She told him she had requested the consultation because she had become aware of a lack of appropriate emotional response to the loss of her leg. In the physical therapy exercise room and on the ward she met other persons with amputations. She recognized their losses as often worse than her own. They grieved for the loss of part of their body; she remained cheerful. She felt that she had not faced her situation and was going on as if nothing had happened.

The psychiatric consultant agreed that there was non-recognition of the implications of the amputation and explored some of the circumstances of the accident. He recognized defensive operations of thought-stopping and inhibition of communication, but did not know what thoughts and feelings she might be warding off. Moreover, he felt uncertain about disrupting her denial at this time. She was in the midst of active physical treatment and cooperating well with it. True, the loss of a leg in a young, attractive, unmarried, and uncommitted young woman would require psychological work in reorganizing her body image, self-concept, and future plans. But should this work be done now, or after she learned to use her prosthesis successfully? When is denial useful and when does it impede adaptation? After appropriate discussion with her and with staff, the resident psychiatrist referred the patient to a stress unit therapist for further exploration and formulation.

This therapist then interviewed Xalia on the orthopedic ward. She was pleasant but urgent in her self-presentation. She communicated a feeling of pressure that could be verbally described as, "You really must help me right now."

Here is a transcript of that interview, and the one that followed. They will be interspersed with commentaries on meanings and implications of what is being communicated. The psychiatrist has already introduced himself and obtained consent for tape recordings and their use in research and teaching.

FIRST SESSION

T: (Therapist) Why don't we start with you telling me why you asked for a psychiatric consultation?

X: (Xalia) What I asked for a psychiatrist for?

T: Yes.

X: Because, um, I think that I need somebody to help me.

T: Uh-huh.

X: Um, because uh (pause) well, since the accident and my stepbrother was driving, *I start hating him later (pause) and I don't want to hate him.*

Note that, almost at once, Xalia presents a new topic that was not mentioned to the consultant. This hatred of her stepbrother is a complex of ideas and feelings that intrude upon her: "I start hating him later and I don't want to hate him." She had told the first consultant about a complex of ideas in a denial phase, that is, her intellectual observation of the absence of appropriate reactions to missing a limb. The present psychiatrist had, of course, not heard of the hatred theme from the first consultant. He listens attentively to her further development of this theme.

T: Yes.

X: I don't want him to think that, um, it was his fault, but (pause) or, um, something 'cause, um, well, I don't want him to. And, ah, sometimes, well, I feel like yelling it to him and telling him it was his fault and, uh, that he can get out of that game (pause) so, um, so I just don't want to tell him never.

T: Yes.

X: Not even to my family 'cause I'm the only one who knows.

T: That's something we might be able to talk about. Anything else?

X: Mm Mm.

T: Well, tell me what happened. I know you've had an accident but I don't know anything else.

X: Well, um, we went to a dance (pause); I was, um, two of my stepsisters and me, we went with my stepmother and father. It was a dance for Andy, my stepbrother. So, after the dance, my parents were going to go somewhere else, so they told us to go with Andy in the car, and, um, (pause) oh, yeah, and then when we were, we were going just to (pause) go in a street, it was a blind intersection. It was like this.

T: Yes.

X: And, uh, and uh, he, he was, um, my, I think he was drunk and um, I was, I was talking with my stepsisters in the back, I was in the front seat and, um, and then I saw that, that he didn't put no brakes on and we were going to, getting to the corner. So, um, I saw him, I was thinking that was really strange. We were almost at the corner. He didn't put the brakes on and we were going to crash. He didn't, he was just smiling, that's all I remember and then I, I woke up in the hospital (long pause). Well, they were trying to save my leg for two weeks. And Dr. Smith told me that he was going to amputate it and, uh, (long pause) well, my parents didn't tell me nothing, you know, about Andy. After, only when I was over here, about a month and a half later since the accident, she told me that (pause) he was very, very, um, very bad, that he was (pause) um, crying all day in his room, (pause) that he wasn't eating or nothing, that he thought it was his fault. And she told me it wasn't his fault, it was the brakes' fault. (pause) But I knew it wasn't the brakes. I mean, I told, I told the police, I told the (pause) the, um, insurance man, everybody, that it was, uh, it was the the brakes. 'Cause I didn't realize before; I still don't realize that I, I don't have my leg. And um, more, I guess I feel funny about it.

T: Yes.

X: See, I don't realize, I don't care. Right now I don't care about it, 'cause I don't realize that I need it.

T: Yes.

X: But when I was at home last month for a couple of weeks and, uh, Andy was going out (pause), he was going to take the car and, uh, and then I was thinking that, uh, how could, how could my parents let him drive again. How? And how was he going out and I was staying, it was his fault. And I felt like yelling and telling him it was his fault, but I don't want him to blame himself.

T: Yes. But you're one of the only people that realizes how much he was at fault.

X: Yeah. I'm the only one who knows that it was his fault.

T: Yes.

X: See, 'cause I told the other people that it was the brakes' fault too.

T: Yes.

X: 'Cause I didn't want him, you know, if I'm, if I'm like this right now, I don't want another person to get (pause) hurt, or losing his feelings.

T: So, then, there are two things that you recognize might be helpful to talk out. One would be that you don't quite realize all the implications of what's happened.

X: Mm.

T: And then, you have this load about your stepbrother. You want him to be punished, but you don't want him to be punished. When did all this happen?

X: September 12th.

T: Uh-huh. And how long were you in the hospital the first time?

X: I was in the hospital there three weeks. Then I came (pause) for about, for about a month, then I was home for a month, then I came here.

T: And you've been here for 15 days now. Does Dr. Smith see you here?

X: Yeah. He's my doctor.

T: I'll give him a telephone call and see if it's all right with him that I talk with you. Would that be all right with you?

X: Oh, he's on vacation.

T: Well, I'll do it when he comes back and we'll just talk, anyway.

X: Yeah.

T: Now, what's your mood been like all that time?

X: My, um, what do you mean?

T: Oh, what has it been like for you day in and day out when you go home? Have you been cheerful or sad or numb or waiting, or...?

X: No. That's strange. I live with my father and step-mother.

T: Uh-huh.

X: I lived in Canada, but I came two years ago here to study. And, uh, I don't know, I feel like, a little like, right now, I don't want to go home.

T: Yes.

X: My real mom was here since the accident. But right now, I don't want to go home. I would prefer to stay over here, and now, not to go away. I don't know why and, well, sometimes I start to get angry at my father and my stepmother, even my stepsisters, and I feel guilty for it.

T: Just since the accident?

X: Mm-hm.

T: You get angry at them and irritated?

X: Yeah, it's funny because they think that, that Andy's very innocent and he's a very good boy and like he is sometimes, but (pause), I don't know.

T: Yes. You know something they don't know.

X: Mm-hm.

T: Okay. Well, you get around pretty well in a wheel-
chair and on crutches too?

X: Yeah.

T: I can't stay too long now. I just came up to see you.
But could you come next door to my office? Would
you mind coming over there? I think we'd have a
quieter room. We could just set up a time and then
we can just have a little longer to sit and talk this
over.

X: Yeah.

SECOND SESSION

T: I'd like to know more about what you've been thinking about.

X: (Pause) Well, (pause) I already told you, well,
(pause) mm (pause) I think that I love my father
and stepmother but at the same time I don't. I don't
know.

T: Uh-huh. You get angry with them.

The therapist has already noted that instead of saying she is
hostile and instead of describing family members as bad she will
inhibit her communications and presumably her thoughts by trail-
ing off and saying "I don't know." She has, of course, made critical
remarks about her brother, but she experiences such revelations as
lapses in control. Knowing that she has such feelings is experienced
as a threat to her sense of well-being. The therapist wants her to
discuss her conflicted feelings, so that they can examine them together in the therapeutic situation. He knows hostile ideas are at
the surface because they intrude into her awareness. He refrains
from questioning her about her warded-off ideas and feelings. If he
were to say here, "I wonder if you are possibly angry at your father
and stepmother?" It would be her style to answer either "I don't
know" or "Yeah, I guess so," in a passive manner. Instead, the
therapist labels her thoughts in a brief, firm, and direct way. He
does this in order to clarify the thoughts and to establish a ground

rule that in this situation there is to be open communication of those ideas and emotions that are usually suppressed in social situations.

X: A lot, yeah. (pause)

T: And yesterday we talked about your stepbrother and you.

X: Yeah.

T: How old is he?

X: Eighteen.

T: So he's a little younger than you are.

X: Mm-hm.

T: And what's he like?

X: (Pause) He's very tall, strong, (pause) mm (pause) very nice guy. Mm (pause) Kinda crazy (pause) mm.

T: Kind of crazy? How?

X: Well, you know, always drinking and, uh, with me, I mean, he was my favorite.

T: Uh-huh.

X: And I was his favorite too.

T: Uh huh.

X: So, we were always going together; well, you know, when I first came from Canada, then, uh, well, he was, uh, the first one, that, um, if one of my stepsisters came and started fighting with me or something, he came and told them to leave me alone, that, you know. And then, uh, he taught me how to drive, he taught me how to get around.

T: Mm.

X: The city and all that, uh, well he was—(trails off)

T: He was very close to you.

X: Yeah. (pause) Sometimes.

T: Right. So, maybe right now we could talk about the business with your stepbrother not pressing the brakes and then telling the police and everyone else that he did press the brakes. Maybe we can just see where we can get with that right now. That seemed to be a problem that you had coming back into your mind.

The therapist seeks to explore the more intrusive theme. He watches her facial expression as he talks. He slowly adds each new phrase until he sees that she is ready to take up the topic.

X: Yeah, I just remember that, um, that I, um, I thought that it was kind of strange when we were going to turn around the corner he didn't put the brakes on. (Pause) And then, I suddenly saw he was smiling and, uh, well, at the dance, I don't (pause), or I was sitting with some friends, so I saw that he was drinking. But, well, he always, he always drinks, but he never got, gets drunk; you know what I mean?

T: Yes.

X: So, then we get—got out, um (pause), then, uh, some friends were outside and, and they told him to, you know, how 'bout a race? He goes, "Oh, okay."

T: Mm-hm.

X: So, we left from the dance and the car was working pretty good. So then, we left them and we were going to go home and, um, (pause) well, he didn't put the brakes on.

T: Uh-huh.

X: And he was going very fast.

T: Was there a race going on, a play race?

X: No, yeah, well, it's kinda, it's kinda a park and, uh, it's named Boyle Park.

T: Uh-huh.

X: And, um, (pause) they have a big place where they have bands some and, uh, oh, yeah, they have a space to drive there (laughs) and, uh, (pause) well, when we were coming back home, um, he was going kind of fast. Well, he, he admitted, he told everybody he was going very fast. (Pause) He was going over 80 miles, close to 85. So, um, then, uh, well, I didn't get scared or nothing; nobody did and, 'cause he always goes that fast. (Pause) But then, um, like, my stepmother told me, um, later that, and, uh, asked them when the car was there and then I w— a lot of, you know, uh, the police and fireman, doctors came to take me out of the car and then, that he went out running into the car kind of crazy and that he was crying and all that, that it was his fault. So, partly because of that, I didn't tell them nothing 'cause I felt, I don't know, that, like, um, I was going to blame myself forever if I, I tell them the truth or something.

T: Yes.

X: So, uh, I didn't say nothing and, uh, oh, when I went home, he was very nice with me. He didn't tell me nothing, though. One time when I was here in the hospital, I called home and he answered the phone, so he knew it was me and he started crying, telling me that it was his fault, to forgive him, and all that. And, uh, I told him it wasn't his fault and (pause) you know, to realize that it was an accident. But I, I wasn't thinking that.

T: Yes.

X: I would think that it was his fault but I shouldn't tell him. And then when I'm home, I feel like yelling at him, telling him, you know? And I'm always in a bad humor sometimes and I, I never was like that.

T: But you haven't told him?

X: Mm-mm.

T: Now there's something there, because, you see, while everyone else may not know, he knows. He knows what happened. And you've been very close with him.

X: Yeah.

T: So, you must be the kind of people who talk to each other. And you know something and he knows something, but you don't tell him.

X: Yeah, but he knows this, but I think that right now, he thinks that it wasn't his fault.

T: Ah!

X: Because, you know, everybody was telling him that it was the brakes. But it wasn't.

T: Yes.

X: The brakes were okay and he didn't even put the brakes on.

T: Yes.

X: So, it wasn't the brakes. Now he probably doesn't remember because, oh, yeah, he said that, uh, well, yeah, it sounded like he was drinking, so he's probably been remembering.

T: Yes.

X: And, uh, (pause) well, everybody's saying, you know, nobody mentions it anymore.

T: Well, do you have the feeling that maybe they're trying to protect him?

X: Yeah.

T: And that they're telling you that you're supposed to protect him?

X: Yeah.

T: And you want to protect him too. . . .

X: Mm-hm.

T: But, there are different levels of protecting. He's actually feeling very badly.

X: It doesn't sound like it. (Angry outburst)

T: It doesn't? He's not feeling very badly now?

X: Mm-mm.

T: You told me that he was crying?

X: That was at first.

T: That was at first so he's forgetting about it now?

X: He forgot all, all of it.

T: Uh-huh.

X: That was about two weeks, three, a month. About a month. But now, well, he doesn't remember or nothing. That time, that time when we, we go out, I told them, well, everybody was kind of afraid that if they told him to take me out that I was going to say no, or tell him I wasn't going to go with him because I was afraid and all that. So, my parents and, um, everybody, every time that I had to go out, they took me and they didn't tell him. Even though I told them that I was—that I want to go with him.

T: Driving in the car?

X: Yeah.

T: So you don't get to have as much time with him.

X: Yeah. And then that, um, well, one time when we were alone, then I told him, why don't we go over there, you know? And he goes, "Okay, you want to; you want to, okay." So we left. He was very happy, I mean probably because he knew that I was trusting him again.

T: Yes.

X: And then, he started asking me when I was going back to Canada, what I was planning to do and, uh, how I felt. But he didn't say nothing about the accident or anything; he didn't mention it.

T: Yes. Well, the accident is kind of like a taboo subject right now, isn't it?

X: Yeah.

T: No one's supposed to mention it.

X: Nobody. (Laughs.)

T: But I guess what I'm wondering is if your father and stepmother don't want you to talk about it, if they want it to be all over and done with.

X: Mm-hm.

T: But I wonder if that's they way your stepbrother feels. I'm just wondering about the idea of you and he having a very private kind of conversation about this.

In what may be too rapid an approach the therapist is trying to suggest a move towards completion by interpersonal working through. He believes she is in conflict between her anger at the stepbrother and potential guilt if she expresses her resentment.

He has not picked up the clues, at this point, that she is also feeling that the local family wants to get rid of her, as in "he started asking me when I was going back. . . ."

One problem will be that she is only conscious of resentment based upon her limitation of activity, being forced to tell a lie, and at being no longer rewarded for going along with the story. She is not yet in touch with her potential rage at her stepbrother as the cause of her loss of a limb. The loss complex is still warded off by inhibitory processes.

X: (Long pause, voice very soft.) Be very painful. I mean he was—(pause)

T: I'm not sure you should either, but I'm just entertaining the idea. We'll just think about it; you don't have to do it, or anything. What do you think would happen if you were to, in some very private way, have an opportunity to just talk it over with each other?

X: He'll probably tell my stepmother that I was thinking it was his fault. And then that was going to be a big problem because they were going to, um, going to tell me that it wasn't his fault, then I was going to get mad. I was going to tell him the truth (voice intense) and then, my mom was going to come and tell them and then there was going to be a big ton of trouble.

T: Yes. You've already thought about what would happen.

X: Yeah. (Pause) So, I don't want it to, I don't want it to happen (laugh).

T: But let's just see what that would be like if it were like a script, you know, written out for a television program. You would have this talk with your step-brother. He'd get mad, I guess, and he'd go tell his mother that you were blaming him for the accident, and then they'd make life miserable for you?

X: Mm-hm.

T: And then what would happen? Would you have to go home to Canada? They'd kick you out? Or they'd be mean to you?

The earlier clues have registered in the therapist's mind.

X: (Laughs) No, well, they're not mean with me. We only don't, um, you know have a good relationship; well, we do, but (trails off).

T: You do and you don't.

X: Yeah, we do and we don't. Well, I was always, I was always thinking that they prefer, well, it does (pause) that's um, logical, that she prefers her sons and daughters, well, yeah. I was the stepdaughter only. And, uh, well, (pause) they didn't let me do nothing, not even to go someplace, because they said that they were responsible for me and that if something happened to me, they were, it was going to be their fault, their responsibility. That's, that's right; they don't like it.

T: Yes.

X: So, mm (pause) you know, they wouldn't tell me to go back to Canada, but I would (laughs). I would feel—

T: You would feel you had to go back?

X: Yeah, 'cause I, if I, I won't feel good staying there.

T: Well, what would going back feel like? What would you go back to?

X: My real mother.

T: Yes, well, I don't know what that's like.

A sign of this patient's immaturity and dependency is seen in her talking to the therapist as if he knew her history. The telling of her story to many persons in a university hospital contributes to this effect, but she reveals in many other ways a psychological, developmental level of less than her chronological age. Her deportment, posture and mannerisms are those of an early adolescent. The therapist believes that this is not merely a regression due to stress and hospitalization, but rather, continuation of a pre-event character structure. Other thoughts strike him; that she probably has an incompletely developed feminine self-concept and body image, is sexually conflicted, may use the injury as an excuse to avoid sexuality and may have unusual problems in working through the sexual and other implications of the body loss. The stress, were this substantiated by later material, would be a complex of the new event, prior conflicts, and impeded psychosexual development.

The patient gives background history at this point which indicates that she feels like a second-rate child with both her real mother, who remarried and had more children, and with her stepmother and real father. She came from Canada when she had difficulty in high school and felt excluded from her family there. She hoped to make a better home with her father and to form an attachment with her stepmother and stepsiblings.

The accident disrupts the refuge she found and she is frightened that they will exclude her because she "knows too much." She must stifle her rage to avoid this threat. She reveals this story but is not actively aware of the psychological meanings, a relatively hysterical style of "not knowing." Nonetheless, this material is at the surface and is clarified by the telling process.

The therapist then summarizes, as the transcript continues:

T: There are kind of two things that are problems for you now, that you wanted to talk over. One is the business with your stepbrother, you know, your anger where you can't win, no matter what you do.

X: Mm-hm.

T: And the other was your feeling that you don't quite realize what it means that you were in the accident and that you lost your leg. And that's probably going to be a pretty gradual thing as you get used to using your new leg. It may feel artificial and funny at first before you get used to it. Do you want to talk at all about that today?

X: Well, you know, lots of people, they lost their leg too and they were very sad and, uh, (pause) even, because I saw a man down in physical therapy who lost his finger. He was crying. (Pause)

T: Yes.

X: And he was very sad and I lost my leg and I didn't realize it. I was very happy. Well, I always have been happy; I never get mad or anything and, um, well, I was thinking that probably I'm not normal. (slight laugh.)

T: Uh-huh.

X: Simply 'cause I don't realize it.

T: Well, you know, I've seen people who've lost different parts of their body and everyone doesn't get sad about it. It's not necessarily abnormal or crazy or anything like that. Some people just take it and go on with their life.

The therapist has made a rapid decision to support her denial of the limb loss complex for the time being and focus on the family support system, establish a therapeutic alliance and then see what happens.

X: Yeah, but I mean, not even crying? Not even that?

The therapist realizes by her response that he may have erred: Supporting the denial sets up a therapeutic misalliance that will perhaps disrupt therapeutic possibilities. He tries to reverse himself.

T: Well, let's find out more about it, though. Do you find yourself having any dreams about yourself?

X: Yeah. (As if disappointed.)

The therapist persists in his error by asking too peripheral a question. Dreams are important for the self-concepts contained, but the timing of this question is poor and based more on the therapist's discomfort than the need for this information at this point. It would have been better to have ended the remark at, "Well, let's find out more about it."

T: What are you like in your dreams?

X: (Long pause) Like I was before.

T: Uh-huh.

X: Dancing again and then, uh, I see myself in a place and all my friends over there.

T: Uh-huh.

X: And then, they don't go over there to ask me for a dance 'cause they know that I have an artificial leg or something like that.

The therapist obtains useful information. In spite of his procedural error, the patient goes ahead.

T: Yes.

X: And then, I see my stepbrother dancing (pause) and I don't know, I feel something against him. It's not, it's not only 'cause I don't have my leg. It's because I don't like the way it looks either.

T: Yes.

X: To say to me they had to do two, some operations and I didn't li— I don't like the way it does.

A typical avoidance of words to clarify her repugnance at how her leg looks. The therapist decides to ask for details to see how deep-seated this defense is.

T: Would you describe it to me? Of course, I haven't seen your leg.

X: Well, it's kind of, um, well, they took skin from here to go over here.

T: Yes.

X: So, it's kind of, uh, looks black and all that.

T: Mm.

X: And, uh, well, I thought I was going to be, you know, there was, they were just going to amputate my leg and that's all.

T: Yes.

X: It wasn't going to look like that, but it does. And every time that I, I w-, I just saw it last month. The doctors wanted me to see it, but I didn't want to, and I said well, if they're going to do another operation, plastic surgery, it's not gonna look the same; it's not necessary for me to see it right now. So, I wait. And I thought I was going to look better.

T: So you didn't look at it then?

X: Only one time and I, I didn't want to, but I did. And I didn't, I didn't like it.

T: Yes.

X: That's the only time that I cried for it and then, uh,—

T: You did cry though?

X: Yeah. (pause) Only because it looked like that (voice tone insistent).

T: Yes, but that's part of the sadness. It's partly there. These things come in doses. But tell me more about it.

The therapist means the sadness is partly there and will occur in doses, but as often happens, his own primary process echoes the patient. "It's partly there" is what is wrong with the leg. These slips are not uncommon in the treatment of persons with stress response syndromes. The therapist unconsciously sides with the patient's avoidances, feeling that the loss is so real that reminders hurt the patient. He also, at a primary process level, explores his own reactions to the universal threat of body injury. The conflict in the therapist to express and to avoid expressing the loss leads to parapraxes.

X: I will cry too because, uh, well, I am (pause), all the time, you know, when I saw people in the streets on crutches and things, I felt (voice very soft) ashamed.

T: Yes. (Empathically)

X: You know that? And, uh, (pause) when I was, when I was over, I didn't want to go to the store or something like they were going to bring me, just that I don't want to, people to feel ashamed of me; something.

T: Yes.

X: That's why I didn't go to graduation, either.

T: Oh, you didn't?

X: Mm-mm. Well, I wasn't, I didn't have to.

T: Yes, but you didn't want to go because you thought—

X: No. (Interrupts)

The patient gets the incipient thought and wants to prevent the clear statement, but the therapist persists.

T: —people would look at you and—

X: Well.

T: —think you didn't look nice?

X: Y-y-y-eah, but (pause) I didn't like myself, you know, people staring at me 'cause I only had one (pause) leg.

Possibly identifying with the therapist, the patient does add the descriptive word "leg," after a pause. Previously, she had used the label "it."

T: Yes.

X: So, um, (pause) well, I didn't want to go.

T: Yes. (Pause) So, this is something that's still tender emotionally for you. (Pause) And you don't like to look at it, don't like how it looks.

X: I do now.

T: A little better now?

X: (Laughs) Yeah, I guess.

The interview ended with formulation of an agreement for brief therapy, to extend beyond the point of discharge from the hospital. During the therapy, discussions were similar to the above material in that the relatively greater focus was on working through her rage and only a little time was devoted to the sadness and shame over her loss of the limb. In other words, the accident and amputation set in motion at least two main cycles of thought and feeling, both in a state of non-completion at treatment onset. One was more intrusive, the other still in a phase of denial and numbing.

All such statements are relative. For example, she did have thoughts about being different after the amputation, or finding the stump unpleasant looking. But many more reactions lie ahead before she adapts to an altered body. In comparison, the impulses to castigate her stepbrother are urgent and conscious, as is the opposing aim to maintain family harmony at the price of silence and thereby avoid both guilt over harming her stepbrother, and fear that she would be sent back to her real mother and stepfather in Canada. Of course, discussion and working through of this conflict involved a growing recognition of the implications of losing a leg.

One explanation for the inhibition of personal loss and the emergence of interpersonal anger lies in the association of personal loss with a more profound threat. There was a brief emergence of this theme during therapy when she told of intrusive ideas that came very briefly into her awareness; of wanting to be dead and of persons on TV who killed themselves. The implication was that if she were to fully realize her personal losses (of leg, as well as of family closeness), she was afraid she might commit suicide. The profoundness of this threat is one reason why techniques that would thwart or skirt her defensive denial are not indicated. The time to master these issues will come later, when rehabilitation is more advanced, when her social support system is stabilized and when she has a well established relationship with a therapist.

The rage at her stepbrother, a theme dealt with immediately in therapy, was not instigated solely by the accident. While very close to him, Xalia also resented his being the complete child of her stepmother and the prize male in a family oriented to sons. In addition, ambivalence and competition between siblings was a major theme in the extended family, going back three generations. Work in this area involved recognition of major themes of conflict present before the stress event.

SUMMARY

The case of Xalia illustrates intrusive thoughts as well as denial. Two complexes, activated by the accident were described and, at a given moment in time, one was more emergent, one more successfully inhibited. The inhibited complex, revolving around sadness and shame over bodily loss was not "purely" denied, but was partly recognized and contributed some intrusive thoughts. Nonetheless, therapy focused mainly on the more emergent themes, following the patient's leads. These themes involved pre-existent conflicts.

CHAPTER THIRTEEN

Visual Shock and the Compulsion to Look

With the assistance of Erik Gann, M.D.*

A YOUNG MAN WALKS DOWN a Chicago street. A woman jumps to her death from a window high above him. Her body smashes into the pavement just behind him. He turns to find her mangled corpse in full view, her brains spattered on the cement and on him. Stunned, he experiences a compelling impulse to stare at the woman's remains. Simultaneously, as he continues looking at the body, he feels an equally disturbing sense of transgression.

Experience of this event did not result in a stress response syndrome of sufficient intensity to motivate this man to seek consultation. Instead, other events led to an interview two years later and provided an opportunity to see what happens to such a memory, independent of treatment issues. The result is an illustration of (1) the enduring intrusion of images from traumatic perceptions; (2) the interaction of the repetition tendency with aims to inhibit such intrusions and pangs of emotion, and (3) the compulsion to look at stressful scenes as it conflicts with social taboos against doing so.

Daniel, the young man, had been interviewed by a physician as part of admission procedures for a medical school in Chicago. During the course of the interview, he described

---

*Dr. Gann is a Staff Psychiatrist at Mount Zion Medical Center, and Clinical Associate at the San Francisco Psychoanalytic Institute.

220

the incident as it had occurred two years earlier in Chicago. A young, Latin-American secretary working for the same firm as he, threw herself from the building, landing very close to him as he passed on foot below her. The memory of this event was still vivid in his mind. He often found himself talking about it or thinking about it. He had not sought psychiatric help, however, for the recurrent, disturbing memories, nor for any other problems. The physician was impressed with the intensity and peremptory emergence of this memory during an entrance interview. She suggested, and he agreed to an interview with a psychiatrist who had a research interest in this type of situation.

During the subsequent interview, it became apparent that this event had several ramifications for Daniel. First, he was immediately thrust into the midst of several universal responses and conflicts. He found it imperative to look, to discover what was going on, and to attempt to comprehend the meaning of what were highly unusual and disturbing visual perceptions. There seems to be a quasi-instinctual need to look at such things; e.g., the uncanny fascination of observing accident victims, looking at executions, watching horror films. In addition, he became aware of his concern about the woman who was essentially unknown to him. This appears to be connected to a common response of identifying with the victim. Finally, another conflict was aroused; that of the guilt of the survivor. These universal conflicts became enmeshed with his own personal conflicts.

After an initial agreement concerning the exploratory and investigative nature of the interview, Daniel was asked to tell of the incident in any way he wished. He responded as follows:

> "I've talked about this a lot. (Pause) I was very upset when it happened. (Pause) A woman jumped out of a ten-story building; she landed next to me. *I don't really remember. I didn't see her.** She landed about ten feet

---

* Italics added to emphasize certain phrases for the reader.

away from me. *I don't remember* any sounds except the blood rushing in my ears, which I guess *didn't happen* 'til I turned around and saw what happened. She was lying on the ground with her head facing me. There was a large hole in the top of her head. (Pause) My first reaction was that she had fallen down, that she had tripped on the sidewalk or had a heart attack. My first reaction was, what could I do to help her? You know, what's the smartest thing to do—cover her up with a blanket, give her artificial respiration? That was my immediate thought, even though I saw that there was nothing in her head . . . just a big, empty hole. (Pause) I stood and *stared* for quite a long time. I remember one of my thoughts was that, *I shouldn't be looking at that,* but for *some morbid reason, I wanted to look at it and kept staring at it.* Then I noticed her brains were all over the sidewalk. Some was on me too, and that upset me. Initially, people just walked by . . . (pause) that really upset me too. Nobody stopped and I started crying. I walked closer and *looked more.* (Long pause) I noticed her right leg was split open. She was wearing big, black boots about up to here, and her right leg was split open through the boot and the next thing I remember was that people started to gather around. I walked off quite a good distance and then *stared again,* again for awhile; I don't know how long. It seemed that what happened was that everything stopped and I couldn't hear anything except the blood in my ears. I wasn't aware of anything going on except this one scene with nothing moving and then I turned around and *stared again* and the same thing happened, and then I left. I got on the bus and kind of *looked* at people; I'd been in Chicago about eight months then. It was starting to bother me because people were so unfriendly there. And I *looked* at them (on the bus) like, well, at least now, be friendly; at least now, open up; but I didn't say anything to anybody."

He then added that what had occurred did not "hit" him at that time and, at first, talking about it did not affect him terribly much; he "just forgot about it." However, not long after the incident, talking about it made him "nervous" and, in fact, the phone conversation to set the appointment had left him feeling "nervous."

One aspect of the scene that was still quite troublesome for him was an image of a passerby stepping on a piece of her brains. He stated, "that still bothers me. I don't think I've accepted that. It upsets me when it comes to my head; I immediately shove that out of my mind. I say, 'how could that have happened' and then say, 'okay, that happened; forget about it.' "

At this point, still early in the interview, Daniel spontaneously reported a dream he had approximately two weeks before (between the medical school interview and this one). He was reminded of it in this context only because his girl friend, an aspiring psychologist, told him it was related to the suicide incident.

"I saw a man get killed in a car accident in the dream. Something that I flash on when I see, picture what happened, was that hole in her head (the girl in the stress event). That was empty and in this accident, the man had his legs cut off, but I could see all the way up into his body cavity and it was all scooped out. I could see all his bones and everything; it was as if the legs were part of the actual body cavity."

At this point, he paused and remained silent for a minute or two. The psychiatrist asked if that was the whole dream and he replied, "Yeah; there's more detail, but *I don't know if you want to hear the whole thing.*" When interest was indicated, he proceeded:

"I was walking over an overpass; there had been an accident. There were police around and I saw the man lying there, and he looked kind of *plastic*, like he had *black*, plastic hair, very *smooth olive skin*, but looked like he was android or plastic. He had a shaft in his chest; it looked like a metal shaft had gone into his chest and had broken off about there, (gesturing). And blood, kind of, on his chest. And when I walked by, I noticed that his *legs were cut open;* of course, I just saw a *cross-section of his legs,* the muscles and the bone, and then it turned into the part where it was all *hollow.* And I could see his spinal—his backbone and his rib cage, but it was covered with—you ever see the inside of a fish? It's kind of silvery, a silvery coating? Well, it (the man's backbone) was all covered with that kind of silvery coating. And then the man started squirming and blood started gushing out of his mouth and would kind of cover his face and run off very smoothly and I could kind of *put myself in his position* and I knew he was in a great deal of pain and I knew he was saying to himself, 'I just wish this would be over.' And I knew he knew it would be over very soon."

He continued immediately by reporting that his girl friend had said that the dream was probably related to his having observed a similar occurrence. When asked for his thoughts about this comment, he replied, "It (his girl friend's statement) didn't click with me; I don't think it (the dream) had anything to do with it (the stress event), but it might. I've never had a dream like that before, where I've seen somebody actually in the process of dying. And when I saw the woman jump out of the window, it was about two years ago—so, I think that was a pretty long time ago. The dream doesn't bother me, though when I had it, I just said, 'okay, you've had this dream.' "

For the remainder of the interview, discussion focused on the immediate and long-range impact of the event. Daniel reported that the time spent in Chicago came during a period in his life when he was somewhat depressed and lonely and he was struck by his experience of the city and its inhabitants as indifferent, cold and uncaring. The woman's suicide was "the last straw" for him. He decided to leave for the west after that.

Immediately after observing the body and the ensuing scene, Daniel had gone to his residence. While on the bus, he caught himself *staring* intently at a young woman across the aisle and became "self-conscious" and felt he "*shouldn't have been staring*" at *her*. For the next several days, he felt numb and somewhat withdrawn and then began noticing a need to tell people about it. There followed a period of intrusive thoughts about the incident, which he kept trying to push out of his mind. After approximately a month, he would not think about the event unless something brought it to mind.

Daniel became essentially free from intrusive images of the scene, unless he heard very specific topics mentioned which would trigger a series of images. He would then feel compelled to review this specific set of images in his mind and would often experience the need to describe the whole memory to someone. He was aware that hearing of an incident in which someone was *hurt or mutilated* or hearing anything concerning Chicago would initiate this conscious and compulsive repetition of the imagery. However, hearing about *death*, suicide, or accidents in general, would not have the same effect.

When his memory was triggered by one of these cues, Daniel would envision the following sequence: first, an image of the woman lying on the ground with the *hole in her head;* then he would see "her face, which was flattened because she landed on the back of her head." This was followed by an image of the leg, "split, with no blood in there either, and white"; and finally, he would see "a piece of brain on the sidewalk and I remember thinking, it must be a part of her medulla because of the convolutions." The images would make him "nervous" and "depressed," because they were "close" to him and occasionally evoked his own vague thoughts of suicide.* Over the two-year period, Daniel felt that he had achieved some conscious control over re-experiencing the imagery at any given moment. That is, he could choose either

---

* It should be noted that although Daniel has experienced episodes of mild depression, he has never seriously entertained suicidal notions, nor has this depression ever interfered with his functioning.

"to push" the thought out of his mind, or to think about it and, inevitably, to experience the above cycle of images.

In general, he had not noticed the onset of any other symptomatology since the event. He was not aware of any other intrusive imagery nor of experiencing any difficulties with sleeping, eating or sexual functions. The only behavioral disturbance he remarked upon involved his reactions after talking about the incident, when he would invariably feel "spaced out . . . my mind just goes out of focus . . . feel emotionally like being about to faint; conscious, but as if there are no stimuli coming in." This feeling would persist for about thirty minutes after having described the scene and the unbidden images, and he reported having experienced this sense of dissociation during the present interview.

In addition, he reported two other significant consequences of his experience. The first involved driving past an automobile accident about six weeks after the stress event. He saw a man on the side of the road holding his bleeding head in his hands. He then noticed that the top of the car was smashed in and that there was a baby crib in the back seat. Upon observing the crib, he suddenly became upset and began to fantasize about the baby or the man's wife being trapped in the car. Then he was struck by the thought that *"it was unnecessarily morbid to fantasize about it and I should stop."* Whereupon, he consciously and with difficulty, forced himself to cease thinking about this episode.

The second occurrence involves an extended fantasy, a story that he had evolved over time about the suicide victim and her reasons for killing herself. She would have many children and was working hard to support them. The children were too much to handle and her husband had left her. She felt *alone, alienated from* her children, and as if she were fighting the whole world alone. This was too much for her, so she killed herself.

In fact, the subject did not know her and knew none of

this to be necessarily true, but he told me, "*I had to give myself an understandable reason why she'd do that.*"

In the final minutes of the hour, Daniel spoke of his fears about this interview. He found that he was more nervous discussing the incident in this instance than at any time in over a year. He was worried that the psychiatrist would notice something that was bothering him but that he was unaware of and would not care to admit, such as the idea that the incident had affected him more than he thought it had.

The psychiatrist observed aloud that Daniel had been able to continue his life with a minimum of disturbance, despite the occasionally troubling thoughts. He offered him a chance to return to talk about it and to be treated briefly for help with the recurrent distressing visual images. Daniel thanked the psychiatrist and said he would call if the need arose.

DISCUSSION

From his own subjective memory report, one can reconstruct the behavioral and ideational contents of Daniel's immediate response to this terrible scene. Perhaps it would be best to begin by placing the whole stress event in the context of this lonely period in his life when he was mildly depressed. A manifestation of that mood was his thought that one is not cared for in Chicago. In this frame of mind, he had an incredible experience.

Suddenly "something" made him turn around as he walked along the street. He reports not *remembering any sounds* except "the blood rushing in my ears." One must surmise that he heard the awful sound of the impact of the body which probably would have resulted in an explosive-like noise. But Daniel has either repressed this entirely, or else did not record the initial impressions in memory. He was then presented with an awful sight—a dead, mutilated, female body with a gaping, empty hole in her cranium. The shock of this visual perception may have eroded preliminary codings of the auditory percepts. Next, he was aware of a thought—"she has fallen down; (perhaps) has tripped on the sidewalk or has had a heart attack." He wondered what he should do to aid her and yet was aware of the irrationality of these thoughts in the face of observing simultaneously "that nothing was in her head." His mind rapidly appraised alternatives along multiple lines of associations. He tried to disavow the terrible finality of bodily destruction but concluded with recognizing its reality.

He was frozen into a state of *staring*. Then after a moment, he became acutely uncomfortable with his awareness that he was staring and he thought, "*I shouldn't be looking at that.*" Then he found himself caught in a conflict; he "shouldn't" look, "but for some morbid reason, I *wanted* to look at it and kept staring at it." A large part of what followed, according to Daniel's description, involved both his *looking* and what he saw.

One source of disturbance stemmed from the incongruity between Daniel's ordinary schema of how bodies should look and the way this particular body looked. Bodies are supposed to be intact, shaped in an ordinary manner, and the insides are not to be seen. This body was misshapen and the insides were visible. In order to resolve this incongruity he instinctively needed more information and his eyes were glued to the body by an automatic tendency to obtain that information. In addition to this automatic tendency, there may have been psychodynamic factors such as body schema developed around fearsome but unconscious castration fantasies.

The compulsion to look is thus an adaptational function based on a need to find out about possible danger in novel situations. But self-awareness gives new meanings to automatically instigated staring. Daniel feels that looking is socially taboo. Customarily, eyes are averted from dead bodies; corpses are covered up as rapidly as possible; children are protected from them. He feels guilty for having looked and wants social confirmation of his act. Since the event, he has relived the horror of looking, the compulsion to look, the aim to never look at such things again, and the wish for social sanctions.

Another facet of the scene is his observation that *other* potential onlookers are *not looking*, an aspect of the general tendency towards denial of threat. People walk by, stepping on pieces of the brain and, incredibly enough, disregarding the body. These other people, then, represent the opposite, or mirror response; the need to not look. For Daniel, cognitive and emotional processing of the event includes not only appraisal of the meaning of the woman's body, but understanding, integrating and accepting his own immediate responses and those of other persons who, in a sense, socialize his reactions.

While riding the bus, he catches himself re-enacting what has just occurred as he *stares* with tears in his eyes at the young woman opposite him. Perhaps he is identifying with the dead woman as he thinks, "Well, at least, now, be friendly" (to him). He is also asking, non-verbally, if looking is all right.

Despite his identification with the plight of the dead woman as being depressed in Chicago, there is probably a counter-theme of relief that it was *she* who died and *not he;* that she is mutilated and he is intact. This thought could only serve to reinforce his sense of guilt.

By this time, Daniel is already manifesting a stress response syndrome. Over the next several days, he forgot about it and felt depressed in a vague way. This represented an initial period of denial and numbing, which soon began to alternate with a need to tell what happened. He also began to experience intrusive imagery and was most aware of this when exposed to one of the trigger stimuli; hearing one of a set of words or seeing events such as the automobile accident. In general, he was preoccupied with the presence of the memory of the event and with his efforts to prevent it from coming to mind. He was also trying to ward off affects of guilt, fear and depression associated with this memory, and one would imagine it is the discomfort of these potential emotions that prompted him to actively attempt to suppress the images. But two years later, he still has intrusive images of the event after certain specific triggers, such as the word "Chicago."

The Meaning of the Interview and the Dream

Daniel's dream occurred some time after the medical school interview, where he had somewhat impulsively told his story, and while he was anticipating the interview reported here. It occurs, probably, as these stimuli activate unworked-through aspects of the memories, and represents a continued ideational cycle responsive to the stress event. His decision to follow the medical interviewer's suggestion and to come for the interview with a psychiatrist may also carry a covert wish to continue with and complete the cycle of thought initiated by the stressful perceptions. He continued to deny, however, that he was bothered very much at this point by the memory of the event. Accordingly, he does not view the dream as connected to this memory or to the recurrent, disturbing, intrusive imagery he still experiences. Instead, his girl friend suggests it and he finds that the suggestion "doesn't click." He maintains his denial despite his report of an association in the initial part of the dream presentation that confirms his feeling that the dream *is* related to the stress memory. He associates the exposed body cavity of the man with the hole in the woman's head. However, after the addition of more detail in the second part of the dream, he tells of his disagreement with his girl friend's interpretation.

It will be helpful to briefly examine the form and content of the interview in this context. Daniel begins with a description of the stress event. He emphasizes the impact on him of the woman's empty cranium, the brains splattered about and his own behavior, looking and staring—first at the body and then later at people on the bus. He immediately presents the disturbing conflict as his desire to look, and his guilt about doing so.

Soon afterwards, he mentions having had the dream, offers a description, concentrating on the part concerning the body cavity that was "all scooped out" and the association to the woman's empty cranium. Then he stops and is silent. The interviewer inquires if that was the whole dream, and the subject replies, "There's more detail in it, but I don't know if you want to hear the whole thing."

Interactionally, he is asking if the interviewer can stand seeing more detail. The interview process is a reliving of some aspects of the stress situation with externalization of some of his quandaries to the therapist. He presents the distressing images to the interviewer in a forceful way and watches his response. If the interviewer preserves equanimity, then, by identification, Daniel too can remain unperturbed. If the interviewer does not criticize or reprimand him for staring, then the compulsive looking is made socially acceptable. If the interviewer expresses his own wish to see and know more, then Daniel can feel less guilty about looking.

Several references have been made linking his dream to the stressful event. What is the evidence for this? A connection between the man's body cavity in the dream and the woman's cranial cavity in the perception has already been asserted. The view is reversed, from above and downwards to below and upwards. Daniel said the man in the dream had been in an accident, a term he had used during the interview to refer to the woman's fall. The man's legs were cut off and the bones could be seen, an image similar to that he had received when looking at the woman with her leg split open.

After learning that the interviewer wanted to hear the details, Daniel reported the second part of the dream. "The man looked kind of plastic, like he had black, plastic hair . . . looked android or plastic." The woman had worn black (patent leather or plastic) boots, probably had dark hair and her face, flattened from the impact of the fall, may have looked "android" or unreal and plastic. The man had "very smooth olive skin"; the woman was Latin-American. In this second telling, Daniel again describes the man's legs . . . "cut open . . . I saw a cross-section of his legs, the muscles and bone." This is an even stronger suggestion of his image of the woman's leg "split open." He saw the man's "spinal—his backbone." He had described a part of the woman's brain as being quite identifiable as her "medulla." The "silvery coating . . . like the inside of a fish" in the dream is probably associated with the luminescent quality of the meninges, which he might have observed on the brain parts. Finally, in the dream, he speaks of putting "myself in his position." The woman has become a man in the dream, as her suicide was "very close to home" for him. The dream, in terms of manifest content, contains images derived from the original stress event and occurs in expectation of reliving the event in the forthcoming interview.

To recapitulate, two years after a frightening experience, images of that experience continued to have an intrusive quality, emerging in spite of suppressive efforts when certain associational triggers occurred. In addition, there was a continued need to retell the story while both awake and asleep. Even the process of the interview itself has aspects of re-enactment. This is by no means an unusual story, and serves to illustrate the endurance and intensity of a response to stressful events in a normal person.

CHAPTER FOURTEEN

An Automobile Accident

With the assistance of Richard Olsen, M.D.*

JANE IS A TWENTY-THREE-YEAR-OLD WOMAN who developed a relatively severe reaction to an automobile accident. Her therapy was completed in five interviews and these will be reported in detail here as an illustration of process in the treatment of stress response syndromes. Relevant issues are the succession of intrusive and denial signs and symptoms, a technique of limited abreaction, and the interaction of the external stress event with her current tasks in life and her personal development.

Six weeks after her automobile accident, Jane called asking for immediate help because she was tense, nauseated, and unable to eat or sleep. She had been seeing a doctor for neck and back pain, and been placed on medications for pain, muscle spasms, nausea and insomnia. Nothing helped, and her physician had called in to see if psychiatric hospitalization was in order. It was suggested that she be referred to the stress clinic for evaluation. When she telephoned, she sounded tearful and desperate, and complained of extreme nervousness and preoccupation with the accident. An appointment was made for later that same day. After a discussion of the research and teaching aspects of the clinic service, Jane gave informed consent for participation. The following interviews then took place.

---

*Dr. Olsen is presently Clinical Instructor in Psychiatry at the University of California, San Francisco.

FIRST SESSION

She appeared for the first session looking pale, tense, and wearing a protective collar around her neck. A slender and moderately attractive person who dressed modestly, her face was rigid and she moved in a guarded and halting manner.

T (Therapist): What's up?

J (Jane): I'd rather you didn't ask me that leading question. (She appears to be very tense.)

T: Well, you called this morning.

J: My doctor thought I'd better call because I was getting more and more anxious and I couldn't eat. He knows— he's treating me for a whiplash . . . (long pause).

T: Yes.

J: . . . and it brings on the pain . . . (long pause).

T: What does the not eating. . .

J: What does it do?

T: Well, how does it come upon you?

J: Well, whenever I get upset, I slow down on whatever I'm eating. I never have had an appetite too much. And when I got upset this week, I just began to vomit in the morning and couldn't keep anything on my stomach.

T: Well, that was just this week that you got upset?

J: Well, yeah, but this is like I've been upset before.

T: When did it seem to start, being upset?

J: I've never calmed down since the accident, not completely. I've been on the medication ever since.

T: What medication is that?

Ordinarily, at the very beginning of the contact, the therapist would not focus on a detail such as medications, but would instead encourage reports of more central material. This focus is made in order to help the patient establish a therapeutic alliance as well as to evaluate the current situation. She is quite tense, resistant to the idea of communicating with the therapist, and focuses on somatic issues. She has not presented psychological reasons for coming. At the same time, she is indicating non-verbally that she is in great need and wants to be taken care of. A somewhat tangential discussion may establish a model of successful communication, provide a calming effect to counteract the extra stress of a first therapeutic contact, and pave the way for freer communication of the more central details.

J: It depends on what week you're talking about. He's been changing it as I change.

T: Uh-huh. Have you been taking tranquilizers?

Her remark, "it depends on what week" is sarcastic and the therapist knows that the state of her relationship with her doctor may be important. Her dependence plus irritation towards her physician already impresses the therapist. He expects that there may be a potential for this sort of transference in the therapy, and considers the possibility of its relationship with her reactions to the stress event. He chooses to persist in finding out the answer to his earlier question, "What medication?", in order to establish the model for therapeutic communication mentioned above.

J: Tranquilizers, pain killers and a joint deflamatory medication 'cause I messed up my hips as well. I have to wear a lift on my shoe now.

T: Who is your doctor?

J: Doctor Smith.

T: What kind of a doctor is he?

J: He's an M.D., internist.

T: Uh-huh. Are you seeing him privately, or are you a clinic patient?

J: Privately. He is the one who I went to after the accident 'cause he was my doctor.

T: And he suggested you come here?

J: Yeah.

T: When was that?

J: I went to him Tuesday because I had missed work. I just started substituting as a nurses' aide and I was really upset with some nurse and I had to have the head nurse find another substitute at the last minute because I got all the way down to Zone City where I'm working and I couldn't stay. And I went to his office and I slept there for three hours while I was waiting for him to come. The receptionist let me sleep there. And then he changed my medication and by Thursday, I was in the same state all over again. I got through Wednesday somehow, but by Thursday I couldn't, so I didn't even leave and go to Zone City. And I called him and he started making arrangements, so he contacted the clinic.

T: Yes, right. So, here you are. Well, this is what we'll do now. I'll just try and find out what I can about you this time and maybe another time. Then, we'll try and assign you for appropriate treatment. It already sounds like something is indicated.

J: What?

T: I don't know, but something.

J: Something?

Her rejoinder is subdued sarcasm and is provocative. The therapist again has the impression that Jane will tend to set up a passive dependent or passive-dependent-aggressive type of transference situation. She is challenging him to do something before he knows what is going on. She has not said clearly that she is in psychological distress, but presented only physical complaints. He is comparatively certain that she is in psychological distress and chooses to focus on this issue. His next remark will, therefore, be made as a statement. This again points toward developing a therapeutic contract. The therapist illustrates his intentions here; he will clarify and interpret, but not assume responsibility for her life. He already has a hunch that the physical complaints are both real and used as a defensive denial of emotional responses to the accident. He is, in a mild way, undercutting that defense by focusing attention on the area of warded-off experiences. These early choices are often quite important. Unfortunately, they have to be made on very little data.

T: It sounds like you are in psychological difficulty.

J: Yeah, I know, it has to be psychological. There is no other reason to have all these problems at once. (Long pause.)

T: Well, I'd like to know much more. Where do you think would be a good place to start; would it be to tell me about the accident, or—? (Trails off.)

The patient is still resistant to telling the therapist what kind of difficulty she is experiencing. The therapist now senses that this is not simply a high level of anxiety or inarticulateness, but that there is also an element of defiance. Perhaps he is being equated with the referring physician. She may be covertly communicating an accusation that would go something like this were it to have been expressed verbally rather than non-verbally: "You see, you won't help me enough: I still hurt, and so I won't cooperate with you. Let's have you make me do what you think will help. Then we'll see that it won't help either. That will prove that if anyone is to blame, it is you, and not me." To avoid this type of transference, the therapist backs off a little from the firmness of his earlier remark, "it sounds like psychological difficulty." He places the responsibility for choosing their next topic partially with her.

J: Well, the accident stopped me from doing all kinds of things. On the day of the accident, I was on my way to an assignment to substitute in Zone City. And I took Banning Road because the school was near Banning. I never take it unless I have to, and in the fog, someone rear-ended me at a stop light. And after that, after I gave out flares and told everybody that my neck hurt, we moved the cars because other cars were bearing down and nearly hitting them again. And a policeman came and passed out flares and put them out on the highway and another car came and smashed into my car and I went into shock. And I was just like a robot from there until a few hours later when I came down again.

She does not mean physiological shock, but rather a direct entry into a numbing phase of response to stress.

T: Uh-huh. You were driving alone?

J: Yeah, I was on the way to work. I have to be alone to get there because substitute nurses' aides never know where they're going to be. But the doctor kept me off work for a month. And that same day, I was supposed to go to an interview for a regular job, and they were good enough to hold the job open for me. And I had to wait until I could find out whether I would be able to work. They decided that I could work and so I went to work with my collar on, about two and a half, three weeks ago. But they placed me in another ward, with new people because there was a rule about two people in the same family on the same service and my sister-in-law was working on that service. I'm supposedly teamed with two other aides, but they are very, very close and are roommates as well so that they are together all the time and they are actually teaming and I am way off and I see them only during report.

T: Yes, so you are kind of isolated?

J: Yeah.

The theme of people letting her down is repeated again: The nurses, nurses' aides, her doctor and (by inference), the present therapist. The therapist gently affirms this feeling by saying she is isolated and she carries on with a freer description of how tough things are at work. She says she broke down one day recently but does not reveal what that means. Only in later hours did she describe what had happened. She had grown so irritated with a complaining, senile patient that she slapped him. She was terrified that she would be reported and lose her registration as a para-professional, as well as the immediate job. After adding details about work, which seem to smooth out the communicative feeling with the therapist, she continues as follows:

J: But after I got myself upset Tuesday, I couldn't get myself calmed down, and I dragged through Wednesday and I couldn't make it Thursday, and I stayed off today.

T: Yes. Well, can you tell me what being upset and nervous is like inside you? How is it going in there?

J: It changes. It started just to be stomach trouble, but along with it, my stomach would hurt and my bowels would be loose. The stress would go into my back and now the small of my back and my hip joints and my neck all hurt, and just about every single muscle hurts by now. I haven't eaten enough in so long that I'm just exhausted, and—

T: How long has it been since you've eaten anything?

J: I eat little bits 'cause every day is like a cycle. In the afternoon, I'm pretty good and by evening, I might even be able to eat solid food. But in the morning or the middle of the night if I wake up, I can't stomach anything and I'll just be sick.

T: Will you throw up if you try to eat?

J: Yes. Or right now, I was throwing up on Wednesday before I went to work and I got it into my nose and I always get sinus problems anyway; and I was sneezing all day and I didn't think about it, but that evening, it drained back down and burned my throat. I haven't been able to shake that yet; I'm still—like I was crying all day yesterday and the night before and the more I cry the worse it got. So, last night, I woke up hysterical; I couldn't breathe 'cause I couldn't clear my throat and I had a pain in my chest and it turned out to be that I was sleeping on my side and a muscle had tightened.

During the therapy, this patient has symptoms related to her joints, bones, muscles, gastrointestinal system, eyes, and upper respiratory system. None of these are malingering; she tends to develop psychophysiological reactions under stress. Such symptoms should never be regarded in an unsympathetic manner. It will be seen that Jane has conflicts between dependency wishes and strivings for independence. She has already presented herself to the therapist as both needing to depend on someone and not wishing to depend on anyone. The somatic symptoms are presented as a reasonable basis for obtaining sympathy and attention, but they are presented in such quantity that the therapist is made uncomfortable with the load. He changes the topic, perhaps too abruptly, but does try to find out more about what may be real aspects of her dependency-independency situation.

T: Are you staying alone?

J: No, I'm with my father and my stepmother.

T: Yes.

J: But I don't get on with my father. He is an alcoholic and we have what he decides is a mutual agreement: we talk to each other as little as possible because if we say more than three words, there is an argument.

T: I see. Then it's somewhat of a tense living arrangement.

J: I wanted to get out of it before the accident. I had planned to leave in either August or in October, depending of whether I could sign a contract for September or not or get some other kind of work. I was taking typing lessons in case I couldn't find a job as an aide. But now, I have to stay home until I'm well 'cause I have no place to go and no money.

T: Did you finish training just recently?

The therapist notes with interest that the accident forces her to stay on with her father. She had planned to separate from him, a more than appropriate move for a 23-year-old. The psychodynamic possibilities demand further exploration, but the therapist delays this because a therapeutic alliance is not yet established and because she is so distraught. He already believes dependency-independency conflicts may be important. He believes that establishment of a therapeutic alliance, in and of itself, will offer enough support to enable the patient to improve, not require hospitalization and probably not need medications. After details about her current work and training situation, the therapist tries a gentle return to the situation of living with her alcoholic father.

T: Do I gather that you had a kind of plan of getting a job and then moving out?

J: Uh-huh; pretty soon.

T: Yes, well, (long pause) so, there seems possibilities of that, but getting into the accident really set you back?

J: Yeah, right after the accident when I was pretty medicated, I felt really, really good because the pain hadn't set in; it took a few days. A job possibility came up for just the kind of job I wanted. Only it was a rumor; it was something the nurses were pushing and the nursing director hadn't set her mind on it yet and she had just asked around for nurses and aides to transfer into those positions who were already employed in the hospital. And so, several people contacted me who had been contacted by her saying, "You really fit into this one." But in the days after that, my neck got tighter. I couldn't drive myself down to Zone City, so I couldn't go to an interview. And since that time, the woman who would have interviewed me committed suicide.

T: Now, what's been on your mind in terms of the accident itself? Does it come back to you at all?

It is advisable to ask directly about intrusive phase symptoms, as the patient knows them consciously, but often does not know how to report them.

J: The only time I really think about it is when we're commuting on the freeway and someone changes lanes or does something stupid. Then I feel that it's about to happen because I saw the guy coming when I was hit. I could see him in the rear view mirror and he was coming too fast. That's the only time I really think much about it.

T: Yes. And you said you don't drive now?

J: Yes, I do. I don't drive to Zone City because it's too far to go, but I drive around the city. Today I'm not driving because I haven't eaten in so long that I'm too weak.

T: And what is keeping you from eating? Is it lack of appetite?

J: Well, I don't have any appetite and my throat was really sore, and my stomach wouldn't take food except for a few hours and then it won't take much. But I talked to my doctor again; I talk to him every day, and he has prescribed something so that my stomach will remain calm so that I can eat. I just picked it up before I came here.

T: What is that?

J: I'd have to look; it's in my purse. Do you really want to know?

T: No, just if you knew. Are you taking any other medicines besides this one you're going to be taking?

J: Uh-huh; I was taking Valium right after the accident, with the other medications, and then I went off of it last Tuesday. Then he put me on Compazine. That Compazine puts me to sleep. When it hits, I'm out. So today, he put me back on Valium and he doubled the dose.

T: Does that help you?

J: Yeah, the only thing that bothers me is that it dulls my mind. After having studied medical stuff like anatomy, that just freaks me out because I like to be able to think clearly and know stuff. Like I couldn't even keep my charts. I had them all messed up as to which patients had what temperatures, which had movements, and all like that.

T: So it would be important to get through this stage that you're in—

J: Right. I really don't like to be on any kind of medicine at all and I usually have to be coerced by the doctor to keep on it. I keep wanting to go off of it and stay off of medication. It scares me because I've seen too many people with problems.

T: And what did you do at home yesterday?

J: Well, first I typed a couple of letters and the phone was going all day with the doctor trying to find out where he could put me in. And the people were calling me who were concerned.

T: Where he could put you in?

J: For psychiatric help.

T: Oh, I see.

J: He had thought he could put me in Acme Hospital. And I'm—

T: That didn't work out at Acme?

J: No, I'm out of the district. I'm reading a book and was watching T.V. And I've got a dog and I usually walk her every day, but when my hip joints hurt, I don't want to walk. Yesterday, by late afternoon, I was feeling good so I took her for a walk.

T: And do you have difficulty concentrating, like when you try to read or watch television?

J: It depends on what it is. Like, I was reading a medical book the other night and I kept having to put it down because I couldn't imagine the parts that you should imagine as you're reading. But when I'm reading really light stuff, like from the *Reader's Digest* or something, then I have no trouble concentrating.

T: And do you see anybody?

J: My family keeps coming in and out, but most of my friends are—like when I was working full time and she's (her girlfriend) staying hopped up on uppers to keep working. And she doesn't really want to see me† because I make her unhappy and mess her up. And another friend just took off† for the country, and another one is leaving† for back East and she claims that she is really busy. And really, those are the only people I see much of; I don't see a lot of people.

† More desertion themes.

T: No boy friends?

J: Not right now.

T: In the past?

J: Not lately, but, yeah.

T: So, you're feeling pretty isolated except for your family? Why does your girl friend say that you mess her up?

J: We act rather strongly against one another; we have different beliefs, but we're willing to be friends. She, right now, is kind of selling what she wants to be and what she wants to do and trying to convince herself. She's going around spouting it out to everybody. She has already tried it out on me and knows that I disagree with it. She doesn't want to be near me because she's trying to convince everybody that the things she's going to do next are right, and I don't believe her.

T: How would you characterize—or how would she characterize you; what are your strong attitudes?

The therapist is after more data on her character and level of psychological development.

J: Most of my friends, including her, say that I'm stable. Doesn't sound like it now, but I'm usually stable and very—if I do something one way, like help out in a strange situation, I can figure out ways to get out of them. And I'm always there when anybody wants to get out of that kind of situation. Like the car breaking down; I'm really mechanically inclined and if it broke down and I was there, I would probably open the hood and, if it was simple, I would put it together or I'd know how to call for help.

She seems proud of having independent skills.

T: Right. Any other strong attitudes your friends would say you had; that would characterize your personality?

J: People who don't know me very well think I'm an egghead or that I'm cold.

T: But it's not true?

J: Well, I've got other friends who say they thought that and then when they got to know me, they found out that I wasn't. So, I don't think it's true.

T: Okay, let's go back; do you mind talking more about the accident? It's seems like it's really centrally important.

This is a firm attempt to set a focus for a brief therapy. The therapist has gathered some general data and tried to foster a therapeutic alliance in the conversation so far.

T: You were going to work and you saw this car coming at you and you knew it was going to hit you. Could you, could you just tell me all the details from there?

J: I had come to a red light and one car had stopped in front of me and I was stopped and waiting. And while I was waiting, I caught an action in the mirror and so I watched it and saw the car coming at me too fast and tensed up and then he hit. And the first sensation after the numbness, the first numbness went away, was that my shoulder and neck hurt. And after the person in the front had seen my car jump, he came back and said, "Are you hurt?" I said, "Yes" and he stayed to help us. And the man behind me, the one who had hit me, he took a look around and came up to see me and says, "Are you hurt?" I said, "Yes, my neck is hurt." But I had checked myself out and I could tell that was the only thing that was hurting; nothing else was hurting at all. So, I got out of the car and looked at the situation, then I crawled into the back seat and got some flares out 'cause nobody had anything to mark off this accident and it was in heavy commute traffic and deep fog. So, I used the flares and said, "Has anybody called the police yet?" Nobody had; nobody knew where a phone was; it was really eerie because we were completely fogged in. You could see the road but you couldn't see anything else because it was really, really fogged in.

Her willingness to relate the details and her pride in taking charge of the situation (independence) are both noteworthy. She became vague and distracted as she said "fogged in" and that prompted the therapist's next remark. She seemed, in a way, to be re-enacting the accident.

T: You probably started feeling unreal.

J: Yeah, yeah. Then the man who had hit me decided that I was shaking and we couldn't decide whether it was cold or pain. I didn't even know which it was, so he put me in his car and we traded information. Then he left me in his car and went to use the phone, and after he came back, I decided we'd better move the cars, because I kept hearing cars braking to avoid my car. We moved them and I left the engine running and lights on and I moved it into a zone that was painted off, a safety zone next to an island, a right turn island. And he moved off to the shoulder and we got back into his car to keep warm. My car was still in a more dangerous position. And a police car came and he said they had trouble figuring out what county we were. So a police car came and didn't seem to see us. It came from the other direction and it made a left turn and stopped. And then, after a long time, the policeman that we saw came, and he pulled around and came and talked to us and pieced together the accident. Then he put out his flares and was going back to get this report book when we could hear this other car approaching and we all turned and watched the next collision, which threw the car about eight feet out into the intersection, because he was going mighty fast. And then that man got out of the car and exploded and he just ran and he swore all over the place. He stomped around—

T: Angrily?

Her facial expression and vocal inflection indicate a great emotional involvement in this new person, and the therapist intuitively picks out a central aspect.

J: Yeah, he was as mad as he could be. I wanted his name before he went anywhere. He said, "I'm going to find a phone." I insisted and so he threw his license at me and stomped away (she is very indignant). And the officer was out of hearing range by then and he came back and they started calling tow trucks and stuff and then they had to decide whether to send for an ambulance for me or whether I knew someone I could notify, because I was the only one that was hurt. I said, "I'm really not hurt bad enough to call an ambulance; I can walk around and I can sit without hurting myself. If I think for a minute, maybe I'll figure out somebody I know who can come and get me." And I thought about it and tried my brother-in-law and he was home because it was finals week and he didn't have a final that morning. So, he came to get me and he

handled my towing service and some of the policeman's questions about me and stuff while I wrote out
a report. Then after we had checked the car and
left it in an empty lot, we called my doctor and took
me in. But my doctor had two other emergencies that
morning in his office and they left me sitting in the
waiting room for an hour and a half. Then they decided, after he looked at me for one minute, he needed
an X-ray before he could decide anything. So, he sent
me over to X-ray which is in the same building. I'd
been there before because I had had back trouble before and I had X-rays and retakes and stuff. And I
went back and he decided there were no fractures and
no nerves pinched; it was just a severe strain. He prescribed tranquilizers and pain killers and a prescription
for the collar and I went downstairs and got the collar
and I got the medications and stayed home. But my
insurance company sent a field representative to my
house that afternoon. And I was really, really—not the
same as I am anxious now—but excited more and I
called a friend to stay with me and my family kept
dropping in and the house was full of people and they
had like a party and joked a lot, having a good time.
And then the guy with a tape recorder came and taped
my version of the accident and he wanted a medical
release and—

T: And so your family didn't realize, because there was
not any big deal like bandages, they didn't realize that
you'd been hurt.

The therapist is picking up on her vocal tone which indicates her
hurt and anger that she got so little attention.

J: Right. And then when I started to hurt, it really scared
me 'cause I didn't know it was going to start to hurt.

T: Right, and that was really frightening.

J: And then the following Tuesday, I started therapy,
physical therapy. But a few weeks later, I had to call
my doctor about pains in my hip joint. It was just one
at first, and I've had something related to that before,
but it wasn't the same; this was stronger. And he didn't

understand what it was and couldn't find out and so he looked up my old X-ray and found out it was in my other hip, so he went for another X-ray. And he then said that the joint didn't show anything, but in the days that followed, it got worse and has gone to the other side. It turned out that I was sleeping on my side. I always slept on my side before this and so I was sleeping on my side. I was sleeping on my hip and it was getting irritated. And then I'd turned over to the other side and done it to the other one. So—

T: How did you feel about seeing your doctor repeatedly?

J: Well, he had me down once a week and it turned out that I made the once a week appointment. I might not have a new complaint every week, but I just got in on a once a week appointment until this week.

T: How did the relationship go between you and your doctor? Do you know what I mean?

J: Yes. Well, he is almost argumentative in manner, but not that strong. I don't know where—well, if I ask something, then he asks something back and we go back and forth. And it isn't as if he's trying to explain the whole thing to me; I need to ask him to find out how things are going to go.

T: Right, just like being surprised that it was going to hurt. Doctors sometimes feel, "Well, I won't say anything because I don't want people to imagine it." And then what happens is what usually happens in these things. Delayed symptoms come up, and then you're surprised. But I get the feeling throughout that your feelings are badly hurt, as well as your neck.

For her, this is a major interpretation. It is also a second round in trying to establish a therapeutic contract for exploring her ideas and feelings.

J: Uh-huh.

Her response is vague, so the therapist tries to gently rivet her attention to the issue. She has not yet fully agreed to the exploration of psychological issues.

T: Does it make sense to you?

J: My feelings hurt?

T: Yeah.

J: I'm awfully disappointed that all my plans got wrecked.

T: Yeah, but I don't think you've been able to tell anyone that.

J: But I talk to my sister-in-law all the time. Only thing is that she is talking about other things when she talks back, so I don't know if she's hearing. (Long pause.)

T: Well, I think there's some working through to do about talking over these things. That, at least, I see as being real essential for you to do. Anything else?

The therapist is once again working towards establishment of a therapeutic contract centered on psychological issues.

J: Oh, on the day before the accident, I hadn't been called to work. And I have a choice; I can call in at the City Hospital where I used to work and say I'm there, or I can do what I please. So, I decided it was about time I got myself another car 'cause I had sold my car about a month before when it was beginning to give me trouble. It was a '60 Toyota and parts were really hard to get 'cause mine was made for the Canadian specifications. So I sold it and was still convinced that Toyota makes a good car for an economy car. It is big enough not to scare me. I know that Volkswagons blow around on the freeways; that scares me and being in an accident scares me. This is before the accident, I went down—I saw an ad in the paper and I made phone calls; then I went down to Danville where there was a good dealer. I won't trust the guy locally 'cause I've heard what happens. And I test drove a car and I said, "Yeah, I'll put a down payment on it." Then I told him that there were a couple of things that needed work before I would pay for the car, and he wrote them up and then I had the accident the next day. I was supposed to pick it up on Saturday and I had arranged financing independently on my own through their bank

which they had set up for me. But it was my own
financing. I got home and my father said, "Oh, no, I'll
pay the whole thing for you; you can just pay me
back." Which is the arrangement he did with my sister
and since I'm financially in a rotten position anyway,
I decided, well, money is going to help me get out of
the house faster; I'll do it. And so I canceled the loan
financing and I got all their correct numbers and had
my father write up a cashier's check 'cause he has the
money in the bank.

Dependency on her father and the link of cars to her father will
turn out to be an important dynamic issue in working through the
stress event.

Saturday, I really freaked out about picking up a car
'cause I couldn't drive; I had the collar on and the
pain was getting bad and I was taking codeine and
was too doped up to drive. I convinced my brother and
my brother-in-law to come along. They took me down
and they were really nice; and they took me in a car
with back rests in it, shoulder harness and drove real
careful. And when we got there, they test drove it for
me. They said they'd take it on a rough road and really
see how it was doing but the salesman who was selling
it to me and told me he'd be there wasn't there, and he
turned me over to the manager.

The desertion theme emerges again. Note that she is talking
more openly to the therapist and in a pressured manner.

And the manager needed all the details because the
salesman had left in a hurry. And we made the arrangements finally and signed the papers and gave him all
the money and took the car home. And since then, problems that I stated on the first form weren't solved.
Today was the day we finally had an appointment to
have it done so I sent my brother down again and he
just got the car back, but I haven't had a chance to ride
in it or drive it myself yet to see if it really is repaired
or not.

T: So you have that hassle. Well, look, we have to stop. I'd like to see you again before we decide anything. But, you know, I think we've already decided that whatever else, there is some talking to be done.

Yet another effort to reach agreement on a therapeutic contract.

J: Okay.

T: You know, I hope this won't interfere with you working.

A suggestion that she is well enough to work and should go on rather than regress.

J: I work in the morning only.

T: Oh, well, let's see what we can do in the afternoon.

J: It would have to be after 1:00 o'clock.

T: Um. I could see you if you could come Monday at 2:30. Would that be okay?

J: Okay.

SECOND SESSION

She begins by saying that she has done quite well over the week-end. She feels that the first hour helped her: "It just worked, I don't know what it did. I know afterwards, I kept thinking, 'I sure didn't say a lot of details that were there that I could have said,' but at the time, I didn't think." This suggests to the therapist that she was in a denial phase of response. The hour helped both in the sense of socialization, discussing the accident with a therapeutically-oriented person and, in a general way, raising her concerns to a reality rather than fantasy-oriented level.

She goes on to add that she has moved out of her father's house. She has asked her pregnant sister to take her in, and that had been an improvement over eating with her father who tends to vomit at meal times because of his alcoholism. She indirectly attributes the idea of this move to the therapist's remark, in the first hour, that the situation at home was tense. Probably this repetition by the therapist of what she herself had been saying, acted as permission for her to become more assertive.

She was worried about being a burden on her sister, but said, "I'm going to turn it around and I'm going to help her and I'm helping because I don't have to be the one that everyone else is helping. It puts me one block away from the person I was commuting with, my sister-in-law. And I'm going to see if I can commute alone pretty soon, 'cause I don't like to be driven. I'm going to try it one time with her sitting beside me and if that doesn't have any problem at all, then I'm just going to commute by myself."

The therapist is pleased to see the reassertion of her striving for independence and activity. He has also been impressed by both regressive forces leading to searches for dependency as a secondary gain from the accident, and the loaded but unexplored issue of her deterioration at the accident when yelled at by the driver of the second car. Also, she was at the point where her doctor was considering psychiatric hospitalization and she was showing many somatic as well as psychological complaints. He favors further work rather than a termination at this point. His feeling that the improvement is, in a way, a relationship cure, adds to this decision to continue. First, he asks more about what seems to be a fear of driving and then asks an open-ended question.

T: Well, what about cars and driving? How has that been on your mind the last few days?

J: Well, I drove here. I drove all over this morning doing stuff, getting keys made and stuff.

T: Alone?

J: Sure. Ever since the accident, I'm always able to drive short distances alone; no problem at all. The only problem that still scares me is getting on the freeway in heavy commute traffic, where mergers are going on.

That part scares me. But I think if I was behind the wheel and not having to watch somebody else do it, I could handle it fine, because I did it since January and never had an accident, or even a close call. You know, I know how to do it; just whether or not I'm scared or not.

T: Okay. Well, where should we go from here?

J: I don't know. I'd kind of like to find out why I get into such deep depressions and can't get—well, this time I couldn't get myself out, because I wouldn't want to go into it again. If it ever happened again, it would screw up my career in nursing, being unable to attend or just breaking down like that. I mean, if I couldn't have pulled out this week, my contract probably would have been torn up and destroyed and my record would have been messed up, you know. And I really would like to get to the root of why I throw myself into depressions.

T: Okay. That's something then that we should explore a little bit more. Maybe we'll have time now. But I wanted to ask you also where the memory is with you right now about the accident.

J: I can remember it fine.

T: Uh-huh. Does it come back to you when you don't want· it to at all?

As mentioned earlier, intrusive phase symptoms are often not reported spontaneously by patients. Risking the danger of suggestion of a symptom, the therapist asks pointedly after a common response to accidents.

J: No. I think—I don't usually remember what I dream. But since, like the last week or so, I have had nightmares, usually right when I wake up I remember something, some piece of it and I think sometimes I have nightmares about the accident because it scared me so bad.

T: Yes. But you don't remember what they are?

J: No. Never have. (Laugh.)

T: Do they sometimes wake you up out of your sleep?

J: Well, it is a combination because I move around if I'm having a nightmare and then I don't know whether it's the nightmare or laying on a hip joint or bending my back or what it is that wakes me up. But I wake up, and I can remember a piece of a bad dream and being in pain at the same time. So, I don't know, is it the night—you know, I'm so wrapped up in too many things at once—I can't say. Like last night, I slept fantastic—no problem at all. And I know I woke up on my side which is supposed to be a no-no until the hips get better. And this morning, this hip joint was irritated, but after I was up and moving around and took a hot shower, after about 45 minutes, it's okay now. So I think pretty soon I'm throwing the book away and forget about it so I can sleep like I want to sleep.

T: Uh-huh, and during the day, you don't find you're having thoughts about the accident coming in on you when you don't want them to?

J: The only time they'd come in on me is if I associate with something happening right now, like in the car—

T: That might trigger it?

J: Yeah, trigger it.

T: Well, you know thoughts like that are always surprises.

This is a "moving closer" type of remark, meant to reveal empathy with the patient. The patient responds with associative memories.

J: Yeah, definitely. Well, I know, well, I mean, I kind of compare it with my mother's death a long time ago and for a long time after that, things would trigger that memory, you know. And now it's so long that—and I used to counsel at the York Avenue place with the kids who had a lot of trouble. A lot of them had fathers who disappeared and people in the hospital dying and things like that and I could handle that fine for them, too, you know. And I got out of that and I'm confident that I'll be able to get out of the accident myself. But something else is still triggering depressions on me because I still get into them.

T: Well, there may have been a clue to that in our discussion Friday. It may not be the right one, but it might be there. I kind of got the idea that you experienced the accident, in one way, as just another insult.

J: Yeah.

T: Does that seem to fit with you?

J: Uh-huh.

T: And maybe there have been a number of other ones in your life and this was just. . . .

J: Another one; yeah.

T: . . . just another one to hit you. Of course, it had that kind of rippling effect in that it interfered with so many of your plans.

J: Yeah. It meant nothing in particular. My car, I hadn't paid for it, I was right in the middle of it. And that afternoon, I was supposed to go for planning for the summer. That particular day, I was doing a million matters of business and none of them could be done . . . (long pause).

In an event-centered therapy, one might not wish to stray too far afield. But she calls her psychological reaction a depression and seems to recognize a recurrent pattern. The therapist believes this must be explored to understand her character, pre-existing conflicts, and the meanings attached to this recent event. As she pours out a tale of losses, the therapist realizes the importance of accumulated stresses and the "last straw" effect in this case.

T: Okay. Well, tell me a little bit about some of the other depressions that you've had. What kind of things seem to trigger them?

J: I think most of the other ones were triggered by people dying, because I've watched my mother go into a depression when her mother died. That was when I was five; I was just a kid and I don't know what I was doing. I used to throw tantrums, but I don't know what else I was doing. But when I was 12, she was ill and she had been ill for years and died of cancer and that threw me. They had to take me to a doctor and start giving me vitamin shots to pull me back out because I was wasting away, losing too much weight.

A few years after that, my favorite aunt died and I went into another one. Shortly after that, one of my best friends died and then I went into one again. One summer, in fact I think it was the summer my aunt died, there was a dog we bought the year after my mother's death—and she always thought a dachshund would be a nice kind of dog because they're clean. So, my sister helped find one and everything, convinced my father who was against it, and we bought a dachshund. It turned out that the dachshund was pedigreed and he was overbred and he had come out with a mean temperament. If a professional had been the breeder, he probably would have been destroyed because of his temperament, but it was a non-professional person who sold it to us, and he was like a one-man dog and we didn't know it. He could have been trained maybe to be a watchdog; otherwise, he should have been destroyed because he was mean. But we kept him for six years and we had to do all kinds of things all over the house so that the family could protect people from him because he was moody and temperamental. He hurt people and I got into all kinds of trouble because I was sitting for people at the time. I had to take a little girl to the emergency hospital and nearly landed in a lawsuit because her eye got scratched and all kinds of problems with him.

But anyway, that summer he fell down the back stairs and dislocated his back and paralyzed himself from the shoulders back with some control of his internal organs. I had to take care of him 'cause I was the only one home and I nursed him, and nursed him, and nursed him and finally I was just getting really tired of it. My parents were going to be on vacation and I said, "Is it okay with you if you'll take along the dog? I'm going to take two weeks off and visit a friend in Tahoe." They said fine. And I call and they say everything is fine and I came home and found that they had run out of pain killers and didn't know that pill was important and hadn't gotten any and the dog had been in pain for eight days and just shaking with the pain. So I took him to the vet and we had to have him destroyed.

We had two dogs at the time—my other dog caught one of the infections that the dachshund had and she had to be nursed back to health. After all that happened, after I went into a depression—it wasn't very long or very strong, because I had to do so many things right then and get back to school and stuff, but it seems they're all tied up with someone dying.

T: Losing something you like or are attached to?

J: Yeah. And then after that, there was—last summer was different. Last summer, I was taking courses, that's the last thing before you student nurse and go out. One of the people in the courses said, "I know you're really good" 'cause I was helping her out. She said, "I've got a job possibility for you" so I went and followed it up and got the job, only the job was really something I wasn't quite ready for and it threw me for a loop. I was tense because I had to learn how to deal with unusual patients and all of this on a semi-volunteer, possibly with money coming through and me in debt for a car that I had just bought, all at once.

And so, I got all upset and Dr. Smith treated me then with tranquilizers and I got through it and we had a glorious summer, no matter what. (Laughter.) But about a week before the end of it, my mother's last surviving sister died of a brain tumor and her daughter is a dwarf, who is slowly becoming—well, now I guess you'd call her a hermit. She has withdrawn from just about every living soul in the world. I happen to be one of the few people alive that she'll talk to. There is a handful of people; my sister, her sister, her brother and a couple who she'll talk to on a very superficial level. I was trying to see if I could help her out but, of course, she wouldn't accept it. And also, having lost my aunt, I went into another tailspin but I came out of that one quick; it was short. I just got mad at the whole thing and said, "I've got to live for me and get out of this mess."

Since that time, there's just been like little short things like the pressure of substituting. I'd get myself worked up in the morning waiting for that phone to ring and wouldn't be able to eat breakfast until after the phone rang and I knew what the day was going to be. I was just waiting because at 6:00 a.m. when it could ring, I'd have to wait until 8:30 to know for sure whether it's going to ring. And then, on three occasions, they called me for emergencies, so I really was never sure. So, I made it a policy that if it didn't ring by 8:30, I just left and I either did volunteer work or I did something else, 'cause it was driving me crazy to wait for the phone.

T: Well, you're a very strongly motivated person to get out and do things.

J: Yeah, well, I've had to.

T: It is related to what you've said; you've decided that you're going to survive. There are a number of messes in your family.

J: Definitely. Yeah. My mother taught me from the time I was very tiny, because my sister told me not too long ago that my mother had arthritis before I was born. And before she was ever pregnant with me, they told her that she shouldn't carry another child; it would hurt her too much, she had arthritis in her back. When I was very, very small, she would be in bed in the morning and she would tell me how to do things. I would have to go and do them and then come back to her and see if they were done correctly. Instead of having her show me, she would just tell me and I would have to go and do them, like getting ready for school in the morning, getting breakfast and that kind of thing. So, I had to learn how to do things independently.

Then, it got to the point where her arthritis would get worse and she wouldn't be awake and I wouldn't want to wake her, so I would do them all by myself and if something new came up, I would sit down and think and see if I could figure it out so I wouldn't have to wake her up. But the older I got, the arthritis got worse and then—I don't know, something happened when I was about eight. It improved for awhile and she got out and got a job. And then we had to take on the whole thing about fixing dinner and buying food while she was out working. Then the cancer started and she stopped work. Then she got really, really sick. Finally, because my father doesn't believe in hospitals, he insisted that she die at home and she died at home from cancer and from all the complications from it.

T: Were you nursing her?

J: No, they wouldn't let me because I was the littlest. They had locked me out. That hurts sometimes (crying). They'd send me away so I couldn't see her very much. Because she was so sick, they didn't want me to be scared, but it's scary not to know.

T: It can be harder than knowing the worst, sometimes.

J: I don't know. She finally died of dehydration; not from the cancer itself, but from what it caused.

T: I get the feeling that you never had a chance to say goodbye.

J: No. She said something once that sounded like goodbye, but they never told her she had cancer and we knew for awhile. She was smart and knew it. 'Cause she was taking cobalt treatment and anybody would know. But (silence) one time she did say something that was like goodbye. But that was months before she died. But I always have to—in my own family—I have to fight for the right to be treated my own age because I'm the littlest. My father wants me to be little and protected.

The regressive trend may have an oedipal overtone, as suspected in the first hour. The accident made her ill and a stay-at-home like her mother. Later material will show that there is an ambivalent attachment toward her father in which they each can play either role: he babies her or she nurses him. Her progressive developmental strivings were leading to a healthy separation from this bond, with external sources of potential gratifications providing the enticements that would allow her to leave her father. The accident upset this forward movement and is a variegated type of loss, as subsequent material will show.

J: I usually win, but it's always a big hassle. Like he didn't want me to go to the funeral. I told him—I was going to a parochial school at the time—I told him they're sending 100 school-age children my age to sing at her funeral and they're my classmates. And if my classmates can go, there's no good reason why I can't go. He was convinced and I went. Had he left me out of the funeral, I don't think I would have believed that she had died.

T: Yes, I think you were quite right to have gone.

In hope of a rapid restabilization at her most progressive level, the therapist has decided to directly support her independence. He means this support also as a counter to the undercurrent of her potential dependent transference.

J: After that, after my father married Joan, she is fabulous; she came in and we tried to make her fit and she tried to fit. It was a strain for awhile, but it all worked out really beautiful. But then Dad began to drink more and more.

T: That's something more recent then?

J: Well, I can't remember how many years they've been married. He drank heavily after my mother died. My aunt, the one who's dead now, was trying to get all the kids placed somewhere else. They wanted to take me away from my house and place me with family or in an institution or something 'cause he was drinking too badly. But we proved to her that we were old enough to run a household whether he was well or not, and we did, 'cause he couldn't do anything. He was drinking really, really bad.

And then, for awhile, he sobered up, and he met Joan and he was well and healthy and doing all kinds of things. Like he's really handy around the house; he fixes everything, or he did. And it was then that she knew him when he was happy, a whole person.

But not long after the marriage, he began to go to pieces again. And a couple of years ago, her son was in Vietnam and he had a few more months before he came home from Vietnam and we had a long time to wait before we could see my brother. So, we planned a vacation 'cause she was getting so anxious for him to get home. We would drive to Arizona and visit my brother and by the time we got home, it would be close to the time for her son to get home.

Shortly after we left, they notified our household that her son was killed in action. My sister was the only one there and she tried to notify us on the road and because it was a military matter, the highway patrol wouldn't help. We got all the way there and my brother told my father on the phone and Joan collapsed and we had to carry her to the car. He knew she was upset; she started saying all kinds of things against everybody.

She reports another loss. The therapist notes similarities but cannot be sure if they are of any relevance. Joan "said things against everybody," which may be like the second man's anger. In what follows, her father insists on sticking to the cars instead of going with Joan. Cars are very important to him. The therapist recalls how in the first hour, Jane spoke so proudly about taking care of the car, putting out flares, but does not yet know what to make of all this.

J: Then we got to the base and my father wouldn't let us abandon what we were driving, which was a car with a trailer. I wanted to abandon the whole thing and take a jet home and comfort Joan and he wouldn't let us do it. So my brother got an emergency leave and we put my stepmother and brother on a plane and they got to San Francisco and they have lots of family and friends here to help them out. But then, my father and I had to take the car and trailer back home. I knew how to drive; I had a license and I was experienced; more experienced than he realized because he doesn't hear me when I say things—he discounts what I say. But he wouldn't allow me to relieve him at the wheel.

T: He tried to drive it all himself?

J: He did. And finally, a gas station attendant took one look at him part way down and said, "Hey, you guys need a rest." My dad told him, "Yeah, we have to get home to a funeral, but I guess I do need a rest." One time, we tried to stop and find a motel, but we couldn't. But finally, a gas station attendant let us sleep in the back of the gas station. I could sleep, but he couldn't and he stayed so wound up; he was wide awake waiting for me to sleep so that I wouldn't fall apart. I woke up and I had to talk to him all the way to San Francisco 'cause I was so scared he would fall asleep at the wheel. He wouldn't let me relieve him at all and he knew I could drive the car even with the trailer on it, 'cause I knew how to drive a car. I knew quite well; I had driven tractors and all kinds of things before that. But when we got to San Francisco and got home, he got sick all over the place and collapsed in a big heap; he had no control over his vomiting, diarrhea and yelling and screaming, and he just fell to pieces.

An important memory contains cars, yelling and falling apart. This memory would be reactivated by her more current accident. Note how the patient is using the hour to go through an association which she may have been warding off in her own thoughts and which would be difficult to talk through with her family members.

J: And he won't allow any doctor to ever touch him and we didn't have anything in the house that we could calm him with, except alcohol again. And there he went again on alcohol. From there until now, he's become an alcoholic only he won't admit it and he won't accept any help of any kind and he won't see a physician of any kind.

Note the implication that she is partly "responsible" for his resuming alcoholism by not driving, needing sleep and giving him alcohol.

J: But, we went to the funeral and it turned out that my stepbrother's wife had sent him a "Dear John" letter and he had volunteered for a dangerous mission and that is how he had gotten killed. Right after the funeral, she was living with another guy and getting the money from the government for him and buying a hot rod and just running all over. Joan was so upset that the household was just in a turmoil for months and months and months. She was bitter all the time. And even today, we all know that we can't say President Johnson in front of her or she'll become upset, and we can't say Vietnam in front of her or she'll become upset, or we can't say the name of the girl he married or see anybody drive a red sports car or any of that because she's still very upset about it. When things happen to make her upset, she sits and cries about her son who's gone, because her husband died and her son's gone and he was the last one of their family.

T: So, this kind of series of events you think might contribute to your vulnerability to getting depressed when an event happens? And there's another element in it that sounds like it is very important, which is your determination to survive and get out from under.

J: Be independent, is all I want. That's the one thing my family always hesitates about, always, is for me to try something. They're always beholding me, saying, "Well, are you sure, are you sure, are you sure?" I finally get myself convinced and I'm ready and confident, and they put all the doubt back in me.

T: Yeah, but you seem very successful when you do things. Like just moving out now; it seems like it's really an important step.

The patient has been crying at times during her telling of these stories. This expression of her feelings seems to have been experienced by her as a positive reaction. The therapist offers an appointment one week off, to see how things are going then, implying by inflection that he expects them to go well.

THIRD SESSION

Jane was to return for her next appointment on Monday. She called before, on Friday, asking to be seen because she didn't think she could get through the weekend. A brief appointment was scheduled for later the same day.

T: Well, what's up?

J: I'm getting all keyed up again.

T: Uh-huh.

J: And the thing that scared me really bad is in the pediatric ward. I've hit two patients. The first one was before; I hit an old man who kept touching me. And then it happened again this morning with a child. It is just terrible. But this kid kept picking at his burn. I couldn't get his attention because my voice keeps fading. My hearing is also shot. Doctors say I've got both eustachian tubes blocked, so when I get all frustrated and something is about to go, I overreacted.

She goes on with details about the patients, crying at times and searching the therapist for his facial responses. He responds neutrally.

T: Yes.

J: And I'm physically getting myself tied up again. This morning I couldn't eat anything again (spoken very slowly and deliberately). I don't want to do that Saturday and Sunday and Monday. So when I left work, I decided that I'd call you and see if I could see you. The first time I saw you—after that I could eat again. (Long pause.)

T: Yes. Why don't you just try and tell me whatever comes to you right now?

J: Well, I'm shaking. (There are tears in her eyes.)

T: Uh-huh; well, you're also crying, aren't you?

J: Yeah. Okay, this morning I told my doctor that I wouldn't take anything that had any depressants in it, 'cause I was scared of getting depressed again. And I have an infection, but he's treating it with antibiotics. He said, "If you won't take any depressants, will you use steam?" I've got an old vaporizer that I used to use when I'd get these things before. I'm staying at my sister's with her husband in their flat. They put me in the spare room that's going to be the nursery in

January when the baby is born. It's just an old flat, but the vaporizer last night was too strong and loosened all the dirt on the wall and this morning there was just gobs of greasy dirt dripping down on the walls, all around. That's what I woke up to. Stupid stuff that's nobody's fault; just keeps happening, but when it does—

T: Did somebody blame you for that?

J: No, they kidded me about it, but they couldn't laugh about it because I was too tied up already and they knew it.

T: Yeah.

J: And then I woke up even before I saw the walls, with some of the paint which had been doing—and once I saw them, my stomach was out of control. I took stomach medicine that I'd been taking and I got up and got dressed and went in and they were having breakfast. I couldn't bring myself to eat anything because I just kept feeling so rotten. After they were gone, I was sick. Then I pulled myself together. My attorney wants me to write a diary, so I wrote an entry in the diary and left for work. (Silence.) That's just today. Today's worse than yesterday which is worse than the day before.

T: You have an attorney?

Litigation is always a concern because compensation can provide secondary gain for continued suffering.

J: Yes, he's on vacation this week.

T: What is he going to be doing for you?

J: He's going to handle the medical costs of my accident.

T: Uh-huh.

J: But it's kind of ripped up; we don't know a lot of things yet. Because I was a substitute, we don't know if there's any way to collect compensation for loss of job.

T: Yes. (Silence.)

J: Other things that keep bugging me is on my own ward. I don't—can't think of things far enough ahead—can't plan ahead, so many things, I can see how they should go and can't make them go. Things turn my head in another direction and I can't get back fast enough.

T: Tell me more about your reaction with your patient.

Jane then gives a detailed description of how frustrating the child patient was to care for. She does not label her affect with words. The therapist provides the label as the transcript continues.

T: You must have felt angry at him.

J: Yeah, repeatedly angry at him. But I have to watch it because he's so destructive of himself and won't let himself heal.

T: Yes, but right now, anger is especially hard for you to control because you're also angry at those people who. . . .

J: Yes, angry at the nurses who won't help enough.

The patient interrupts the therapist. He had intended to link her anger to the auto accident and to the various people who had blamed and deserted her. Deciding this link is probably correct and that she is warding it off by her interruption, he persists with his intent. He feels she will be able to tolerate this confrontation.

T: Well, you're also susceptible to anger now because you haven't had a chance yet to work through and work out anger at the people who got you into the accident.

J: Yeah. Something happened yesterday that got me started off last night. There was a continuing education thing at the hospital. Yesterday's film was a thing on policemen and first aid. It was how a patrolman saw an accident happen and what happened after it. I really got upset during it, but I got myself all together before the lights went back on and helped clean up and everything. I've been having lunch with the ward clerk and went out to see a friend of mine in another ward and talked with her. She is going to try and help find me someplace to stay besides where I am.

But that accident flashed back on me again last night during dinner. My sister and brother-in-law had been riding in their car. They witnessed an ambulance accident and right in the middle of dinner, they were telling me about it. They didn't know it, but I couldn't take it and I just stopped eating and right then, I began to get sick. And I don't want to make my sister any more upset so I just slipped away. They know I don't have any appetite anyway, and they weren't very upset.

Intrusive episodes are now very apparent. While intrusive signs were present before as bad dreams, the earlier interviews basically represented a denial phase. In Interview One, she was in an unstable denial state with loss of concentration, bodily symptoms, anxiety and tension. In Interview Two, the denial phase was more stable. Now, by Interview Three, it appears that ideational repetition has become more prominent and is contributing to her discomfort.

T: But you didn't want them to know that their talking about the ambulance triggered the memory?

J: Yeah.

T: Were you ashamed to let them know, or you thought it would hurt their feelings?

J: No, my sister is pregnant with her first child and we were very, very scared that she would lose it and she wouldn't let us tell anybody for weeks. She's just—I don't want to upset her that much either, because she was upset already about it, worrying about it.

T: Yeah. But last night they were talking about this ambulance and then you began—

J: Thinking about the morning I reacted in my own accident. And then I stopped eating and (silence) and later—

T: And you were feeling frightened when this happened?

J: Yeah.

T: In fact, very frightened.

J: But I couldn't really say anything because I was also afraid to get her upset.

T: Yes. (Silence.) Well, that may have been a trigger to your reaction today, you know.

J: It acted like a trigger.

T: Do you know that this is the sort of thing that happens after accidents?

J: I figured it would, but I never heard it said.

T: Yes. People often go through a period when things are kind of out of mind. Then they come back, especially if there is something that hasn't been worked through about it. For you, there are a number of things that haven't been worked through. You're frightened. Even though you don't rationally think so, part of your mind thinks that it might just happen again.

This is essentially a supportive remark aimed at reducing fear of symptoms and at sharing an understanding of what is going on.

J: Well, it was the kind of accident that could happen again and again because, I was saying, that it was the other man's fault, and I had no way to get out of the way. But I have to commute now because—the only arrangement I had before was riding with my sister-in-law and I reached the breaking point with that. I can't ride with her anymore because I get just as scared watching her drive as not going at all. I'm better when I'm in control of the car.

T: Yes, I'm not surprised to hear that.

J: But even like coming over here. A couple of times I checked the mirrors and ahead in merging traffic, and I look, and there's somebody too close behind me and I have no idea how they can get that close unless they are coming up too fast, which is what happened before.

T: Yes, so there is this constant expectancy below the surface that is frightening you. And the other thing I think that will need some working on is your anger. You feel very badly about having it, and you're trying to do things, like with your sister, by not even letting her know that this reminded you of your accident.

J: That's why I want to stay with somebody else besides her.

T: Are you sure she's so delicate?

This is an indirect challenge directed against what the therapist intuits is her own defective or vulnerable self image. The remark, at an unconscious level, may be received as "maybe you are not so delicate and can see yourself once again as a capable, grown-up woman."

J: Well, she was a few months ago, and she tells me she's not now. But it's hard to believe.

T: Well, for her to know what you're going through might not injure her in any way. You might just let her know what you're going through.

The therapist ordinarily does not give direct suggestions, even in brief therapy. But, in this instance he does, because he believes that less inhibited communication with her sister may help her to work through the meanings of the accident more rapidly. As with his previous statement about the delicacy of her sister, this comment has an indirect meaning: "You can take knowing what is going on and it will also be all right to let others know how you have responded."

J: The thing is that she's a personnel worker for the phone company and she's getting people like me all the time and she's always saying she works because she has to. I don't want her to be pressured at home, too. But she really should stay out of that job; it's not doing her any good.

T: Well, we have to stop now. We can continue on Monday at the time we scheduled. So, see you then.

J: Okay, at 3:00 o'clock.

FOURTH SESSION

She reported feeling gradually better over the weekend, but she was still shaky and awoke early. At the beginning of the hour, she and the therapist again reviewed her reaction to the movie on accidents and her intrusive thoughts about her own accident. She then talked about wanting to avoid discussing the accident because she is afraid if she does get into it again, she will become upset and not do well at work. The therapist is inclined to deal directly, even abreactively, with the accident memory, again in a denial rather than a completion phase, and he wants to work the memory through to the point where she will not be upset by reminders. The hour proceeded with the following discussion of whether or not to focus further on the accident.

T: Yes, that's the decision we have to make now. Should we do that (not dwell on it now), while you try and get through, or—sooner or later, I think it has to be talked out.

J: I know it does, because it scares me when it happens.

T: Yes. So I think your intuition might be best. My intuition doesn't say for sure, so let's go on yours. You decide whether we talk about it now or make another appointment and talk more about it.

J: It's kind of weird because it's hanging over my head if I don't do it. And then I might just start thinking that way and go round and round again.

T: Well, I wonder if you're not in enough control so that we could do a little bit, kind of a small dose, and then just stop.

J: Okay.

T: Want to try that? Let's say you can stop any time you want.

J: Okay.

T: Okay? So, I'd like you to do this feeling as relaxed in your body as you can. Why don't you try and just see if you can't really relax yourself, okay? Then we can spend a little time talking about it.

The suggestion to relax is used because the therapist believes it will be helpful with this particular person. Other patients tense up with a directive to relax. The suggestion, covertly, is that she will be able to talk about the accident with the therapist without getting too frightened. In what follows, the therapist continues talking until he feels the patient is in the mental set where she can recall, and yet retain a sense of control.

T: Okay. Here's what we're going to do and all we're going to do. We're going to go back to the accident and have you remember a little bit of it and just see what springs to mind from it and perhaps it will be something that will make you re-experience some of those emotions. As it happens, you'll try and keep relaxing and we'll try and talk about the ideas and feelings as they come to you. You'll try and keep putting the feelings into words and I'll try and understand them, as best I can. We don't have to do a big chunk of it today; we can do a portion. That way, you'll learn it's safe. I think it might help to put it all in your control, keeping it from coming back when you don't want it to. Does it seem reasonable to you? Any questions? Okay, let's just go back to the accident. One thing that struck me about it was that man who came out yelling at you.

J: Yeah, he was the second guy.

T: Yes, I thought maybe that was upsetting you, especially upsetting. Was that so?

J: I could feel myself just going out of awareness when he was doing it. I mean, just slipping into shock or whatever it is; just the more he yelled, the farther away from him I got until I finally just yelled at him, "You're not leaving the scene of this accident until I get your name!" So he threw his license at me and left anyway. But that was a long, long time because that collision was a half hour after the first collision.

T: Now, try and just go back and remember what he said and let's just see what comes to you.

J: His thing was how he had appointments to keep and I couldn't hear a lot of it. He sees the wreck and yelled and screamed and then he turned to us. But to us, he just says, "I have to go find a phone as fast as I can." And it turned out that he was in very much the same situation as I was in: he works in a hospital the same as I.

T: He was going to work?

J: Uh-huh. He wasn't a nurse, he was a student lab technician. But it's hardly any different. He had the same need to be on time that I had. But then he stomped away from the scene and I don't even know where he went because you couldn't see in the fog. I was mad because I had stuck to the scene of the accident and I wanted to see a doctor because my back was hurting, and he stomped away right away! We had the policeman; we could have settled it and I could have been on my way if he had stuck around. And I was standing around shaking and hurting and he was gone.

T: And what's this; he threw the license—

J: Threw it at me.

T: At you?

J: Because I was the one that protested.

T: And   where did it hit you?

J: I think I caught it.

T: And then what happened to his license? He drove off without his license?

J: No, he couldn't drive his car; his car was demolished. He walked away fast from the scene, but you couldn't see more than 20 feet in the fog, and he went to a phone, which I should have done long before that. But since my neck hurt and I knew I was numb every place else, I was afraid to walk as far as it was to a phone. I didn't know how badly I was hurt.

T: And you never saw him again?

J: No, he came back. In fact, a few minutes later, the policeman had his report and stuff together. I got confused then, and I gave him the other man's license instead of my own because he wanted a license. And then I left to phone Zone City to tell them I couldn't come. By then, they had already talked to me about an ambulance and I told them I didn't think I needed one. So I called my brother-in-law to come and take me to a doctor.

T: But this other man came back?

J: Well, I missed him somehow. I'm not sure if he came back by the time I came back.

T: And did you have any more to do with him?

J: Yeah. We climbed into the back of a patrol car to fill out all the forms because it was really cold and he kept borrowing pens and being obnoxious to everybody. He had to ask his questions whether you were in the middle of saying something or not, and this kind of thing. I was the last one to finish the report because I had the two collisions to report.

T: How was he obnoxious to you?

J: It was just his general attitude, I would suppose. His standard behavior. Instead of asking for anything politely, he would just demand it. Like if another officer asked a question about the tow cars—I called for a 3-A truck because I know 3-A's come faster and I'm personally in 3-A, even though my Dad's not. So they had three different trucking companies, two trucking companies coming. A tow truck arrived and he assumed automatically that it was his. And I listened, and understood that it had to be mine. But he butted in already and I couldn't out-speak him; I had to wait until he was finished and then explain it to them that it was my tow truck. Every time there was any question, he was right there for himself.

T: So you feel he was being selfish?

J: Yeah.

T: And his selfishness was hurting you worse.

J: This was the wrong time to be selfish. He should have been—like the police officers; there were two of them there, let them direct it. And before that, when they weren't there and they weren't in charge, he didn't take any effort to lead it, you know, like direct the traffic or put out the flares or that kind of thing. But when somebody else was there, he would compete with them —just standing in our way.

T: So, he was obstructing your getting help?

J: I wanted to get out of there as fast as I could and find out why my neck hurt so bad.

T: Let's try and go back then. We know a lot more about your neck now than then, but let's go back then; let's see if we can reconstruct your thoughts about your neck.

J: Right after the collision, I was numb and in a few seconds, the only feeling I had was my neck on the right side and in my shoulder. And it hurt, I couldn't feel anything else at all. Then the driver in front came back 'cause he could see I was just dazed and looked straight ahead. He had seen through his mirror my car hit. He came back and said, "Are you okay?" And I said, "No." He said, "How bad?" I said, "I think it's only my neck, but I'm not sure." Then I waited and I could tell that the rest of me was okay. I felt okay.

T: What thoughts were going through your mind?

J: Well, I know that if you're hurt and you get into shock far enough, you can be badly hurt and not know it, and walk around with it. That's what was going on in my mind. It just feels like my neck, but I'm not sure.

T: So you were thinking that you might be badly hurt and you might not know it, and you might walk around and hurt yourself more.

J: Uh-huh. But then, I looked at the situation and I thought, if I don't move this car from where it is right now, somebody is bound to collide into it again. So I got out of the car anyway and got into the back of the car and gave them some flares to pass out. Then I looked at the situation and said to the other man that I think we'd better move our cars because we're at the top of a grade by a red light on a really foggy morning and it's going to be a ten-car pile-up if we don't. So, I moved into a safety zone near an island and he moved all the way off to the shoulder. I left my car running with the lights on so that people could see it.

T: Could we go just a little way in your imagination and imagine what didn't happen, but what you might have thought might happen? Which would be that you would walk around and your neck would get hurt worse. Just imagine—

J: My neck or my back?

T: Yeah, imagine that. What would you imagine would happen?

J: Well, I've had back trouble before and when it got bad enough, I was told not to move until it relaxed. And I would imagine that I would get paralyzed.

T: Where would you be paralyzed?

Because of the patient's neck pain, other somatic complaints, and her mother's severe illnesses, the therapist wishes to explore for cognitive elements of somatic localization that occurred at the time of the accident.

J: I don't know.

T: Your legs?

J: Well, before it would have been my legs, but I don't know about this one.

T: What was the back trouble before?

J: I have one leg shorter than the other and I repeatedly strained muscles because of the imbalance so it's been different muscles getting strained. One time I did it real good; strained it on the job and had to stay still for awhile until it eased up.

T: And if you didn't, you might get paralyzed?

J: No, just that it would stay, the pain.

T: The paralyzed idea was during the accident?

J: Yeah.

T: Okay. Any other thoughts about your body; anything you can remember? Try and go back in your mind to the accident.

J: Well, after the accident, after the first collision when we were waiting, we were sitting in his car, I got double vision. But that's not unusual for me; I have a muscle problem in my left eye. I wondered about it, because I didn't think my head had gotten hurt.

T: But it might mean that you had a head injury?

J: Right.

T: At least, that was your thought then?

J: Yeah, but I get double vision under stress, no matter what's causing it. Can't think of anything else.

T: So, you were worried then that you might be—your back might be broken or something and you might get paralyzed if you moved. And then you were running around putting out flares.

J: Well, nobody else would do this kind of thing; nobody else was thinking. You know, I'd ask a question and there wouldn't be a response because they couldn't think of an answer for it.

T: Well, maybe you felt that they were fools. You had to risk yourself because they were so foolish.

From listening to her vocal intonations, the therapist has a growing conviction that she is struggling between impulses to express rage and a need to inhibit such expressions. He is attempting to get at a clear expression of ideas that might lead to anger as well as ideas that might be theratening, were she fully aware of them. At this point he is trying out certain labels with her, and more importantly, encouraging continued expression by actively receiving her communications and not being critical. In a sense, he has just said, "It would be all right with me if at the time of the accident you thought the people around you were fools, or were afraid they would think you were a fool. I'd like you to freely tell me that sort of thing, even if you feel badly about it." As it happens, the label of "fool" does not exactly hit on a central ideational complex, but the feedback from the therapist sets up a dialogue that promotes fuller expression.

J: Well, I had to save myself anyway, because they weren't going to move their car, his car. Nobody else wanted to—like—like direct the trucks that were bearing down. You know, I said, "Well, listen, I've got a flashlight in the glove box with a red cap on it; if you swing it, they can see it and get around us." Nobody wanted to do it and my arm was stiffening up and I was about to stand out and do it because I—

T: What do you mean, "no one wanted to do it." Who was that?

J: Well, the man in front of us who had stopped and the man who had hit me.

T: Why didn't they want to do it?

J: One man was ready to leave for work because he said nobody is really badly hurt. And the man behind me had to leave to telephone his place of business to tell them he wouldn't be coming in. And nobody was around who was not busy.

T: So you were just left. Were you all alone?

J: Yeah. I was sitting in the car of the man that hit me because his was in a better position by then.

T: So you were kind of left alone with no one to take care of you?

J: Yeah, but then I could sit up straight and I knew that if I didn't to anything, nothing horrible was going to happen to me like that.

T: Did you feel it was unfair though?

J: Yeah, and I asked him to make a phone call for me and he came back and said, "Oh, I forgot."

T: He forgot?

J: Yeah.

T: That must have made you angry.

J: I don't know if I felt angry. I felt like desperate—like, how can I make that dumb phone call.

T: Yeah, but you'd been left out again. Do you remember that moment, when he came back and said he forgot?

J: Kind of; he was back in the car again.

T: Now, you seem pretty relaxed talking about all of this. Any side thoughts?

J: No.

T: How are you feeling right now?

J: A little bit tense.

T: A bit tense? Where is the tension?

J: It's all over.

T: Yeah, describe it though.

J: I wouldn't know how.

T: Is it in your muscles?

J: Yeah.

T: Do your muscles feel tight? Okay, try and relax them. Does my asking you about it make you more nervous?

J: About relaxing?

T: Yeah.

J: Well, it's just that that's the one thing that everybody is telling me to do.

T: Everyone tells you to relax?

J: Yeah. You can't exactly do it without knowing how.

T: Have you ever learned how?

J: I don't know. I guess I did a little bit. I used to take Yoga for awhile but I can't relax myself when my mind isn't relaxed.

T: Well, let's see if we can find where the tension is in your mind right now. What are you doing now? What are you paying attention to?

J: The back of my head.

T: Uh-huh. (Long silence.) Well, one way to find out about such tension, for us to use right here, would be for you to say whatever comes to your mind now.

J: I'm getting scared; I'm not wanting to talk anymore.

T: Yes. What would happen if you were to go on talking? Do you think you'd get more scared?

J: I don't know. This is the same way I feel when I wake up, feeling sick.

T: Uh-huh. Is it a scare that something is going to happen?

J: I think it's more that something is not going to happen that should happen.

T: Uh-huh. That would mean that there'd be no help for you?

J: Yeah.

T: Okay. What do you think should happen?

J: I don't know.

T: You know, the idea of no help for you runs through a lot of this. Nobody being able to help you; your family not being a help to you; the other drivers not helping you; maybe my not helping you.

This labeling of her sense of not being helped seems to make her feel safer, and she goes on with considerable additional material, without responses from the therapist.

J: Something else: when I made the phone call, a male operator came on the line and I didn't recognize the voice as an operator's and I thought it was Bob, which is my brother-in-law and so I spoke to him as if he were, and then we figured each other out. We were both mixed up. He took the message wrong, too. Then I told him the number and he connected me so fast that I didn't recognize the change in voice. And so, when Bob answered, my message was all confused. I know it made him upset, but the more I said anything, the more confused I got and I couldn't get it straight.

So, it turns out that after he had hung up, he didn't know how badly I was hurt so he called my sister at work and all he told her was that Jane's been in an accident and I'm going to pick her up. I'll call you later.

After the accident when we were trying to arrange a doctor and stuff, he told me about it, about her being notified. And I said, "Aren't you going to call her back?" He said, "No, we'll wait and see how you are." When I got to the doctor's office, he had two other emergencies ahead of me and so I waited in the waiting room for an hour and a half and then I waited in an examining room for 15 minutes, and then when he saw me, he sent me to X-ray. The doctor in charge of X-ray had to look at the X-rays that were taken.

And it wasn't until after all of that, that my brother-in-law told my sister. She had been sitting there all morning not knowing, just knowing that I was in an accident. That bothers me because there have been other accidents in the family. There was one when my stepbrother died in Vietnam and my sister was the only person in San Francisco, so when the call came through, she knew and we were on our way to Arizona. Nobody would notify us because it was a military matter and the Highway Patrol wouldn't stop us so we had to get all the way there where my brother was and he had to tell us. It was just her sitting there again, waiting and not knowing.

T: So that happened to her with your accident.

J: Yeah.

T: That's upsetting for your sister?

J: It's upsetting for both of us because after that, I was in Arizona with my father and we put everybody else on a jet; my brother got emergency leave, and *my father refused to let the car sit and go back with his wife.* He insisted that we drive back to San Francisco. And I had a driver's license and was perfectly capable of driving, but because there was a trailer on the car, *he didn't trust my driving and he wouldn't allow me to drive.*

Here is a compulsive retelling of the story of the trip with her father, discussed in an earlier interview. The timing in this hour and her general demeanor indicate the importance of her father in the associations to the accident.

J: So, for the whole trip back, I really was tired and very, very worried so I kept tuning in radio stations and talking so that he wouldn't fall asleep. And he wouldn't pull over and he wouldn't rest until finally, I convinced him that we needed to stop and we stopped in a town full of motels and all of them were closed for the night. So we had to go on or sleep at the side of the road and refused to do that. Finally, a gas station attendant let us sleep in the back of the station but he didn't sleep all night; he only did it for me, and I barely slept and then had to get up again.

T: How do you know he didn't sleep?

J: He told me he didn't and he'd been sick. He had vomited all over the trailer. He told me he hadn't slept at all. I told him I was in better shape to drive, but he wouldn't let me.

T: That still bothers you?

J: (indignantly) He still doesn't believe I can drive. He won't ride in the car if I'm driving.

Here is an important meaning of her accident. Her father has criticized her driving. Right after the first collision, one association would be something like, "Oh, no, my father will say this is all my fault!" This thought would already be on her mind when the second collision occurred and the driver of that car angrily screamed at her. In a larger sense, she anticipates that her accident will give her father reason to say that, not only can she not drive well, but she is not an effective, grown-up woman and must remain his dependent and subordinate little girl. She anticipates his rage and depreciation of her. Responding to this prophecy, she is hurt by him and angry at him. The various rejections and desertions she experiences from other persons involved in the accident and its aftermath serve to justify these feelings. Frustration, sorrow and anger are also activated by the disruption in her life plan.

Rage at her father cannot be expressed or experienced directly because that would make her feel guilty. She already feels badly at not having rescued her father from his alcoholism relapse after the long drive following her stepbrother's death. This is part of a general ambivalent attachment to her father. While these formulations are oversimplified and incomplete, they represent the therapist's working hypotheses at this point in therapy. He follows her statement with an exploratory question relating her father to the recent accident.

> T: He thought that if you drove, you might have an accident?
>
> J: Uh-huh. Any car that I've bought, he's never stepped foot in.
>
> T: And now, you've had an accident.
>
> J: Uh-huh.
>
> T: Maybe you were worried right at the accident about what your father would say. There you'd gone and had an accident, even if it wasn't your fault at all.
>
> J: Yeah! Later that day, I let my brother tell my father; I didn't want to tell him.
>
> T: Why didn't you?
>
> J: Because if I talked to him on the phone, we don't get along very well at all; but if I talked to him on the phone, I would probably get upset enough for him to worry that I was hurt more than I was—just because it's so hard. He doesn't usually hear my voice; he's deaf in one ear and hard of hearing in the other one. He usually—I either shout or he reads my lips. And on the phone, it's impossible with two of us, but it's always a strain for me to talk to him. But on this occasion, I just said, I can't do it at all. Somebody else has to do it.

Her initial response here is probably partly defensive in function. Other evidence suggests that she was primarily afraid of her father raging at her. But she seems to undo that fear by saying that he will worry unduly about her: "I would probably get upset enough for him to worry that I was hurt." This also suggests another defensive operation. If a person presents signs of physical harm, then one shows concern and does not blame them. She goes on to develop a covert complaint about her father's neglect: "He doesn't usually hear my voice." After these remarks about her father, she then expresses her own anxiety over confrontation with him: "It's always a strain . . . I just said I can't do it." The therapist chooses to focus on this self-experience.

T: Were you concerned about what your father would say?

J: Well, I didn't want him to come walking home from the bus stop and see the car all smashed up.

T: Yes, what would he have thought if he had seen the car all smashed up?

J: He would have wondered where in the world I was, what had happened.

Once again, she presents a worried and concerned image of her father rather than that of the enraged accuser. She continues along this line.

J: I didn't think he should do that. I would rather that he be told on the phone than when he comes home—

T: Well, he would think that you'd been in an accident.

J: Yeah. Well, one time before, I messed up the front end of a car and he went on for hours about "why didn't you tell me." So I knew I had to tell him, otherwise we'd go through that again.

Here is the associative meaning to the man yelling angrily at her. The important and, as yet, undisclosed detail that the car damaged in the current accident belonged to her father follows after the therapist clarifies that the car she dented earlier also belonged to her father.

T: Was that his car?

J: Yeah, *these were both his cars.* Because I had sold my car a few months ago.

T: Oh, so this was his car in the accident?

J: Yeah.

T: And the new car you bought was going to be yours?

J: Uh-huh (very softly). I sold my car when it started giving me trouble.

T: Yes. So maybe you felt badly that it was your father's car that was damaged.

J: Yeah. We never agree on that car anyway. He won't keep it up (very angry)! He won't, like, put the tires on soon enough when they're wearing out or get stuff done that needs being done. It's always run down. And like, he rebuilt the engine and put it back in; he didn't put the transmission back in straight so when you start it, you have to know how to force it into drive to get it started. I usually get frustrated with the engine; you have to sit and wait and then get it started. I am— every time I get into the car, I'd get mad if I couldn't happen to get it started right away because of the way he fixed it; only half way.

T: Yeah.

J: He did that to the exhaust system, too. It sounded horrible to drive. They'd give you three clamps; he'd put one clamp on and put the tailpipe on and it would rattle all over the place. It'd get a hole in it and was worn out.

T: Yeah, he really didn't take very good care of the car.

J: He took as little care as he could. He insisted that no work be done that needed being paid for. He had to do the work.

T: But then he bawled you out when you got in an accident?

J: Yeah.

T: What did he say to you that other time?

J: That was the car before this. That was my fault because I had a sinus infection and was all run down.

Once again, physical illness is presented as a way to avert blame.

J: I had a choice of public transportation and getting on the medicine and not being able to drive 'cause it makes me drowsy. So, I decided to drive and not take the medicine but I got too tired anyway and I missed a turn in the parking lot and hit a cement wall at a low speed and punched in the front end and one side. So we all knew it was all my fault, but he refused to accuse anybody. He just went wandering around junk yards trying to find a replacement for the front end of the car, and he never found one.

T: Huh. What did he say to you though?

J: Well, by the time that he saw me, I was upset enough and my face was swollen enough that he didn't want to say anything. I loosened my front teeth and I couldn't talk by the time he saw me, 'cause my whole face was swollen.

T: But he was angry?

J: He didn't show anger or anything; he just stomps away and gets a drink because he's an alcoholic; but he doesn't say anything.

It is possibly relevant that she uses the same word, "stomping," to describe her father as she did to describe the driver of the second car that hit her car, because the present accident is a repetition of the earlier accident. Since she is physically hurt, she does not receive the direct brunt of her father's anger, but instead, is made to feel guilty that she has hurt him and caused his drinking.

T: But did you feel worried about how he would react before he reacted?

J: Yeah.

T: Were you very concerned in your mind?

J: But then he doesn't really react; he runs away from it.

T: But beforehand, you were worrying about how he would react?

The therapist is holding here to the topic and trying to obtain clarity about her feelings about her father's potential or actual anger at her.

J: Yeah.

T: I wonder if you had any thoughts about your father right during this current accident?

J: I don't remember thinking about him. I do remember thinking, "Well, at least this car is gone now; nobody can drive it; he'll be forced to get rid of it." And it turns out he's not; he's taking money for it and says he's going to put it back together again. Since then, when we got it home, he made me drive it one afternoon. I told him that the doctor told me to leave the collar on and if I needed to drive, to only go a short distance and take the collar off to drive so I'd be able to turn my head. I said I didn't feel like turning my head enough to drive that day, but he insisted.

She is talking about how her father hurts her. The role structure is that of one person hurting another and she can place herself in either position. She is afraid both of her accusations that he hurts her and of the possibility that he will accuse her of hurting him. Her communication is devoted to obtaining a verdict from the therapist that she is "not guilty," has been hurt more than enough and deserves tender attention. She may also want the therapist to be angry at her father. This would be anger on her behalf and she could avoid guilt. She continues with evidence that her father gave her a bad car.

J: So I drove it and I'd been complaining about the car down-shifting suddenly on hills 'cause the transmission still needed work. It took a really good hill to do it and there weren't any near the house so I took it to the best hill nearby and it didn't do it. He still doesn't believe me and he's not going to work on that part of it. But what used to happen was, if I took it to work in Zone City, it doesn't have enough speed to make merging easy, so I would go wandering freeway to freeway in a way that I wouldn't need to merge so much. I would get onto highways that weren't freeways.

And one of them was Pickwood Drive which is really steep, and up near the top of it, the car would downshift suddenly and then shift back up and just jerk really, really bad. He had never experienced it because he doesn't drive at all like I drive. I kept telling him that it would happen and that it needed something so that it wouldn't happen, but he wouldn't fix it. So, that's why he wanted me to drive it. He said there's nothing wrong with the car. The whole tail end of the car now is out of alignment; it doesn't even travel on a straight line anymore but, according to him, there's nothing wrong with the car anymore. He's going to drive it that way.

But every time his job makes him travel, because his job changes, he takes the other car.

Throughout these sections, she is expressing anger at her father as shown by her tone of voice and her non-verbal communications.

T: Which other car, the new one?

J: There's another car that he owns.

T: He owns two, a better one and this clunkier one?

J: Yeah.

T: And you got to drive the clunkier one?

J: I was not allowed to drive the better one.

T: Why not?

J: He didn't want me to.

T: He wasn't using it at the time; he was taking the bus.

J: That's right.

T: So why doesn't he want you to use it? Is the idea that you'd get in an accident?

J: I'll do something to it. I'll scratch it in a parking lot, or whatever. That one was special; this one is the one that I was allowed to use. It was the one I had driven before that, anyway.

T: But you resented it.

J: I hate that car to begin with! And every time I had car trouble, they'd tell me it's just because you don't like the car and are not willing to put up with it. I said, "Why can't you get me in the situation where I can get another car and I could put up with that." Like, I'd wear the battery out trying to start it and I couldn't keep the transmission in drive long enough to get it started.

T: Okay; well, it seems to me that we were able to talk about the accident and it wasn't too dangerous to talk about here, so we might go on and schedule another appointment to do that a little bit more.

J: Okay.

T: Does it seem reasonable to you to do that?

J: Yeah.

T: Okay. How about next Monday at this same time?

J: I can make it any time; I'm out of work by then. My job ends Friday.

T: Okay, let's make it 3:00 next Monday.

FIFTH SESSION

During the fifth session, Jane indicated that she felt she was back to normal. Her physical symptoms were much improved. She was sleeping and eating well, and no longer felt tense and anxious. She did not have intrusive episodes or moments of intense irritability. She still had some pain in her neck and in her hip joints. She felt that things were going smoothly for her. Three topics occupied the session; relationships to her father, her mother and the therapist.

During the week, she had entered into a dispute with her father which, due to her assertiveness, was resolved to the satisfaction of both of them. Her father wanted her to sign a release so that payment for damage to his car could be obtained from the insurance company of the other driver. She refused to do this, pointing out that the medical liability was as yet undetermined. She consulted her attorney who backed up her position. Her father became "pleased that someone more responsible than he or she was looking into it." She felt relief at living out of the house, since her father was drinking heavily during their discussions. She had resolved her guilt feelings over living with her sister by working at sewing maternity clothes for her.

The therapist felt that the restoration of Jane's equilibrium was the result of many factors. Time had passed, some working through had taken place in the therapy and concurrent with this, her improvement might have been motivated by a desire to reduce the need to explore the relationship with her father. The presence of unresolved conflicts and ambivalent attachments would not, however, be an indication for the continuation of a brief therapy aimed at restoration of a balance disrupted by a stressful life event. She had moved out of her home environment and was continuing her work; she could pursue her life plan. The therapist continued the interview by asking about the status of memories about the accident in order to see if there were further intrusive episodes. This would be an additional sector of information relevant to a decision about termination.

T: Any memories come to you about the accident?

J: Today's weather reminds me of it: looks the same.

T: But have there been any other events, like the conversation with your sister that triggered it?

J: No. I've been feeling people being more sympathetic because—even though, like I've had to miss some days at the hospital, one of the other aides came up to me and said that her mother had had the same thing. Only she said that her mother had to have special shoes made and I kind of smiled and said, "I'm wearing special shoes, too." Other things—we had a ward party and people came and talked to me and stuff.

She went on to talk of how her body was feeling better. She was afraid that any tension might make her stiffen up again.

The therapist offered a kind of summing up of one aspect of what had happened:

> T: One of the psychological problems for you was that the accident let you know in a way that your body was vulnerable to injury. When you didn't get better rapidly, you got frightened that your body was even more vulnerable.

> J: It made me think of something. My mother used to have arthritis in her back and stay in bed in the mornings. I found myself doing the same thing, just like her. I was staying in bed because it was the most comfortable place to be. I didn't want to get up and move and walk around. I just kept thinking of all the things I was doing then and that she was doing that when she hurt from arthritis in her back.

> T: Yes. She kept on going also?

As before, a covert encouragement and support of her thrust towards independence.

> J: Yeah, until she had cancer and she died of cancer.

The therapist believes that one function of this remark is to test him for a transference potential. If he feels sorry for her and gives her attention for being sick, then she may be tempted to adopt that role more durably in order to obtain the gratification of sympathy. The therapist believes Jane is covertly asking if she really has to get better. He wants to give her the support of saying "yes," which he does with a repetition of the same type of remark he made when he said, "She kept on going."

> T: So you feel kind of brave at times?

> J: Sometimes, but sometimes I feel dreadful because I know, uh—she used to send us away when she was feeling badly so that she could rest. I can't send my responsibilities away.

> T: Okay. Now, have you had any other thoughts, you know, since we talked a week ago, about getting upset because of the accident? Have any other explanations for that occurred to you?

J: I think it was a huge disappointment that stopped me from everything I was trying to do. It was at a time when I was trying to plan moving out of the house and getting a permanent job and just changing everything around me. And all of a sudden, I was frozen where I didn't want to be.

The remaining part of the hour dealt with the idea of termination and the possibility of a transfer to long-term therapy if she wished to explore further her vulnerability to depressions after losses. Since she did not express feelings about the separation other than gratitude, the therapist asked her directly:

T: Well, maybe you'll be sad not to see me anymore?

J: I think so. (Pause.) Yeah. (Pause.) That's been happening this last month to everyone I'm around though. Well, one friend who took me out to dinner really doesn't want to see me. It's happening all around me. I'm beginning to get used to it. The patients, you get to know them and they leave. It's okay.

She later accepted the idea of long-term therapy and continued to see another therapist twice a week for five months. By the onset of that therapy, she had essentially recovered from all symptoms related to the immediate stress event. The physical symptoms that had gone into remission remained absent. The residual pains in neck and hips improved by the end of one month. An exception to this marked improvement was continued difficulty with her eyes, a symptom corrected by a new prescription for glasses. The central issue of the therapy was that of loss and neglect with the attendant fear of not getting enough care in her relationships with other people. She kept her angry reactions to frustrations in tight check. These themes were worked on in relation to obtaining medical treatment for the eye symptoms, legal manipulations around recovering medical costs after the accident, relationships with her family members, and in the transference.

DISCUSSION

Were it not for the accident, Jane would most likely have continued her progress toward independence. By establishing social and professional ties, she would have been able to continue her development throughout young adulthood. If not beset by stress and the disruption of interpersonal relationships due to her neurotic potential, she probably would not have sought psychiatric treatment. At a crucial time, however, the accident activated unresolved conflicts about her own bodily integrity, degree of dependency and the validity of what might be called her "self-righteousness."

Her concept of bodily integrity was related to her mother and other relatives who had severe bodily misfortunes. She, herself, had a slight leg deformity and a tendency, when stressed, to a disruption in optic focussing that was also apparently based on a mild congenital anomaly. She was the baby of the family and was raised during a period when her mother was an invalid. Thus, she had a special vulnerability to feeling a defective identity and body image. The physical trauma and fears of even greater injury enforced on her awareness by the accident, served as reinforcements of the defective self-image as it stood in conflict with more recently developing womanly and intact self-images. Such an accident threatens the sense of invulnerability of all persons, but she had a less stable adult self-image to use in mastery of this threat. Working it through on her own was impossible. The therapist supported her adult self-image by his encouragement of her continued efforts to work and cope.

The ambivalent ties with her father were rapidly conceptualized by the therapist in establishing a working model for the therapy. This rapidity carries more risks of error than the more temperate inferences possible in a long-term psychoanalytic therapy where more associations, memories and fantasies are gradually accumulated. Basically, it seemed as if a variety of factors had combined to develop a self-image as "hurt, little and in need," one that was in conflict with her developmental progress toward a more mature self-image.

Her mother had been too ill to provide complete maternal care, or even a stable identity model. She might have turned to her father, not only as an oedipal love object in a normal, developmental sequence, but as a source of pre-oedipal gratification. She probably developed a role model of an ambivalent sort at this stage of early childhood. On the one hand, she conceptualized herself as "little and in need" and her father as taking care of her with development of a mutual, loving attachment. But, at times, she probably felt insufficiently cared for and had a dyadic model in which she was "little and in need" and her father was neglectful. Rage at her father would stem from this latter version.

Because of such rage, she would also develop a model of herself as destructive in her relationship with her father. In conflict with her ideals and morals, this image would generate a tendency to feel guilty if she were placed in the role of hurting her father. To avoid guilt, to gain the stronger role for herself and quite likely also to replace her mother, she would tend to conceptualize herself in the care-taking role and her father in the role of being in need. Later material supported these formulations. Her father turned to her for care at various times, but he also rejected her when she assumed a care-taking role. During her adolescence, he fostered her regression to a pre-adolescent stage of life and rejected her efforts to care for him. He belittled her attempts at this and in general, undermined her efforts to gain a sense of womanly competency.

The accident heightened the not-so-latent ambivalence between them which already had "cars" and "accidents" as a theme because of the previous dented fender, the long, traumatic drive he refused to share with her, and his reluctance to let her drive the "good" car. As soon as the accident happened, she knew that blame would enter the picture. Her father would blame her and she would blame him for blaming her, and for providing her with a bad car. The second man, who yelled angrily at her, became a symbolic father-image for her, and gave the ambivalent role fantasy a terrifying reality.

The accident thus became an event that gave rise to fear over her bodily integrity, to rage and sorrow over the loss of her plans for independence and to anger and guilt, entangled with a wish to remain attached to her father. Perhaps the most important conflict was one of dependency and independency wishes. The bodily symptoms gave her an excuse to resume dependency, and yet led to the frustration of not being taken care of properly. The bodily symptoms also could punish her for her aggressive feelings toward her family. Working through the stress event meant processing these themes. She had to reassure herself, by a re-examination of current reality, that her body could still work and was not under continuing threat. She had to consider the possibilities for resumed dependencies and ties to her father (or father-substitutes such as her doctor) and reject them. She had to re-examine her work and living situation and continue in her thrust towards independence. She had to evaluate the accident and decide that it was just an accident; the angry man just a nasty stranger who behaved badly, and that it was over.

The therapist fostered this working through process by providing a temporary relationship and encouraging continued efforts towards independence. The various themes were not interpreted at a deeper level. Rather, there was an effort to process the details and immediate associations to the accident so that reality could be clarified and separated from fantasy elaborations. The major theme of dependency-independency surfaced in the transference as a tension between an "I don't want any help; I can do it myself" attitude, presented largely through her demeanor, and a subsurface clamor for excessive worry and concern on the part of the therapist. This was countered with a steady insistence on working on the immediate meanings of the stress event. That is, the therapist did not appear worried about the patient, guilt-driven by her remaining symptoms, or neglectful in providing her with help and sympathy.

SUMMARY

Jane drove her father's second, poorly-cared for car to a job that she hoped would enable her to gain her own independence. She was rear-ended on a foggy day. The man who drove into her was so polite that she could not be angry with him, but a second car piled into her already damaged vehicle as it stood by the roadside. That driver, a man, exploded angrily at her. This seemed to induce a dissociative state. Later she had difficulty in obtaining medical attention. She then felt that her family neglected her by turning a post-accident visit (to check up on her) into a party which ignored her condition.

She developed a progressively debilitating syndrome combining somatic and psychological signs and symptoms. She had neck and hip pains, eye difficulties, nausea, upper respiratory infections, and sleep disturbances. She was also affected by dazedness, difficulty concentrating, irritability, intrusive and repetitive thoughts, and episodes of anxiety. Her brief psychotherapy began when she was in an unstably defended denial phase, in terms of conscious ideas and then entered an intrusive phase.

The accident, when viewed retrospectively, could be seen as an activator of unresolved conflicts. Before the accident, these conflicts caused episodes of what might be called a neurotic depressive reaction, not severe enough, as yet, to motivate her to seek psychotherapy. Rather, she was moving forward in her psychological and sociological development. After a turbulent childhood and adolescence, she had successfully completed school and training and was about to engage in a career that would allow her to separate from her family and, especially, to diminish the ambivalent ties binding her to her father. Therapy enabled her to continue this forward course.

CHAPTER FIFTEEN

Multiple Stress Events

With the assistance of John Bebelaar, D.S.W.

LAURA SUFFERED MANY LOSSES in her young life. Such accumulations of sorrow sometimes seem so self-instigated that the person is said to have "traumatophilia," not so much "love of trauma" as a seeming attraction for it. Laura used her youthful appeal in an impulsive manner. She did so to compensate for earlier losses, her limited capacity for interpersonal relationships, and for her impoverished self-concept. Her actions escalated in desperation and culminated in the equivalent of a suicide attempt. She entered therapy in an extreme state; her ability to cope with life had been virtually exhausted.

She improved during brief psychotherapy. Her story illustrates how inhibitory operations can lead to a phase of denial so pronounced that it resembles organic brain disease. In addition to repression, suppression, and denial, she used transference provocations in an attempt to avoid awareness of ideas and feelings associated with the stressful event, to compensate for an immature level of ego development, and to continue a pseudo-active but actually passive-dependent life trajectory.

Laura is a slender, well-formed 25-year-old woman who was deeply involved in the counterculture and drug scene. Two months before the present therapy began she was in an auto-

---

* Mr. Bebelaar is now a therapist on the staff of Highland Hospital, Oakland, California.

mobile accident. Speeding up a narrow mountain road, she tried to pass a slower car. Unable to complete the turn back she careened over a cliff. Fortunately, there must have been only a modest incline at that embankment. Her car came to rest, totally destroyed, with Laura intact, but unconscious from a concussion. She remained dazed for three days.

She recovered quickly in all physical respects while under observation at a hospital. Neurological examination was normal. Her mental status showed her to be dazed and dull, but she was correctly oriented for time, place and person. Her memory was not consistently impaired, but at times, her wandering attention made examinations and communication difficult. A neurological puzzle, she was subjected to extensive diagnostic procedures. An absence of abnormal physical findings led to a discharge to the home of her grandparents.

Over the next few weeks, she seemed to become even more dazed, disoriented, depersonalized and limited in conceptual functioning. She was then re-evaluated for brain damage, but results were again negative.

Remaining with her grandparents, she felt somewhat better, although she describes herself during this period as being disturbed by intrusive thoughts of worthlessness. She felt tense and restless, and impulsively left for San Francisco to live with a male friend who would, she felt, play the role of a good father and not pressure her for sex. This was important because while she had been very active sexually for several years, she now felt "freaky" at the prospect of being touched by a man and had not engaged in any sexual activity since the accident.

The man, Hans, had indeed taken care of her. He noted her continued withdrawal, chronic tension, emotional constriction and cognitive limitations. As she was ordinarily vivacious and dramatic, the change was marked. He urged her to have a psychiatric consultation, and she agreed.

She was seen three times. The consultant felt that her mental status was so decompensated that psychological tests for brain damage were indicated. He also considered in the differential diagnosis that the might have an unusual form of schizo-phrenia. The psychological tests did not conform to any pattern typical of brain damage, but suggested the use of inhibitory defenses such as repression and denial to ward off possible sexual impulses and/or a sense of extreme worthlessness. The outcome of this conflict was believed to verge on an illness of psychotic proportions.

Despite communicative difficulties imposed by the patient's blurring, vagueness and inhibition of thought, additional data had been obtained. Neurological examination was again normal. During the interviews she indicated that the accident happened on the anniversary of two events. One year ago on that day, she had taken a hallucinogenic drug, inadvertently knocked over a candle, and set her house on fire. Exactly two years before, her ovaries were removed because of benign tumors and she in-dicated some sorrow over her inability to have children. (It later emerged that she had already borne a child and placed it for adoption.) With such clues, but a persistent concern for the possible neurological basis for her inability to think coher-ently, she was referred for a trial of psychotherapy in the stress clinic.

Her history unfolded very slowly, but it is helpful to have an advance summary of it in order to grasp some issues involved in the process of her psychotherapy. Laura describes herself as rebelliously separating from her morally rigid and lower socio-economic class parents when she was 15 years old. A crucial incident was a sexual affair with an older boy at that time. She had always done poorly in school, and dating was her main interest. They married when she was 18. Two years later, they were introduced to hallucinogenic drugs. After several "good trips," her husband developed a paranoid psychosis. A tur-bulent period ensued and she left him when she felt he was a menace to otheir infant son.

Laura was able to maintain a job as a clerk in the daytime. She spent her evenings in bars, where encounters with men led to a series of ultra-brief affairs. One more extended episode involved her in masochistic practices with a sadistic man. It was to suit his preferences that she placed her son, then two years old, for adoption.

Thereafter, although irrevocably committed to the loss of her son, she felt very guilty and remorseful. She had recurrent fantasies of kidnapping him from his foster parents, but was frightened by the prospect of life without her lover and without a constant supply of drugs. When her lover deserted her, she entered compulsively into brief sexual liaisons. She was used and abused while seeking pathetically for care, tenderness, and romance. At the depths of this period in her life, she had intercourse in rotation with each member of a fraternity house. Following this, she met Antonelli, a member of the drug scene who was also experimenting with body energetics and meditation. She began living with him in the most enduring relationship she had yet achieved. One weekend after they had been together for several months, he went out of town on an urgent family matter. She felt lonely while he was gone, and slept with one of his co-workers. This man informed Antonelli immediately upon his return. Infuriated, he called her a whore and ordered her to leave his apartment.

The "accident" occurred after a frenzied month of searching for fun and, indeed, any sensation to purge from her mind a sense of guilt, gloom and worthlessness. The night of the accident, she was given Cinzano to drink. It was Antonelli's favorite beverage and the bar also reminded her of him because it had an Italian name. It was in this state of mind that she borrowed a car and the accident occurred.

After the three-visit consultation described previously, Laura accepted the therapy referral. During the initial hour, a contract of time-limited therapy was set up. She agreed to be seen for 20 hours, and if further therapy was indicated, to be referred to another therapist.

FIRST SESSION

Laura presented herself in a seductive manner conveyed by bodily means. She had "cute" and receptive facial expressions and coquettish postures, gestures, and vocal inflections. Her first words to the therapist were, "Ooh, you look nice."

Such a self-presentation is not due so much to any active sexual interest as it is an habitual and stereotyped way to attach herself. For her, to be sexy is to be worthy and is perhaps the only way she has learned. This demeanor is a way to reduce the threat of being rejected and feeling defective.*

She and her therapist covered four topics in their first hour of work together. These included her symptoms, her recollections of the accident and hospitalization, some references to her life style, and expectations from the therapeutic arrangement. During the hour, her state varied suddenly and considerably. While describing her symptoms there was relative clarity of communication and centralization of attention. On all other topics there was vagueness, attention deployment ranging from confusion and daze to sudden episodes of uncontrolled sobbing, and flirtatious interest in the therapist.

This lability is determined by both her character and her response to stress. The sudden instigation of inhibition in order to avoid painful topics leads to communicative blockage and alterations of consciousness. These changes in state of consciousness are minor equivalents of dissociative reactions. Global and relatively undifferentiated controls are used to regulate ideas and feelings. She has historically not developed more differentiated, discreet, defensive manners. This tendency to dissociate presents a therapeutic problem. Although it gives clues as to the degree of threat of a given topic, it limits information. It also limits reception of communications from the therapist. If the therapist says something dangerous, she may inhibit awareness globally and change to a dissociated state of consciousness. Interpretations of warded-off contents will not be processed but instead, will appear to traumatize the patient. Even clarification, as will be seen, can have such effects.

---

*As in previous case vignettes, the change in type face indicates a commentary on the immediately preceding therapeutic process.

In this session Laura described her current syndrome and it appeared, to the therapist, to be a period of oscillation between denial and intrusive phases of stress response. Her principal signs and symptoms seemed to be an extreme form of the denial phase. She described her most pervasive feeling state as "spaciness." It became gradually clear that in this state she was minimally responsive to others, had no sense of reflective self-awareness, little memory for her immediate thoughts; hence, no sense of continuity of experience. Connections between one event and another or one idea and another were not made or, if made, not retained.

She did report waking two or three times a night but was unable to recollect if a dream preceded the awakening. During the day, in spite of a stuporous or languid appearance, she was startled by sudden noises. Occasional painful and intrusive thoughts of being worthless popped into her mind and motivated her to follow through on treatment arrangements. She dramatically stated that she must change or die.

As mentioned, her initial self-presentation was seductive, an opening that represents one type of transference test. If in response, the therapist were flirtatious or charming she would either strive to use him as an object substitute, or be too frightened to continue. As alluded to in the earlier summary, she has never been able to achieve a stable, independent existence. Her dependency relationships are also unstable. Sexuality is used to attract a man, but consummation is followed by rapid dissolution of any bond established. Whenever troubled, she initiates the pattern, a character trait of hers that is repeated in the therapy. Were she successful in enticing the therapist, the therapy would be subverted in order to act out a fantasy of rescue. But she is also extremely vulnerable to rejection. A profound feeling of worthlessness underlies her efforts to engage interest. A therapist who is frightened by her overtures and withdraws from her will be experienced by her as too cool, and as hiding behind a caricature of the ground rules of psychoanalytically oriented psychotherapy.

The present therapist is less reactive than the patient seems to wish, but he carefully maintains a steady interest and connection with her. "Closeness" as discussed in the chapter on hysterical personalities is present in the steadiness of attention and in a gentle (not cooing or seductive) approach, as the therapist uses simple questions and repetitions to encourage continuity. Thus, the main interventions in this hour were an effort to maintain a focus during a communicative process. This therapeutic alliance eventually allowed her to encounter the train of thought avoided by massive numbing and denial, for by herself, she could not tolerate the thoughts.

SECOND SESSION

As is often the case, during the second hour the patient presented herself as more decompensated than during the first hour. The establishment of a therapeutic relationship apparently allowed her to loosen her efforts at controlled self-presentation. While dressed seductively, she impressed the therapist as "blurred" throughout the session. Her speech was slow, halting and weak. Her thoughts were vague and except for a repetition of description of her symptoms, no train of thought was continued for any appreciable length of time. The therapist was more convinced that she had very weak cognitive functioning and extreme vulnerability. The undertone of seductiveness in the first hour had been replaced by one of helplessness. The therapist sensed that he should be extremely gentle.

The hour began with the patient confused about what to do. The therapist quietly told her that her job was to tell him what was going on and his job was to help her understand what it meant. She then repeated the description of her symptoms as given in the first interview. This reduces anxiety because she has already repeated the story in several medical settings. The therapist accepted this and simply asked occasional questions to obtain details or keep her going when she trailed off. Her descriptions then included a report of recurrent, intrusive and "almost real" images of Antonelli.

The process of questions and repetitions from the therapist plus further details from the patient clarified the phenomena and led to the first associations not directly linked to symptoms. Laura talked, in a vague way, of her current relationship with Hans, her sexual inhibitions since the accident, and her feelings of gullibility. The therapist labeled relatively diffused comments as being centered on the theme of "Can I be a good woman?" Laura then said she had been having impulses to try an overdose of street drugs.

Work on this theme led to a murky connection between current suicidal ideas and those at the time of the automobile accident. A relatively "close" interaction between patient and therapist followed the theme of her feelings of worthlessness. As the reasons for this were approached, she became more diffuse, spoke in a detached way of "needing to sort out the past," and gave scattered information about putting her child up for adoption. She then said, in a seemingly disconnected manner, "Who am I?" paused and continued, "Why not kill myself?"

As the therapist, in a simple way, connected the adoption (i.e., desertion) theme and the suicide idea, she expressed her feelings of worthlessness more clearly. The therapist suggested that she call him between appointments if she became too frightened of suicidal impulses. Perhaps intimidated by the implied closeness of the relationship, she then denied the seriousness of all she had been telling him, and ended the hour by saying she might not come to the next scheduled appointment because of a pleasure trip.

During both hours, her expressive style was preponderately vague and inhibited. She spoke very softly and slowly with many pauses and sighs. Her inflection gave an indefinite quality to what she said. It was as if her words evaporated and had no meaning for her after she spoke them. This style provokes the therapist to label and clarify for her. Doing so, he moves closer when the patient is very vulnerable. During this early phase, the labeling or repetition by the therapist encourages Laura to go on for a few more sentences. To continue doing this for her later, when she is less vulnerable, would be an error. Here is an example of what this was like at the beginning:

> L (Laura): I fool myself (pause)—there is nothing to be said (pause)—haven't been able to talk, there is nothing to be said (pause)—nothing a person can relate to (pause)—before the accident.

In spite of the vagueness and scattered ideas, the therapist has developed an inference based on the repetition and juxtaposition of the "nothing to say" statements and the "before the accident" allusions. He therefore suggests a connection.

> T (Therapist): Are you saying that "before" you felt there was nothing to say?
>
> L: (perks up) Yes (pause)—my thoughts go to Antonelli (pause)—I imagine his voice, his looks.

A story line is gradually pieced together in the therapist's mind on the order of: Before the accident, she and Antonelli reached a point where there was nothing to say to each other. She is grieving for him. This "story" remains unclear and is slowly clarified through each repetition during the therapy.

THIRD SESSION

The patient arrived quite early and was dressed in an unusually conservative manner. She seemed stronger and more alert than at any previous time and later said she had been experiencing more capacity for thinking, and was feeling less "spaced out."

On entering the room, she said, "How are you" in an intimate and engaging way. Remarks about whether therapy was or was not going to be of use followed. She revealed that she had polished her nails while preparing to come to the session, then removed it so as not to appear as if she had carefully dressed up. Later, during the hour and as if unconsciously, she started reapplying the nail polish. She also said, offhandedly, that she could make men happy.

These episodes are also transference tests. As before, if the therapist is too responsive, even with a shy smile, then she will be deflected in the direction of seeking a transference gratification by using the therapist as a substitute for lost love objects. The therapist cannot be too cold either—for example, waiting impassively for her to go on. This patient is so fragile that she does not have a secure idea of the nature of the therapeutic alliance and silence means a rejection that is beyond her current capacity to tolerate. The therapist avoided either hazard by speaking simply of the therapeutic alliance.

After saying that she could make men happy, she paused, then said in a provocative manner, "What good is this doing?" The therapist replied, "So far, we have learned that we can talk together in order to clarify what happened to you before and after your accident."

The patient abruptly ceased her efforts to engage the therapist in talking or responding to her, assumed that she had his attention, and spoke clearly of her current symptoms, the absence of sexual desire. She referred to three important relationships with men, one of whom was Antonelli. She asked herself ruminatively if he would want her back and then drifted into an abstract consideration of right or wrong. Here is a transcript of that segment.

L: Is there a right and wrong? It seems like if you do things for the right reason, you'll get a good reaction. Like the accident and the changes I've gone through— maybe I was doing things the wrong way, or not taking full account of everything (laugh). So, I want to think right and do things right. But who decides what's right? I'm beginning to think more concretely. I don't feel spaced out. I feel capable of most anything.

T: Sometimes you think the accident was the result of wrong things you were doing?

L: Yeh. I'm sure. The accident seems funny to me: I was madly in love with Antonelli. And I almost kill myself by getting drunk on Cinzano, his favorite booze, living . . . er, leaving a place called Luigi's right before the accident. Seems funny to me.

T: Like it's too much to be coincidence?

L: It could be coincidence. When I look back at it, I think I lost my touch with reality a long time before that— probably when he told me . . . you know . . . ah . . . or maybe before then, maybe years ago (laugh). I don't know (laugh) . . . but, uh.

An emergent thought about what he told her threatens to evoke too much emotional pain and a characteristic type of inhibition sets in, clouding both her conscious experience and the communicative process.

L: . . . And the accident was right . . . uh, like a final way. Because over this past weekend, I was more aware of what was happening around me than I was the first time.

She has not shifted the topic, but has continued to inhibit aspects of the topical complex. What she means by "the first time" is the period just before the accident. This vague labeling is also both stylistic and immediately defensive.

L: So, I don't know what I was doing the first time—just living it up, I guess. Just like I think about right and wrong, I think about what's important to do.

It would be very hard for the therapist to know what she means because of the vague and somewhat mislabeled concepts. From later material, it is evident that she means that before the accident, she was feeling confused and seeking as many experiences as possible in order to jam her mind and avoid ideas and feelings about the loss of Antonelli, and those of her actions that led to that loss. The "wrong" ideas are allusions to these actions.

T: So you were living it up and feeling out of touch with some part of reality.

L: People can become carried away by their idea of who they are and what's going on, not as aware or thoughtful as they can be of what's happening.

T: You think you were ignoring things you wanted to ignore?

The patient has depersonalized the reference: "People can become carried away." The therapist labels her as the subject of the incipient ideas, "You think, etc." As will be seen, even though she goes on with "I," she is not yet ready or able to experience or communicate the idea that she feels and felt badly about doing something wrong that ruined her relationship with Antonelli.

L: I wasn't really ignoring, I was forming my own opinions. For example, I saw what was going on in the house of one of the people in the place where I was staying. The girl wasn't as aware as she should be of what was going on. She was on her own trip too, and wasn't able to understand why her old man was (vaguely) with her. Or just forming opinions of things, (pause) I'll probably do that again. But it's better not to just accept everybody as exactly who or what they are. That's how I want to be accepted. Like, before I was just being a pretty girl. I wasn't thinking about anything. I was just (pause) you know. And the accident just made me take a really heavy look at myself, and maybe I don't like what I've seen. My 25th birthday is next Wednesday. I think about age a lot. I feel like I've aged a lot physically since the accident. I don't feel sixteen anymore (laugh). Um. Ooh. (Long pause in which she lights a cigarette) I don't like my smoking but it's hard to quit. (pause) Sometimes I suspect smoking cigarettes keeps me from another level of thinking. But then I think the "other levels" idea is just my imagination. But then, I know that's not true. (Very long pause) Hans told me he can't wait 'til I find out who I am (mumbles). (Extended silence)

The patient has circled closer to a repetitive theme of having done something wrong. The therapist attempted to move closer to expression and clarifications of what this was when he asked about what she wanted to ignore. Laura uses inhibition and a scattering of generalities to ward off such mental contents. Nonetheless, each episode of approach to the warded-off contents is progress toward clarification. At the same time, each approach is a check on the situation for safety. Alone, the patient dares not dwell on "it." In the therapeutic relationship, she learns that she can think about "it" and feel the painful, emotional responses it evokes, without the pain exceeding her limits of toleration. Thus, those avoidances ilustrated here do not indicate that the therapy is not moving along.

Following the above excerpt, the patient paused and then denied that she was either crazy or unhappy. She paused again, then remembered experiences of intensive images of Antonelli. She imagined the future in terms of how she might act if she could only meet him once more. She again dropped this theme, spoke in a trivial way about recent activities, and idly began to polish her fingernails and glance at the therapist.

The warded-off pain involves both feelings of guilt that she betrayed Antonelli and, more potentially intense right here, her sense of hunger for attachment. She cannot represent this in words, but instead, behaves seductively in order to replace what is lost, and avoid grief.

The therapist, in effect, waited her out in a calm and stead-fast manner. She suddenly seemed to become more alert, emerged from a blurred state, and talked of how men "came on to her on the street." This was followed by thoughts of an impending earthquake; a cataclysm during which the unworthy would perish, and of how devils existed inside people.

Her thoughts have, as if inexorably, returned to the theme of wrongdoing. But the return of this repressed theme instigates further defensive efforts.

She then said defiantly that the accident had changed her outlook and that she does not want to be fooled again.

This means she does not want to be seduced or enthralled by the therapist, tell all, and then be left in the lurch. Her basic self and object schemas lead her to expect that this will happen.

She repeated the sequence of discussing the accident a little, feeling wrong in herself, blocking, externalizing and talking philosophically and vaguely on the topic of who she is. The therapist then said that she both wanted new awareness and was afraid of the emotions that it would bring about.

FORMULATION

After the hour, the therapist reconstructed in his own mind a sequence of thoughts that Laura has and also has been warding off. She has suggested that the automobile accident was a suicide attempt caused by her feelings of desolation. She felt such despair because of the difficulty of mourning for and recovering from the loss of her lover. Thinking about it made her feel intolerably and abjectly remorseful for having caused the separation by her infidelity. Pre-existing conflicts included guilt and anxiety over sexuality and counterphobic promiscuity; guilt, sadness and rage over separations and inadequate supplies from others; and shame over a defective, worthless self-image. The goal of the therapist was to help her work through the three recent events: the "act of infidelity"; the loss of Antonelli; and her suicide-equivalent, in terms of these conflicts. This therapeutic effort would have to proceed through the filters imposed by her hysterical style, her immature developmental level and her continued search for parent substitutes.

FOURTH SESSION

During the hour, the patient tells of her experiences with Antonelli. She had lived with him for several months. When he was called away on a necessary trip, she felt lonely and deserted, and slept with a mutual friend. The friend told Antonelli as soon as he returned. Antonelli called her a worthless whore and asked her to leave his apartment. She cried for hours and drove wildly about the city, narrowly missing a wreck that night. She then became blurred over implications of this story.

FIFTH SESSION

She reports taking a hallucinogenic drug the previous day.

This is reminiscent of the hierarchy of defense described in the chapter on Harry as a hysteric: inhibit representation, do not translate images into word memories, dissociate, become passive. Here she has used a drug to help her dissociate and also, perhaps, to provoke the therapist into rescue activity.

She tells of having feelings of worthlessness and thoughts of suicide during the hallucinogenic "trip." She had expected the drug to make her feel free and to allow her to be sexual with Hans. Her manner indicates anger with the drug and the therapist. She changes in a labile and partly uncontrolled manner, from feeling worthless and guilty to anger, to seductiveness, to being "spaced out." She ends by observing her own low control and plaintively questions her lack of control when Antonelli was away and she slept with his friend. The therapist commented that asking this question in and of itself showed that she could begin to control herself.

The basic purpose of this comment was to increase her sense of self-esteem. It also contains a covert suggestion that she rouse herself to a sense of active responsibility and that therapy is helpful.

SIXTH SESSION

She is able to assemble her story in its sequential order and in a coherent manner. She experiences guilty feelings and checks the therapist to see if he will be either critical or warmly encouraging. Eroticized transference overtures become increasingly overt, and she is more clearly angry at feeling rejected, allowing herself to pout when the therapist does not take the candy she has offered during the hour. She goes on conceptualizing her story with Antonelli, adding some associations that include warded-off oedipal attachments towards her father and an unresolved sense of symbiotic attachment with her mother.

SEVENTH SESSION

She seems much more energetic and there is little in the way of eroticized transference acting-out. Instead, she reports pleasurable flirtations with men and generally avoids talking of the entire stress event. She does, however, add historical material about her earlier flight from her family into promiscuity and her growing sense of worthlessness at that time.

EIGHTH SESSION

She again deals with the Antonelli relationship. She is more emotional and she also is more deliberately evasive. She inhibits ideas, but does not dissociate. She reports feeling sexually aroused by Hans, making an overture, then having intrusive thoughts of Antonelli and crying. She becomes anxious in the hour as the therapist repeats this sequence, but her thinking is generally much improved. The question of organicity is set aside in the therapist's mind. He helps her to clarify cause and effect sequences in the story.

REMAINING SESSIONS

She continues to feel more energetic and "forgives herself." She imagines meeting Antonelli again and not begging him to take her back at any price. She also discusses her drug history, her feeling of using sex and drugs to escape growing up, and her sadness over the disruption of her marriage and over giving up her child.

She is seductive at times and this leads to memories of her anger with her father when he appeared to lose interest in her as she developed sexual, womanly attributes during adolescence and when he accused her of trying to show off her breasts in a sluttish way. She then grows angry with the therapist and displaces this onto anger at needing therapy. She then cries and talks of her sense of inner deadness. Transference gambits of an erotic sort continue whenever she feels especially vulnerable, but she is more able to control them. For example, she can joke about her feelings: "If I thought the world was coming to an end, what would I do? Seduce you? No." (laughs)

This thought about the world coming to an end referred to impending termination, a topic dealt with in many of the ensuing hours as it related to (1) fears of relapse without the therapist, (2) loss of Antonelli and previous losses, and (3) anger that the "price" of getting better was giving up the therapist. As termination approached, her seductiveness emerged again in a more peremptory manner, and led to further work on her need for attachment, her tendency to offer sex in order to be cared for, and her feelings of inadequacy that are both the cause and the effect of such behavior.

DISCUSSION

The therapy was terminated after 20 sessions. There was a marked improvement in her mental status. Her interpersonal relationships were restored to the maximal level she had achieved prior to the accident. She felt better about herself, was not suicidal, and had worked through several aspects of the loss of Antonelli and her related actions. She had also learned to think about her life and decisions in the context of the psychotherapeutic situation. Some aspects of longing and rage had been touched upon in relating Antonelli to her earlier life, and in working through the prospect of separation from the therapist. Her core neurotic conflicts and incompletely developed character structure were not changed although she had more insight into their existence. Now that she was relatively asymptomatic, she could either resume her life as it was before the flurry of recent events, or accept a recommendation for long term psychotherapy aimed at working through characterological problems.

CHAPTER SIXTEEN

Death of a Parent

With the assistance of Frederick Parris, M.D.*

MARGARET, A TWENTY-FIVE-YEAR-OLD WOMAN, illustrates denial and the resumption of mourning during psychotherapy and the communicative problems imposed by a style in which isolation and undoing are prominent.

She telephoned the outpatient clinic for an "evaluation of depression" because of suicidal thoughts during a period shortly after her mother committed suicide, and fear that "she might do as her mother did." She was referred to the stress clinic and an appointment was made. She phoned and cancelled this appointment, explaining that she was feeling much better. Contact was renewed several weeks later, when Margaret called again, saying she had been feeling better but now wanted help.

FIRST SESSION

She presented herself as composed, unemotional, in control, intelligent and personable. As part of obtaining informed consent, she signed a statement containing the words "Research on Stress Response Syndromes." She began the first session by commenting on this phrase.

---

*Dr. Parris is presently Clinical Instructor in Psychiatry at the University of California, San Francisco.

> M (Margaret): It is important to, uh, to study that, and I think the greatest impact has of course, been on my father.

She refers to the suicide of her mother.

> M: And ah, I read a research study recently in the paper that said that sudden deaths are extremely hard to get over for a spouse, for him, and after they've been married for 33 years, and were very, very close, in the relationship, so it affects me most when I'm with *him*, but when I—where as I'm living my own life out here, and I was living my own life when she died, although we were very close. (pause)

She repeats that her father is the one affected by her mother's suicide. As is often the case, the first minutes of therapy indicate a character trait of the patient. She uses alternative facts ("he is upset") as a way to ward off threatening facts "I am upset"). She goes on to say how days can pass *without* thinking of it before disclosing her own distress.

> M: So I was just thinking recently that sometimes I'm, I'm pretty sure I, I go whole days without thinking about it—and I'm feeling the more direct problems that I'm confronting, you know in my work, which is difficult. I was standing talking on the phone at work yesterday and there was this girl behind me who was cracking up, saying to her girlfriend she felt like committing suicide and, you know, everything was going wrong. And all the machines weren't working and, you know, I was identifying very strongly because that happened to me a couple weeks ago.

Identification with one who commits or might commit suicide inscribes itself on the therapist's mind as a possible key issue. The "universal" stress response theme of fear of merger with a victim is here colored by another "universal" theme, identification with the parent of the same sex.

> M: . . . 'cause all the machines I wanted to use weren't working or I was doing really stupid mistakes. And ah,

it was just before Easter and I had to get something done and, and I was just starting to shake, I was just so uptight, and, so when I first called here I, ah, was in a very, uh, very bad situation, you know, emotionally, I just didn't know what was going on, and I was, I was feeling suicidal and ah, just, for the first time in my life that I just couldn't cope with the things that were happening to me. And I couldn't cope with my own feelings, and I was just, I felt like I was getting out of control. And, when I started realizing what I was doing to myself and to the people around me, notably to the guy I'm living with, um, I realized I had to get a grip on myself, and I have been, I don't feel like I'm freaking out that much anymore. Sometimes I feel, this is why I didn't follow up too closely after I called, I called and, and ah very very urgent at the time and then, you know then I got a grip on myself and ah, I, I couldn't really make up my mind whether or not I should come ah, or whether I was getting back on the road and I didn't have to worry too much any more and still feel alternately one way or the other. Sometimes I feel fine, I feel sane and sometimes I still feel that ah, I need new perspectives and, I really need somebody to um, help, you know put my head right back where it should be, you know, I don't know if I've ever, my head has ever been where it should be. So, um, it, it's also hard. I got kind of nervous this morning when you first saw me because I suddenly tried to put all my problems together, and sometimes I feel I can talk about them very coherently, and I like to, and then it comes out to somebody, who ever I happen to be with at the moment and then, there, I was just afraid this morning on account I wouldn't be able to talk and I wouldn't be able to put anything together. So, I don't know if I can. (pause) But, I guess, it's also hard for me just to sit here and keep talking without any sort of direction, I suppose. So, (laugh) do you have any advice for me?

She has become diffuse and repetitive at an abstract level, over the issue of whether or not she is all right.

The therapist asked her to go on with whatever she felt most distressed about. She talked of her current love relationship with Ned but quickly shifted the topic to her work in photography. She graduated from college with a major in literature, then decided to leave her home in suburban New York to come west. She obtained a very promising job in movie production. It required that she plan her own original work in addition to carrying out certain editing room routines. For the first time in her life she felt that she was embarked on a satisfying and self-fulfilling career, but had difficulty concentrating in the darkened editing room. She retraced her history in order to illustrate her feelings during earlier periods, continuing as follows:

M: You know, I really hated myself all through high school. I thought I was ugly and nobody likes me and I went through all these very unstable things, um, that I started getting over finally when I went to New York State and um, I had a couple of relationships and I met a girl who is now very very close to me. I'm very close to Alice and we lived together for about a year and a half, and have been friends for nearly three years now. And then after I graduated from N.Y.S. as a lit major, um, I worked for a year as a secretary in Central Bookstore which was, it was fun, it was nice but I felt I wasn't doing anything with my life and I wanted to do something more creative and interesting. So I came out here because a friend had this movie studio that was really moving, and then um my father, who is a computer designer, he was working for General Labs in New Jersey and he was pressured into taking a big important job which would mean moving to Philadelphia for two years and my mother said absolutely no, I won't go, I'd die sooner. You know, she's very strong-willed, independent person and ah that upset me a whole lot, like (laugh) my god, my parents are splitting up and for 29 years, and there was no way my father could get out of it so um my mother would go back and forth. She finally decided to go with him, but she was going to stay home in New York for the summer, and ah then she killed herself, it was just as sudden as that. You know, it's very in a way it's very like her because she wasn't a person to make a big show of trying to ah commit suicide. You know, just she did it (ha, ha).

Her laughter is not simply nervousness, it is a way of undoing and averting negative emotional responses. She later reveals that her mother was strongly committed to being "not only a housewife." She had her own career as a free-lance illustrator and had earned substantial sums for many years. For a period immediately preceding her suicide, she had received unusually frequent rejections in competitive circumstances, and was not earning any money. Her mother loved their home, friends, and community. She hated Philadelphia and the idea of tagging along with her husband and was sure that he would have a second and fatal heart attack from the enormous pressures of the new job to which he had committed himself.

M: —you know just a total shock to everybody and so I stayed with my father for a month. Just every day, just trying to see him through every day and ah then I spent the next month seeing him and going, arranging things in New York and and ah relaxing and then going down to Philadelphia and, and then I came out here ah about five and a half months ago, um and started work. I was going to work full time but I didn't, I'm working part time instead. I'm working two days a week, taking some courses, um and that's about it. I don't know if it's given you any insights. It's been a, you know, I feel it's been a pretty normal middle class existence and, ah, up till now I feel I've been coping with everything fairly well. (pause) So, I don't think it's anything unusual, I don't even think my problems are anything unusual and you said it was, um, it was good I realized that it was all going on inside my head, and I do know that. I don't feel that the world is doing anything to me. Um, I feel that, the way I see life is that life is to me, and I can sort of make it whatever I want to, ah so I'm I just feel, I know that whatever I'm doing with my life is totally up here. (pause) So I don't know where to go from here.

She is in a denial phase. After her mother's death she devoted herself to her father's grief. Then she continued with her plans. She is having difficulty at work and with her boyfriend. She plays down the problems in order to maintain her sense of esteem. At this point she is *not* experiencing sadness over the loss of her mother, although the need to ward off such responses may contribute to her problems at work and with Ned.

The therapist then asked a series of questions exploring for signs of depression, suicidal potential, and any abnormalities in her current mental status. When no material of consequence emerged, he requested more details on her present interpersonal relationships. She responded by telling of her difficulties with Ned, of her periodic feeling of jealousy and her worries about losing him. The therapist sensed, because of clues in the flow of her remarks, that it was she who wished to leave Ned but that for some reason she felt badly about this and could not acknowledge it. He did not verbalize this, and she continued to describe now Ned moved in with her.

M: Just after Ned and I started getting a little, very very slightly involved um he was he was forced to move out his apartment and ah so in a moment of rashness, you know, of generosity, I said well you know stay with me if you can't find any other place to stay, as a temporary thing. That's how (laugh) that's how it started. It was really weird and for a long time for about a month I guess, I said ah you'll just have to find your own place as soon as you find a job and can pay for it. And he was saying after awhile, after we'd been living together for a couple of weeks, he was saying, "No I want to keep living with you," and I said "No, I don't want that. I want to live by myself." um And so finally, you know, we worked out things to the point where I decided, after about a month and a half or something, that if if we found different living quarters our relationship, which had built to a certain point, that point would just be thrown out the window because it wasn't the kind of thing that could survive on ah two totally separate um things. It would be a regression, if we lived in different places it would be putting our relationship on a lower level which neither of us thought it would survive. So I decided I wanted to continue with it rather than just completely throw it out. And that's why we got a larger apartment and moved about two months ago.

T: And that's about the time you began to become jealous, had fantasies, and worried?

M: Well, it was also the sort of time when *I stopped being in control of the situation*, because as long as Ned was saying "I want you," and I'm saying "Well I'm not sure," you know, *I was more in control* and as he was always the one who was making the efforts to to adapt to my needs and wants and I needed more time by myself. And ah once I, once I you know, sort of made a turn around and said, "I want you too," then sort of like the balance shifted and ah he became, *he wanted to become more in control.* I've always, I, I, you know, always resist him being in control, you know, and I said I'm the one who's suddenly having to make all the adjustments. I want it to be 50-50 and ah that's when started, um, resisting the security of, the security of the relationship, and, and sort of subconsciously trying to dump on it and *that was when we moved.* So, now, now I, I sort of resent feeling that I'm the one who has to make most of the adaptations and most of the changes. You know, because he's he's still he says, "Well that's the way I am you know. If you don't like it that's too bad."

T: How do you feel about having to make the changes? Are you feeling very frightened that if you don't you'll lose him?

The therapist is aware of the parallel between Margaret and her mother. Both are threatened by lowered controls, possible loss of a man, and loss by moving. He gropes for this connection and her possible identification with her mother in what follows.

M: Yeah. (pause)

T: I'm struck also—I'm trying to tie this in with the "Why now" question I have in my mind. You came west involved with yourself. Everything was going fine. You had your independence but for some reason things have regressed.

M: Mm-huh.

T: Perhaps you feel now the way you did back in high school, that you doubt your own value.

M: No, not, God forbid if I could ever doubt that again. No, I still have a basic sense of my own value and my own worth and and the person I am. I still have, you know, about three hundred percent more self confidence, down basically than I than I did then um.

T: What I was really driving toward was closing the circuit. I was wondering if your mother's death had any effects on you. Here was this case where *she* wanted to retain some control in a sense of not having to make the move, was forced into a corner and, as you said, "She wouldn't make the move even if it killed her," and that's apparently how it occurred. Would you identify with this part or would you prefer to—

M: Ah, I respect her alot, and ah, ah, I respect, you know, the, the strength that she always had and the independence and the the person that she was. You know, she was just a really beautiful person and, ah, I suppose the fact that I had to come to terms with her suicide, the fact that she deliberately took her life in the sense that I respect her so much. You know, so I got to respect what she did, you know.

She does not quite connect with the therapist's communication about identification. Instead she is reacting as if the therapist suggested that she might feel critical of or angry at her mother for committing suicide. She is protesting too much about how wonderful her mother was and how much she respected her. She not only avoids negative feelings, but she avoids them by stating opposite ones. This is a characteristic style for her, akin to the switching described in chapter 9. She does this so emphatically and repetitiously, while seeming ill at ease, that the therapist approaches it in a very gingerly manner.

T: In fact you almost had to respect what she did, so as not to interfere with your image of her as a. . . .

M: Mm-huh.

T: Not to place a value on suicide, but you had it in your mind as respecting her suicide because if you didn't respect that, you would have to question the image. . . .

M: Yeah. Also, um like she couldn't, you know, I can see how after decades of of living with one man and loving him and having a very close, good relationship that they did, she couldn't turn around and say I'm leaving you. You know that. I don't see how any person could really do that.

Hence she cannot break up with Ned, although later in therapy she felt able to do so. One reason for coming to therapy was her conflict over how to terminate an unsatisfactory but close relationship.

M: Whereas knowing how much she hated Philadelphia and the pressure cooker existence, that and the fact that she, she was also very sure that my father, you know, was going to die of a heart attack because he almost did five years ago. And put in a similar situation she was positive he was going to drop dead anyway, once he did that, once he moved. um So, having made that decision, and she she also felt that he betrayed her by doing this when he knew that she she would hate moving so much. But I respected that fact that she wanted to retain her independence and and that it was hurting her pride to have to follow somebody else. You know, like just to be an appendage to my father um (pause). So, she she wrote in her note, you know to my father, "You did what you have to do. I'm doing what I have to do." And, ah, I, you know I've never, I haven't thought of suicide at all since I was about 16 years old. And, you know, the fact that, you know, my mother's, you know, doing it brought it to my attention so much, and having to respect the fact. Like I, I'm, I'm almost positive that's why it seems like an alternative to me now. Um—although I'm, I'm I'm pretty positive that I wouldn't do it. Because I, I don't think that I could face hurting my father that much. I mean I wouldn't have to face it, obviously, but um I just don't think I could. You know, knowing, you know, how much it hurt him for her to die. You know, I just feel it would be another blow that he couldn't bear.

T: I wonder if what makes it even triply hard for you, as sad as you feel, just trying to respect and love your mother, is the fact that she did hurt your father very much in the final analysis.

This is a fairly direct interpretation of her hostile thoughts toward her mother, and of a warded-off hostile component in her reaction to her mother's suicide.

M: No. I know she was a very selfish person and I knew that when she was alive and I knew it when she was dead. Um, it was a selfish thing to do, you know, and she was a very self-centered person and she, I knew, I always knew that. (pause) So *I don't respect her* for being so, you know, that self-centered, you know. *I certainly don't blame my father* either. (pause)

The therapist can infer an unspoken thought, "I don't blame my mother" before she says "I don't blame my father either." This is a sequence of undoing: "I don't respect her (I do blame her). (I don't blame her), (I blame father), I don't blame my father." She ends by denying the impact of her mother's death.

M: But I do feel that I've come to terms with, you know, with her death about as much as I ever will. I don't feel that it's, it's really disturbing me so much now, you know, emotionally, except that there are situations that I find myself in now that I I just say (laughing) you know *"I wish you were here."* You know, because she, you know, she was always a great support for me. She was, somebody who really really did believe in me, and always said so. And, she always tried to put some backbone into me, you know, and she really did. I absorbed a lot of things from her. When I was in a situation where I'd say "Oh mommy I like this guy and he won't ask me out" and she'd say "Well go ask him out. What are you waiting for." You know she was a very aggressive person and she, she pounded that into me. Um, and she was, she was an extremely proud person and she pounded that into me as much as she could too. (pause)

T: Okay. We're going to have to end for today.

SECOND SESSION

She came in expressing ambivalence about her need for therapy. She denied any relationship between her problems and what had happened to her mother and said that she had come back only because she felt obligated to discuss whether or not she needed therapy. She did not like the way the therapist just listened to her, and offered nothing of himself. In various ways, she asked for support and friendship. However, in doing so she was provocative and accusatory. The therapist felt that she was testing him to see if he would collapse (have a heart attack as her father did), become angry and wish to be rid of her, or approach her more intimately and socially, (which would frighten her), or try to control her. He continued with the same concerned, tactful, and objective professional manner as in the first interview. She announced that she was going on a visit to see her father for a few days.

THIRD SESSION

Margaret dealt superficially and unemotionally with the visit to her father. She felt that she was much better and believed her fears of being flooded were related to "a period of identity problems in adolescence." She gave additional history, including a suicidal gesture when depressed as an adolescent. She was agreeable and intellectual during the hour, using undoing, negation, and disavowal to avoid anxiety.

FOURTH SESSION

Margaret spoke of an episode of sadness that occurred while she was developing her own pictures in the darkroom at work. She had taken these pictures during a recent visit home, and had also brought back a picture of her mother that she found there. She talked longingly of missing a girlfriend but, to avoid intensification of sad feelings, she switched to discussing both difficulties and successes with her editing work, focusing on mechanical issues. The therapist, in summarizing her remarks over the hour, mentioned an idea she spoke of earlier in the hour, about going home to be closer to old friends of hers and her mother.

She responded that introspection on such ideas made her "massively oversensitive to any little thing." She related this oversensitivity to Ned, and continued as follows:

> M: . . .—like um—even if, if I feel a I feel affectionate to-
> ward Ned and he just doesn't happen to feel that way
> at that moment, it just sends me I mean right to the
> bottom, or *just looking you know at a picture of my
> mother will just send me into a fit of crying* and this
> doesn't happen, normally. But things that don't nor-
> mally upset me do, things that I just can't, I can't deal
> with them rationally. I can't shrug them off, and I feel
> —in a way I feel a huge loss of self-esteem—whereas
> on they other hand if somebody said, "Do you like
> yourself"—I would say "Yes." It's just one of one of
> the main characteristics of my depression is just feeling
> unable to cope with the complexities and the demands
> of life and the future and making a living and achieving
> something or accomplishing something. It just seems
> too complicated and too difficult and the whole thought
> of it just appalls me.

> T: It's only a hunch but I would think some of those feel-
> ings come to mind when you look at a picture of your
> mother and have some realization of her loss and talent.

The therapist notes the defensive maneuver of abstract generalization, attention to peripheral details, and expansion to issues
too large to contemplate such as "the complexities and the demands of life and the future." He tries to hold her to a topic she
has brought up and is also warding-off, by giving this interpretation.

M: Well one of my one of my strongest fantasies, or actually I have very very few fantasies that, that I wish, but one of the things that has been recurring since she died is wishing that I'm little again—very little—you know like about five years old. And I brought back from the East two pictures, one was of my mother when she was in college, and one was of me when I was five years old and, I'm I'm planning to put them together in a frame because that is my strongest fear (a slip of the tongue), ahh, fantasy, you know, I want to go back to the time that everything was taken care of for me and I didn't have to worry about finances, and supporting myself, and, and a trying to accomplish something in life. Although I suppose you know, the little things I was going to try and survive were just as traumatic as the things I, I might go through now. But that's, that's how I feel. You know, it's not so much that I hate myself, I hate myself, but a feeling of just being unable to cope with all these things because I, I think that the self-esteem, and the, ah, the feeling I like myself, or I wouldn't be anybody else, um, I think that those feelings are very solid in myself. I don't question them, I, I feel in that sense, I always feel very together. . . .

She is switching from her wish to be little and dependent, an idea that makes her feel too infantile, self-critical, and controlled, to assertions that she likes herself. When this undoing operation restores a sense of safety she can resume self-critical statements.

M: . . . But my main, the the main characteristic of my depression is just I hate to get up. I hate to face each day. I hate to—um, I feel that every single day is a struggle and I never want to wake up in the morning, or when I wake up I never want to get up. I just *dread* every day. And that's, those are, that's the massive feeling that my depression consists of. And, ah, I relate *this* to the pressure that has been put on me by my father to succeed—it's not that he's pressuring me. . . .

She is using her characteristic switching maneuver again. She has switched in describing her father and is also using the topic of her father to switch away from ideas and feelings related to her mother. As will be seen, the "mother" topic will return.

> M: . . . but (sigh) he wants me to, you know, for my own sake, be, because he knows, or he's instilled in me, I suppose, the need to feel that I'm accomplishing something in life. But at the same time I've gone through four years of liberal arts college and movies are such an overloaded market that it's *very* difficult and you have to be extremely aggressive to be able to succeed, and ah, much as I want, I still have these ambiguous feelings. I have tremendous fear of not being able to. And, ah, it's just really, that is, that is another thing that's very, very difficult for me to cope with. And, you know, when I got these feelings from him my mother was always the person I was able to go to. She wanted the same things from me but she she didn't express them in a pressurized way. She expressed them in a much more sympathetic way that I could identify with and I've, you know, I always turned to her. And in the years when I was closest to her, I was farthest from my father.

> T: When were those years?

The therapist, sensing she is about to switch away from the train of thought involving her mother, seeks to hold her to this topic by asking a relevant question about her mother.

> M: Oh, my college years and, and, ahh, up until she died —well after I'd left home. She was, ah—um, I feel a lot of sympathy for her, because she, I don't think she was a very good (pause) mother. . . .

This "I feel a lot of sympathy" is a kind of premonitory undoing of the angry feelings that are incipient and emerge clearly in her voice when she subsequently speaks of her mother's terrible temper. Both feelings are really present.

> M: . . . She didn't want to be really (a mother). My father told me this after she died. Especially when both my sister and me were little. She hated having two little kids around and, I mean she loved us but I remember

she had the worst temper, you know, she's used to—I remember when she grabbed me by my hair and shook me like that. Um, I mean she never beat me or you know anything like that but she, you know, she had a *terrible* temper. And this died away very, very much after I left home. And she and my sister, ah, my sister was very unstable and really hated my mother for years even after she went to college, and ah, I don't think their relationship ever really got close, even after that. But after I left home, very quickly I started growing back closer to my parents and, and my mother always, um, (pause) she, she always needed me, and I, I understood that, you know, without ever really talking about it. And you know sort of a feeling she really wanted me to have all the freedom that I could possibly have, even though she needed me, and she wanted me to be near, you know, on vacations and stuff like that. You know and she urged me to move to California even though you know, she would've much rather had me (pause) closer. (pause)

The therapist tries to hold her to this topic with another question, but she deflects to other topics until the end of the hour.

FIFTH THROUGH SEVENTH SESSIONS

The next two hours, the fifth and sixth sessions, deal with ordinary matters at work and with Ned, and avoided mention of her mother. In the seventh hour Margaret talked in a general way, about everyday work frustrations. She then told of how strongly she had felt that she had to get away from Ned and be with a girlfriend, not to "sob on her shoulder, but to get her energy." She "accepted it with equanimity" when the girlfriend was too tired to have her come over. She immediately returned to work topics and expressed righteous anger with her boss. She then criticized her editing machine for being defective and talked abstractly about artistic tasks. One purpose of discussing the boss and the equipment was to show that she was not at fault or to blame for her anger.

She then talked of showing her film work eventually, but in

a dejected manner. The therapist said that she might be asking if it's okay to show not her work, but her feelings, for he could sense that she was depressed. She said she was sad that she had only her work to attest to her worth, and she was uncertain about it. She came close to tears at the end of the hour, but the cause was unclear, concealed by intellectualized generalizations.

EIGHTH SESSION

She began the next session by saying that she had been feeling unstable for the last two days. She had been reluctant to do darkroom work because she was afraid she would be unable to focus her thoughts while there. The first half of the interview was occupied with a long soliloquy about the uncertainty of her future plans and her ambivalence toward accepting financial support from her father. When the therapist attempted to focus her attention on the unstable feeling, she deflected towards continuing these generalizations and abstract ruminations. But she then went on to mention her mother, as illustrated in the following transition.

> M: . . . ah, like last night I got terribly depressed about what I was saying, and I was going through one of my sort of panics, and this time I said "I'm not going to run over to anybody," and in a way I didn't want to, I wanted to just figure it out. And I couldn't. I mean I just couldn't figure out why I was feeling so completely down. I knew when it started though, and, and I have an absolute progression of what happened because I'd been sort of down for two days. *It all started with a thought of my mother, and, ah, I mean everything was fine.* I was feeling really good one evening and Ned and I were just sitting around talking and a song of Joanie Mitchell's came on the radio and all of a sudden I flashed back to this conversation I had with my mother about Joanie Mitchell about two or three years ago, a long time ago, when um my mother was just saying "Oh, it's just her publicity people that say

she writes and sings and plays the guitar and she does everything." I said, "Mother, cut it out, she really does." And my mother said, "Oh." You know, she was she was just thinking I was being naive. And I flashed on that and I got really depressed and into my own thoughts and I sat down and I wrote a long letter to this woman back East, who, um, was my mother's closest friend, and who's like, you know, another mother to me. I just haven't, I haven't been writing letters lately but I wrote her a long letter and (sigh) it was just you know I just went into the bedroom and and sort of sat and thought for a long time. I was, I was feeling down, but not not really terribly bad. I was just thinking and I wanted to be by myself, (sigh) and I was still down will the flu and I was sick of being sick and, ah, and so on. And the next day, the next evening, a couple of friends of Ned's came over. I've talked to you about the problem I have of relating to his friends, and this is his friend Tom, who's a total freak and Tom's, a woman that he lives with. I mean it's a really weird situation; she's a call girl.

T: Can I ask you what the letter was like that you wrote to the friend of your mother?

While the associations may possibly be relevant, the therapist notes the reference to ambivalence about her mother and so he chooses to help Margaret hold onto that aspect of the topic, that is, the issue of missing her mother, feeling frustrated, and wishing for a substitute mother. If Margaret were on her own, as she would be alone at home, she would probably not continue to develop this ideational line because it evokes painful feelings.

M: Oh, yeah um (pause). I wanted to explain to her you know what was going on between Ned and me because I'd talked to her about it when I was back East. What I mainly, what I expressed right away was the fact that I needed, um (pause), ah, somebody sort of to function as my mother, and, you know, she is the closest to me. But she doesn't have the background in my life, and the, the things that you always go through with your parents. (pause) (sounds about to cry).

T: I asked you that very directly because I think you're experiencing a lot of feeling right here and now.

M: (long pause) (sigh) I just don't know if I can really talk about it (almost crying) (sniff) (long pause).

T: What sort of thoughts are you having?

M: I'm not really having any thoughts. I'm just trying to pull myself back together again so that I can talk. You know, it's like I said I don't want to come in here and, and break down, you know, although you said that does serve a purpose (cries). Um, I really want to use these sessions very constructively for my head (sniff). But we are getting very close to my emotions recently, because I've noticed this several times when I've come in here and started talking, just talking, you know, but not about my mother, not about anything, but I feel like crying and it's not as as hard, I mean it's not hard to hold back but but I feel that I'm very close to my emotions (sigh) (pause) (sniff).

T: I think that there's something very constructive going on, expressing emotions here.

This patient has been warding-off crying not only because sadness is painful, but because she believes it is humiliating to give way to emotions. The therapist says this to counter her tendency to feel humiliated. With other types of patients it would be a gratuitous remark that could be used transferentially.

M: (pause) Um it's not that I've been holding back. The emotions that I'm feeling are reactions to what I'm saying um. Thoughts of my mother have been very much with me. Well one way of showing this is a photograph I wanted to make, a self-portrait for my father. What I chose to do (sigh) was use time exposure on my camera, you know you can set it and about ten seconds later it goes off so you have a chance to get into a pose or something, do it by yourself. So I chose to try to take a picture of myself studying myself in the mirror and in the mirror are two pictures; the two pictures that I mentioned once to you very briefly before; one of my mother and one of myself when I was little, and the one of my mother was was when she was about say twenty. And to show that I'm looking at myself very strongly these days, and that these two pictures are um, well, pictures of the little girl, I mean myself as the little girl because that's, as I've said before, that's sort of almost how I wish that I were, was, and the picture of my mother, and it's an old picture. She'd, she just didn't like to have her picture taken so we have very few pictures of her that are recent and of those my father has them. My father's coming this weekend, by the way. . . .

She is expressing the thought "I miss my Mommy, I wish I were a little girl with her again." She modulates the rate of emergence of the idea by use of other thoughts. In effect, these thoughts partially fill cognitive channels so that the previously warded-off thought cannot rush out all at once and overwhelm her sense of control. The other thoughts, such as "my father's coming" may also serve as antidotes for her compelling sense of loss. She continues talking about her father, using his sadness as a vehicle for externalization of her own similar feelings, identifying with both his feelings and his capacity to cope with them, and savoring the continued attachment. Note that she will say she wards off ideas of her mother for his sake.

M: . . . So, I'm hoping that we, as always I'm hoping that we'll, we'll just enjoy each other's company and not (sigh), um, bring too many old ghosts back in. Um, this past week was their anni—, their wedding anniversary and ah I was afraid my father was going to be really down, so I called him up and he was he had friends over for dinner which really made me happy, he wasn't by himself and depressed. *He had been very depressed lately.* I knew that, but he was really pleased and touched that I had remembered and that I had called and that made me really happy and we're both looking forward to seeing each other. But, um *when we're together I try to keep as far away from any mention and thoughts of my mother* as possible because it (sigh) amplifies the feelings *so much* when the two of us are together. I mean I can talk about my mother and I can cry about my mother in front of Ned or you or any one of my friends. . . .

As far as the therapist knows, this is the first time she has cried. To reduce embarrassment about it she declares that she is comfortable with crying and does it all the time.

> M: . . . but with my father, his pain is just so great and so is my own that we just increase each other's feelings. So with him, I just try to avoid every mention of her, every thought, and whether this is good or bad I don't know. . . .

One reason she may feel badly is that she may be pre-disposed to feeling guilt over an oedipal victory. She now has her father and excludes (mention of) her mother. This would be only one factor in an over-determined behavior pattern.

> M: . . . (sniff) (pause) There are, there is this one lady, ah Marion, who is my mother's closest friend. I've known her all my life. She has a daughter who's a year younger than I am, and (pause) you know it's like back home I have a lot of people who who want to function as my special friends and parents and they do, but she's, she's very much the closest . . . (pause) (cries) (clears throat).

Stabilized by discussing her father and perhaps growing anxious about *that* topic, she returns to her wish to attach herself to a woman friend as a mother replacement. The woman cannot replace her mother, she must give up her mother, and so her sadness speaks again.

> M: . . . But what I feel that she has been, she's missing in in her role with me (cries) is you know all the things that are, that go between a mother and a daughter when they're growing up. All the little problems, all the, you know, the adol-, especially adolescence, which has got to be the worst period of anyone's life, but all the things that you know I went through with my own mother and I have never experienced with Marion. (pause) So, one of, I expressed that in my letter to her, saying that I wanted, that there were questions that I wanted to ask my mother about her experiences in life that I had never had a chance to or had never run up against and ah . . . (sniff) (pause)

T: What sort of questions would those be?

M: Well they're mainly ah with regard to ah her marriage. Like I know that my parents went through difficult times and I, I wanted to know how much do you, should you go, I mean it's crazy, nobody can tell you this, but I wanted to know from my mother's experience (sigh) how do you, how long do you hold on to a relationship when it's not good? How hard do you work for it? How, like, like Ned said to me once there are going to be times in our relationship when we'll hate the sight of each other, you know, and, and trying to show that that's, you know, that if you really, that a relationship will go through good times and bad times—and the bad times will be awfully bad but if you can hold on, I mean, the relationship will be very much strengthened, and this is something that my mother had also said to me. She'd, when we'd discussed the relative merits of marriage you know, I've said, you know, what am I supposed to push marriage for, you know, for nothing (said rapidly and vehemently).

She continued talking in generalities about one person hurting another. She then recalled a family scene in which she said she did not want to have children. Her mother took her side when her father was horrified. She went on to talk of her parents' ambivalence towards each other. The therapist summarized by saying that she was talking about expressions of both tender and angry feelings between persons, and added that she too may have angry feelings that cannot now be shared with her mother. She denied this:

M: Um not so much share feelings with her because I always did, and I always did tell her how much I loved her. But I think that's I (sigh), when my mother died I must have been the only person on earth who didn't have guilt feelings, who didn't say "If only I had done this" or, um, I had no feelings that I could have prevented or, or, ah, I don't know, just plain guilt that that she had done it, she had committed suicide, and I still don't have any. I don't have any feelings that

I wish that I had said that I loved her because, you know, I did. I said it many many times you know, starting I remember even years ago. Must have been when I was just about 17 or 18 and, and, ah, about to either just off to college, or about to go off to college, I said, I remember very distinctly saying to her that she had given me so much love and understanding and it was the kind of love and understanding that you can't give back. I mean, I can't turn to her and say "Now, you know anytime you want advice come to me," but it was some something that I could, that I had learned and could hand on to somebody else. And, ah, even way earlier than that *I remember when I was about probably 12 or 13 I had said something meaning to be funny and it was actually very malicious.* I said she was, no I, I must have been about 14, 'cause I remember the house we were living in, and it's one of my really clearest memories (cries). She was, she was doing the laundry and I was sitting at the table and she was singing and I said "Mother have you ever listened to yourself sing" and she said "no" and I said "Well you're lucky" and I was just, it was a stupid joke and years, I remember for years later I always said if there was one thing that I could call back in my life it was that, because it started her crying. I had made my mother cry and I was just, I, I apologized I said I'm sorry I didn't mean it that way, that was really stupid.

She continued with memories of her mother, then spoke of wanting to talk to her father about her mother, but being afraid to do so. Finally she talked again of longing to see her mother's friend Marion, and of being envious of Ned who can still call up his mother whenever he has a problem. At the end of the hour she gestured to the box of tissues and said, "Do you always keep these by the chair?" The therapist suggested that she was asking him to say that it was all right with him that she cried during the hour, and it was all right.

REMAINING SESSIONS

The stress oriented treatment continued for seven more sessions. The above session marked the beginning of open mourning for her mother. The grief process was marked by her loving attachment as well as her resentment and fear of over-identification with her mother. She had a model of her mother that had never before been clearly conceptualized by her; she saw her mother as superficially strong and powerful, but as weak underneath. The refusal to move with her father, for example, she saw as strong in her first conscious thoughts, but she was warding-off ideas that it was weak to have to commit suicide. Her mother was dependent on her father and could not live independently from him. But the attachment was ambivalent and unsatisfactory; her mother felt neither fulfilled by the marriage nor by the children or her creative work.

SUMMARY

Margaret was afraid she was too much like her mother. The relationship with Ned was a psychological parallel for the relationship between her parents. Like her mother, she believed, she could not give Ned up, because she would then drown in a sense of abandonment. On the other hand, she feared marrying Ned because he was self-centered, in some ways unstable, and she did not love him enough. As she could deal more authentically with her separation and independence from her mother, while also accepting the painful reality of the loss, she could risk separation from Ned. She engineered this separation and tolerated it well, while using the therapist as an interim relationship.

In the therapy she also worked through feelings of being neglected by her father, especially when she heard of his plans to remarry a woman younger than himself, who was about her age. Rage at all abandoning figures, including the therapist, with whom termination was impending, was an important topic for working through in the therapy, where she continued to use her style of switching topics or attitudes about the same topic. This characterological defensive style was not interpreted systematically as it would be in a psychoanalysis. The therapist's awareness of it allowed him to help her temper its use; to use it when emotions were too threatening at a given moment, or to not use it, and stay with a topic when the emotions were anticipated to remain within tolerable limits.

CHAPTER SEVENTEEN

The Suicide of a Friend

With the assistance of Robert Hammer, M.D.*

TIM IS A THIRTY-ONE-YEAR-OLD SINGLE MAN whose friend committed suicide shortly after a plea for help. During the weeks that followed, Tim felt so haunted by his dead friend that he was motivated to seek treatment. He was unable to sleep, afraid of the dark, had startle reactions, and unbidden images. During a brief psychotherapy these symptoms were relieved. The suicide of his friend was also linked associatively with the death of his father several years earlier. When a situation of safety was established by the therapist through a tactful maintenance of Tim's self esteem, a mourning process not begun at the time of the father's death, was initiated.

Jack was Tim's friend, and in some ways his leader, for several years. His was the role of a man who knows women and is successful at work. Then, for about a year while each was involved in other affairs, they seldom met. Recently, Jack had called Tim and they spent a long evening together. Jack spoke of feeling depressed and meaningless. He asked Tim to spend more time with him, and hinted at moving in with Tim. Tim inwardly recoiled. He was aware of a strong feeling that he did not want to be sucked in. He did not want to rescue Jack; they had not been that close recently. But on the surface he presented

---

*Dr. Hammer is presently Clinical Instructor of Psychiatry at the University of California, San Francisco.

a friendly demeanor and tried to cheer Jack throughout the evening.

A few days later, Tim received a telephone call from Carol, a woman who was a close friend of Jack's, and a person Tim had recently dated. Carol was worried. Jack was missing and had left a note that suggested a possible suicide. Once again, Tim was concerned but did not want to become involved. Over the next four days Tim felt episodically anxious that Jack might be playing some type of trick to get back at him for not being more concerned. On the fifth day Carol called again to say that Jack had shot himself, and that his body and been found in some nearby hills.

Carol asked Tim to join some friends in a funeral service. Feeling pressured, he refused, but then felt that he had acted in an aloof and callous manner. Within days he developed insomnia, a phobia of the dark, and intrusive thoughts about Jack that at times were so vivid that he could feel his presence, as a menace within the room. Here is the opening of the first interview in which he describes some of these symptoms.

FIRST SESSION

Tim: A friend of mine shot sh-shot and killed himself, I don't know about 10 days ago; *since that time I was afraid of the dark and I'd keep a light on. At first it took me forever to get to sleep, I kept, I'd keep wanting to open my eyes to look around to see if anyone were around in the apartment.*—I experienced periods during the day when I was frightened, felt very empty, extremely alone, (pause) every time I drive by the hills I hate to look in the direction to where I think he was when he shot himself (pause) I don't even want to know the specifics but I have general information about it. (pause) His body was taken to a funeral home which happens to be very near where I live. Every time I go by there I hate to. I just get very uncomfortable and (pause) I don't like dealing with a woman whom he was involved with, who I happen to work with somewhat now; I

THE SUICIDE OF A FRIEND / 339

felt like she was going to suck me in this thing, into a funeral and extend it and that was very upsetting. I had a talk with her last night about how I don't want to have anything else to do with her whatsoever (pause) and then on top of that, I started thinking about my own life and how I am not happy with it. I dislike it, how I want to change certain things in it (pause) how I'm lonely, want to get closer to somebody, thinking about having a family and having a job that I would like to put energy into (pause) but mainly right now I just want to get rid of all these feelings about him (pause). I can't stand it, it's hard for me to, he crops up when I'm alone all the time. . . .

T (Therapist): You mean sort of intrudes on your mind?

Tim: Yeah this morning, *washing my face, I have soap in my eyes, with my eyes closed I keep thinking all of a sudden somebody is going to touch my arm and there's no one* in the apartment (pause) I don't know why I freak out on that; I just force myself to finish washing my face and then I open my eyes and I'm O.K., look around, it's daylight and every thing's fine. . . .

T: How have you been sleeping lately?

Tim: I was sleeping a little better—at first I had all the lights in the apartment on, now I'm down to one in the living room which I'm very much aware of from my bedroom. Until last night I was definitely sleeping much better each night. I wasn't feeling much. I was better, and then I had this confrontation with this mutual friend, this woman and that upset me and I felt nervous in my stomach and it was hard for me to get to sleep. It makes me a little angry, the whole thing, that it should bother me.

T: It makes you angry.

Tim: Angry. I figure the way to get rid of the stress, for me, is to start doing things I want to do that make me happy and to stop sitting around on my ass 'cause *then I just think about him.* But I feel I move like a snail toward things I want to do.

During the beginning of the first hour, the therapist noted that Tim was seductive in his display of earnestness, readiness for "therapy," and a kind of charm that would tend to lure forth smiles, nods of agreement, and reassurances. There were unusually frequent requests for the therapist's interpretations and personal responses, all of which would have been premature or inappropriate. The therapist found it necessary to make some effort not to react with either a feigned warmth or a withdrawal from the patient.

Tim had obtained psychotherapy on several previous occasions. He had entered both individual and group treatment after his father's death, several years before, when he had felt not so much sad as empty, alienated, and aimless. These therapies had focused on his difficulties in maintaining intimate attachments with men and women. Since developing the intrusive images of Jack, he had already gone to a gestalt therapy group. There he had worked on this symptom, and he described it during the interview.

Tim: I took a gestalt therapy group which I haven't found helpful. I wanted more personal attention.

  T: You wanted what?

Tim: I wanted more personal attention. This thing was so stressful for me I felt that I had to get on it now and work on it closely, work on improving my life closely with somebody and I felt that it wasn't going to happen at the gestalt therapy.

  T: Have you been able to talk about this in the gestalt therapy?

Tim: I talked about it yesterday. I had Jack on a pillow, you know, this guy on a pillow, and I yelled at him. I said: "I don't want to think about you anymore. I want to get on to living." Did that whole thing. And I didn't get what I wanted out of there. I was leaving and one of the senior consultants there, I went up to him and I had wanted to ask him for a hug, but I hadn't been able to in the group, well, he said that was fine, he would give me a hug afterward anyway. And then he said, you know—he didn't know what to say. And I interpreted that to mean that he couldn't offer me any help about this thing. And that was, I didn't like that, I felt lonely. I felt like saying (angrily): "Hasn't anyone died in your life or something and haven't you had to work it through? Can't you even tell me that?" I didn't say that though.

He criticized the gestalt therapist for behavior he felt badly about in his own relationship with Jack. "He couldn't offer me any help." Tim also seemed to denigrate the gestalt therapy in order to win the approval of the present therapist, to whom he related rapidly, superficially and projectively. He appeared ready to idealize the present therapist as a shaman who would exorcize the ghost of Jack and diminish Jack as a person with the power to hurt him.

He watched the therapist intently. If he told of his problems to an extent that might be embarrassing, he would then switch to another version of the story which seemed to reflect him in a better light. In telling of his relationship with Jack he spoke alternately of caring and not caring, as if trying to correct from a blame-worthy to a praise-worthy position. The danger of an uncaring and strong self-image was to blame for hurting or using others. The danger in caring was weakness and personal vulnerability. The therapist did not comment on these shifting self-images. He concentrated on trying to develop a shared model of the sequence of events and a therapeutic alliance in which his role would be defined as giving neither blame nor praise but rather clarification of what had happened and was happening now.

Later during the first hour, the therapist was surprised by Tim's expression of intense anger towards Carol, towards the gestalt therapist, and towards others in general. In essence, Tim regarded Jack's death and its aftermath as an imposition upon him which weakened him by depleting his energies. This imposition was personified by others who made demands on him or did not contribute to his well-being. He was especially intense in his anger at Carol, whom he felt was trying to "milk Jack's death for all it was worth" and to "move in on him" in doing so. He minimized all of his own questionable attitudes and displayed Carol in a bad light.

SECOND SESSION

The second hour can be summarized as one of transference testing. Tim reported feeling much better. His phobia of the dark was improved and he could sleep with progressively fewer lights on in the house. This was followed by a eulogy about Jack's good qualities. He then attempted to engage the therapist in sweeping theoretical reviews of his current life problems and to communicate a non-specific readiness for an "in-depth" approach. His wish to please the therapist was clearly apparent but because of his vulnerability to shame, was not interpreted. Instead the therapist diligently leaned in the direction of a continued reconstruction of the stress event, Tim's state before it happened, and the sequence of subsequent events. His benevolent non-reactivity to the patient's provocations for expressions of closeness seemed to be reassuring. Tim then went on to review his life history, commenting on various patterns and meanings himself.

THIRD SESSION

In the third hour the patient seemed to be dejected, closer to the therapist, and again solicited sympathy. He described general feelings of fear and helplessness, and gradually related these to an identification with Jack. The next associations led to Tim's first discussion of his father, who had died of cancer some years previously, and from whom Tim had inherited some money. His mother tried to get closer to him, and also felt that she should have a greater portion of the money from the father's will. His feelings that his mother was "trying to suck him in and being selfish" were linked by the therapist to his reactions to Carol as trying to suck him in after Jack's death.

FOURTH SESSION

During the fourth hour Tim was more defensive than he had been throughout the first three hours, and seemed aloof. He talked earnestly and somewhat glibly about his conflicted attitudes towards women. He enjoyed fantasies replete with sadistic but harmless play. In actual relationships with women he tended to be so submissive that he felt they soon lost interest in him. There was a certain exhibitionistic quality around his stories of sexual relationships, as if he were saying pointedly that he was heterosexual rather than homosexual. The therapist accepted these demonstrations at face value and did not interpret them. He worked to maintain a steady and non-directive interest in Tim in order to stabilize his self esteem.

FIFTH SESSION

A few weeks had now passed since Jack committed suicide. Carol called to invite Tim to join several friends at the site of the death where they would have a final farewell ceremony for Jack. He was determined not to go and tried to make other plans for that day, of a concrete and defiantly pleasurable nature. In this, the fifth hour, Tim spoke with some pressure of how he wanted to avoid thinking of Jack because it "would drive him crazy." The therapist sensed that it was necessary to ask him what this meant in a gradual and gentle manner. Tim, with embarrassment bordering on a sense of deep humiliation, reported that while he had said he was feeling better, he had still been having recurrent intrusive images of Jack. While he could not describe this quite as directly as it is stated here, he had not told of these intrusions because he was afraid the therapist would not be interested or would withdraw from him because he had not improved rapidly enough.

In the intrusive images he saw Jack, still alive and bleeding from his wound, having second thoughts and crying out for help. The therapist quietly said "Jack felt alone." Tim then related "alone" to himself, talked of his own suicidal ruminations, and his identification with Jack. He then worked on the association to himself of "having second thoughts." He had second thoughts that he ought to have been more willing to re-establish his closeness to Jack, and thereby prevent Jack's need for such a desperate escape from loneliness. This line of thought was repeated throughout subsequent therapy sessions and, as he reviewed his acts and decisions, he confirmed for himself that while he did feel guilty, he was not responsible for rescuing either Jack or Carol.

As he returned to the idea of suicide, and whether or not persons should be rescued, he revealed for the first time that his father had contemplated suicide and had himself entered therapy with a psychiatrist. Tim had felt then the way he had felt with Jack, that he should give more affection to his father but did not want to drain himself. He used the treatment as an excuse; he did not have to get close to his father, because it might interfere, in some nebulous way, with the therapeutic process. His father had, at this time, tried to get closer to Tim, but in a needy rather than paternal way. This abortive effort at intimacy or, as Tim experienced it, at using him, had been repeated after the diagnosis of cancer.

In more normal times, the father treated Tim imperiously. A successful businessman, he regarded Tim as an appendage rather than a successor whom he might groom to take on adult work. Tim was placed in a need-fear dilemma. He felt dependent on his father and lonely without his love, but whenever he got close to him he felt used.

SIXTH SESSION

At the sixth session, Tim reported that he was depressed. After the last hour he had felt like talking with his mother. In a long telephone conversation he had both positive and negative feelings. His mother seemed to make herself more available to him and to want more contact, but he was uneasy about becoming more intimate with her and being used. The similarity of his images of mother and Carol, and his fears of being sucked in were worked on. While he feared being used, he also had bad self-images when he backed off from people. He then spoke of also feeling badly when he approached the women. He felt as if he were too strong, inappropriately taking over father's or Jack's woman. The emotions of these "strong" images were isolated, he did not feel virile and competitive, only vaguely disturbed over issues of right and wrong. Avoidance of blame in the imagined eyes of the therapist seemed to be an important motive for how information about these meanings was processed. For example, he readily changed the designation of attributes, sometimes labeling the one in need as himself, other times as Carol. The therapist's interventions were to gradually clarify who had any given attribute in a specific interchange.

He became uncomfortable talking of his mother and Carol and, as an avoidance, began to discuss sports. He described his enthusiasm and vitality while playing ball. He imagined that the therapist was "a fellow jock" who empathized with this, and felt warm and close. The therapist asked if this reminded him of anyone. He then spoke of how he and his father had played ball and of how it was the only time of sharing between them. He cried and spoke of continuing with sports as some kind of celebration of his father's memory.

SEVENTH SESSION

The following hour, the seventh, was characterized initially by flat affect. He talked vaguely of current work and dating problems. The therapist commented that he "seemed to have more difficulty getting started this hour" and asked in a kindly way if they might reflect on it together to see why this might be. With hesitation, Tim reported that he was having "difficulty thinking about his father." This acquisition of the therapist's word usage ("difficulty") was noteworthy. The implicit shield of certification seemed to enable him to contemplate warded-off ideas without feeling like a bad person for having them.

He went on to say that he had been stopping himself from thinking about his father when he was alone. As he spoke, Tim checked the therapist with penetrating glances to see if he would feel that such avoidance of therapeutically endorsed topics was deserving of blame. When he seemed reassured that the therapist was not angry with him, he expressed anger with his father. He questioned the need to let himself feel sad; his father did not deserve his positive and sad feelings because he had given Tim so little during his life. Tim should be selfish too, a person who needs no one. The same held true for Jack. Tim was angry that he had been made to feel as though he ought to be a rescuer. He did not know how to be of help to anyone else and did not want to be expected to try.

REMAINING SESSIONS

In nine ensuing hours, Tim and his therapist worked through his fear of being "sucked in," his anger, and his fear of retaliation for neglecting Jack. A mourning process had been initiated, a process with certain narcissistic qualities. As part of this process there was considerable work done on his feelings towards his father and his father's death, as well as on the symbolic connections between his father and Jack, and between Carol and his mother. The process in relation to his father can be summarized as follows.

DISCUSSION

During Tim's mourning process, the threat of injury to his self-concept was prominent in the themes that were warded off and in the transference attitudes activated by approach to these themes. Rage at neglect was the central theme and it had to be viewed in terms of self-experience as both the neglected person and the person to blame for the neglect. Tim placed himself in both roles in relation to Jack and his father.

When Tim saw his father as healthy and powerful, and when he saw Jack as the masterful leader, he felt anger at their lack of interest in him. When he saw his father and Jack as in need, Tim felt withdrawn and even found them repugnantly weak. He then feared that they would in turn be angry at him. If he were to give of himself, he feared that he would be drained, lose independence, and be doomed to serve the identity of another. By dying, his father and Jack seemed to confirm to Tim that he was at fault.

His problem was to ward off this blame. He expected the rage of others in the form of either angry demands on him or revenge for neglect. This fearful expectancy was represented in the intrusive images of Jack who had, symbolically, come back to haunt, assault, or trade places with him.

As Tim recalled and related memories of being with his father during the terminal illness, he realized that he felt badly that he had not been more giving to his father, just as he regretted not being more supportive of Jack. But this awareness emerged in stages. He softened the potential injury to his self-esteem by first presenting material about how others were to be blamed. By implication he was then not to blame, or not completely to blame. For example, he explained to the therapist that the reason he had not told his dying father that he loved him was because his mother had told him not to do so. Her rationale was that if he told his father that he loved him, it would be an unusual event and his father would then realize that he must be terminally ill.

As he spoke of his regret for not telling his father of his feelings, he expressed rage at his mother. He pointed out to the therapist that she was also to blame for making his father uncomfortable when, because she was worried about money, she would not provide luxuries for the hospital room. Only when he was further along in the working through process could he acknowledge that, as a person in his late twenties, he was independent enough to decide for himself what to say or to do for his father, and that his holding back was related to his own discomfort with closeness to his father and his fear of his father's illness.

As Tim dealt with the issues of himself as self-centered, and related this to the selfishness of his mother and father, he experienced the therapist in such roles. He felt that the therapist would be critical and angry at him for neglecting the therapy and at times tested the therapist for this counter-transference potential.

At the height of this transference, interpretations were likely to be experienced as reprimands rather than insights. He would feel more aloof from the therapist when he thought the therapist was enthralled with the theory that Tim's reaction to Jack's death was connected with reaction to his father's death. Tim could then disavow that such feelings were his own, by believing that he was manipulating the therapist as he continued the theme only in order to make the therapist happy. If he did not feel praised for such continuation, then he would feel the therapist was angry at him. During this period, he felt that he and the therapist were each, in some way, neglecting the other. Rage would be vaguely in the air, never fully attached to either person.

It was necessary for the therapist to avoid direct interpretation of the externalization of blame during the period when this defense to preserve self-esteem was prominent. Premature comment that Tim blamed his mother for what he blamed in himself would have been taken as a slur. Tim was not yet ready to tolerate the experience of bad attributes in himself. He must first contemplate the idea of blame for neglect at a distance, to see if it was safe. Gradually the attribution could move from others to himself.

While the therapist avoided overly direct interpretations, he did encourage this working through process. For example, while Tim talked of the issue of not saying he loved his father, the therapist helped clarify which persons communicated what ideas, what his mother said about not telling his father, what

Tim felt like saying but did not say, what he said to his mother, what he said to his father, and so on.

With such work Tim would present contradictory statements. When he felt too badly about not expressing affection, Tim would say that he had shown his father that he cared. When he felt less threatened he said he had not expressed himself to his father. A tactful approach meant avoidance of confronting Tim with contradictions but rather, encouraging a gradual movement along a train of thought that he had been inhibiting and distorting.

SUMMARY

With this rudimentary outline of some themes, it is possible to assemble them as a kind of sequence of thought. This omits some psychodynamic themes, including oedipal competitions, separation anxiety and object loss, and fears of homosexual love. But it conveys the quality of working through a given cycle of ideational and emotional responses. Some of the prominent concurrent defensive operations are indicated in brackets.

—My father (and Jack) is a powerful man. He does not do to enough for me; I like him but I hate him for that.

—I would like to be powerful like father (and Jack), then I would not need him.

—I will model myself after him while watching out for the danger of being used by him or being sucked in by him.

—He (father, Jack) is not omnipotent; he can feel pain, weakness and death.

—I must move further away from him (father, Jack) to avoid contamination with death or extreme need. I am afraid it is too late, the same thing may happen to me.

—By moving further away I did not save him (father, Jack) or even help him during his suffering.

—Jack, like my father, will be enraged and get back at me.

—These images and my feeling that he is present are either evidence he is out to get me or it shows I am weak and going crazy.

—But I am not to blame. I refuse to believe I should have done more. People are wrong to expect anything of me. I refuse to think any more about this [denial, suppression, disavowal].

—It is not true that I moved away from Jack or my father [slides meanings to alter the story].

—Even if it is true, then others did it too, more than me. They are to blame [externalization].

—In spite of the fact that others moved away and bear their responsibility, I am responsible that I moved away from him (father, Jack).

—While I did not do all that I might have, I am still not a terrible person. My neglect did not directly kill them.

—I miss my father, and am sad that it was not better between us.

—I am sorry that he (father, Jack) died, I wish I had done more. But even though I did not do as much as I would have liked, it is not true that they are now enraged at me.

—Even though it is true that I felt an inner rage that my father did not do more for me, that rage did not kill him (or Jack). So I do not have to bear total responsibility for their deaths.

As indicated by the later items in the condensed ideational line, Tim began to grieve not only for the father he had lost, but for an ideal father he had never had. As one example of this mourning process he had a kind of restitutional fantasy in which he was a surgeon operating on his father and saving his life. This fantasy condensed many feelings; his anger (cutting his father open), his rescue wishes (saving him), his need to be strong and admirable (the brilliant surgeon), and his need to have omnipotence against death.

His symptoms were relieved. With cessation of intrusive images of Jack entering or being present in his apartment, he was able to go to bed with the lights off and to sleep through the night. His anxiety attacks stopped and he felt confident that he had worked through the stress event. He had shown a readiness to deal with his character problems and a wish to advance from his less than optimal pre-stress level of ego development. For these reasons, long-term psychoanalytic psychotherapy was recommended after termination of the brief therapy.

Part VI

CHAPTER EIGHTEEN

Extensions

THIS BOOK HAS EXAMINED OBSERVATIONS and theory within a specific sector. The boundaries of this sector were styles (hysterical, obsessional, and narcissistic), of persons at a given developmental level (adults), as treated by certain approaches (dynamic therapy aimed at completion of working through), for a pathological state (stress-response syndrome). Assertions have been made that are clearly positioned within the frame of reference of these four boundaries.

What is gained through this model is an organization for systematic assembly of clinical knowledge. By placing assertions in such clear conceptual positions, many of the schisms that now characterize psychiatry and psychology will fall away. Disagreements at comparable rather than incongruous levels of abstraction will lead to new empirical observations and reformulations.

The assertions made here can be specifically challenged; general stress response tendencies may not follow the pathways defined, there may be better ways to typologize what was called "hysterical," "obsessional," and "narcissistic," the nuances of focused psychodynamic psychotherapy may be incomplete or inappropriate. A specific site of disagreement can be localized by following the same dimensions used in this model. For example, an argument about a nuance of treatment would have to be connected with a specific kind of person, in an intrusive-

355

repetitive phase after a stressful external event, involved in psychodynamic treatment aimed at relief of intrusions and resolution of the state of stress.

While this model localizes conceptualization, it may be argued that it defines restrictively small areas. Within the general field of psychopathology and psychotherapy there are multitudes of such areas. I believe that the field is so large that many specific subdivisions are indicated, and that knowledge will be accumulated and clarified by this method. The complexity is not overwhelming. The present model can be extended by keeping most dimensions constant while extending the boundaries of only one or two. For example, extensions may involve other variations of personality, other versions of pathological states, and other views of therapy.

OTHER DISPOSITIONAL STYLES

Nuances of technique, such as the importance of clarity with hysterical styles, holding with obsessional styles, and reconstruction with narcissistic styles, were described as variations on the general theme of helping a patient complete the processing of stress related ideas and feelings. A clear extension of the present model for organizing clinical information would be to maintain the focus of stress-response syndromes, and a brief psychodynamic treatment approach, while enlarging upon modes of behavior for other types of persons in the therapy situation.

Other well-known character styles could be examined for particularity of response. Withdrawal in the schizoid personality, splitting in the borderline personality, externalization in the paranoid, counterphobia in the impulsive, and symbiosis in the dependent, are obvious points of departure that could lead to further clarification of both stress-response variants and specific nuances of treatment technique as they are related to the patient's style of processing ideas and feelings.

Dispositional styles could also be examined from the perspective of other theories of personality typology. Levelers could be contrasted with sharpeners, introverts could be contrasted with extroverts, and from the cross-cultural viewpoint, contrasts could be made among members of different ethnic groups.

OTHER DEVELOPMENTAL LEVELS

Examination of developmental variances would be another extension of great interest. Children do manifest phases of both intrusion and denial after stressful life events, but their cognitive characteristics are different from those reported here. Object substitution, regression, precocious development, and splitting all play a larger role. Denial is very prominent at times, especially in adolescent responses to parental death, where there may be an absence of grief work or mourning. Certainly the working through process varies greatly; each period of growth has its own cognitive, emotional, defensive, and relational characteristics, and requires particular nuances within a general rationale for therapy.

OTHER THERAPIES

Keeping a constant focus on stress-response syndromes and hysterical, obsessional, and narcissistic defensive style, another extension would be to examine other modes of treatment in terms of rationale and processes of change. Here, the focus has been on brief psychodynamic psychotherapy with behavioral psychotherapy discussed to demonstrate the application of the concept to other sets of treatment techniques. An extension would include such modes of approach as transactional analysis, gestalt therapy, or conjoint family therapy.

For example, the transactional analysis approach would include the intrasystemic, and the intersystemic conflicts of the person's parent, adult, and child self-organizations in reaction to an attitude about the stress event. In addition, the introjects or imaginary projections of attitudes from both parents, plus the relation of the stress event to the person's life script would be considered. Such labeling might be seen as useful to counteract hysterical vagueness, but as facilitating intellectualization and isolation in the obsessional patient. In contrast, the guided imagery or "empty chair" techniques of gestalt therapy could encourage hysterical dissociation while they might serve to hold the obsessional on a given aspect of a train of thought and so promote working-through and completion. Whether or not such differences in responsivity of various character types would be observed in practice, dispositional variations have to be considered in prescribing a therapy technique. Any comparison of psychotherapies for effects would have to include such variables. Previous studies of the outcome of psychotherapy have been too broad-gauge, according to this model, since overinclusiveness of states and styles leads to a washout effect as positive and negative effects are averaged.

OTHER STATES

Stress-response syndromes were chosen as the focus for trying out this model for the accumulation and clarification of clinical knowledge. This choice was based on the belief that the knowledge of the details of the immediate event provides a useful handle for interpretation of other mental contents, that the phases of response are known from concordances in clinical, field, and experimental investigations, that the treatment is brief with usually rapid change, and that the individual signs and symptoms are significant components of other syndromes. The general concept of a completion tendency and the ideas about nuances of treatment were important results of this analysis of stress-response syndromes.

The theoretical model presented around the theme of a completion tendency is not limited to responses to recent external stress events. The model may be useful for conceptualizing symptom formation and working through processes when stresses are of internal and mixed origin. For example, a nightmare, an obsessive thought, a recurrent emotion, or a behavioral pattern can replace the external stress event as a starting point for analysis of ideational-motivational structure. Similarly, emergence of a strong impulse could be conceptualized as "new information" which is then stored in active memory and which sets in motion a train of thought aimed at revising schemata into accord with the new situation. The interactive model of cognition, memory, affect, and controls might, therefore, prove applicable to pathological states other than those which follow external events such as death, violence, or failures.

The concept of nuances of technique can also be extended for consideration of treatment for other syndromes (Horowitz, 1974). Since the nuances relate to the person's style of processing information, they will be pertinent to any kind of work that involves increased awareness, clarification of patterns, reconstruction, or interpretation.

Sequential Clarification

The essence of this model is sequential clarification. This book provides an early step in the clarification of the interaction of stress response syndromes, styles, and dynamic therapy. While there are extensions possible at these boundaries, there is also a deepening within the boundaries that would involve examination of the assertions for reliability and validity.

At this early step, an effort was made to provide generalizations based on clinical, field and experimental work. The tendency to intrusive and repetitive thinking after stressful life events is seen so consistently in clinical, field, and experimental studies that I believe this observation to be both reliable and valid. The tendency to phases of denial seems to have equivalent stature. Other generalizations include some observations that may be inaccurate or possibly erroneous. The concept of nuances of techniques is especially new and tenuous. Further clinical observations, field studies, and experiments are possible; they will be done with increasing operational definition, controls, quantifications, and checks for reliability. The results will correct errors.

Conclusion

A valid methodology for the study of human psychology at the level of conscious experiences and meanings is to assemble clinical knowledge, as clearly as possible, in a well defined area. The results will be progressively helpful rather than "once-and-for-all-time" proofs. Decisive research designs are not possible in this holistic frame of reference because it is not possible to control enough variables. Human meanings change with history, and are invariably overdetermined. Thus any such assemblage of clinical knowledge will always contain uncertainties. Constant redefinition and revision is the essence of this side of science, and the contents of this book will need to be rewritten in the context of the future.

BIBLIOGRAPHY

Horowitz, M. J. (1974), Stress response syndromes: Character style and brief psychotherapy. *Archives of General Psychiatry,* 31:768-781.

BIBLIOGRAPHIC NOTES

CHAPTERS 3, 4, & 7

Aspects of the phases of stress response syndromes have been discussed in HOROWITZ, M. J. (1973), Phase oriented treatment of stress response syndromes. *American Journal of Psychotherapy*, 27:506-515.

CHAPTER 5

Experimental studies summarized in Chapter 5 are based on the following publications:

HOROWITZ, M. J. (1969), Psychic trauma: Return of images after a stressful film. *Archives of General Psychiatry*, 20:552-559.

HOROWITZ, M. J. (1970), *Image Formation and Cognition*. New York: Appleton-Century-Crofts.

HOROWITZ, M. J. & BECKER, S. S. (1971c), The compulsion to repeat trauma: Experimental study of intrusive thinking after stress. *Journal of Nervous and Mental Disease*, 153:32-34.

HOROWITZ, M. J. & BECKER, S. S. (1971a), Cognitive response to stress and experimental demand. *Journal of Abnormal Psychology*, 78:86-92.

HOROWITZ, M. J. & BECKER, S. S. (1971b), Cognitive response to stressful stimuli. *Archives of General Psychiatry*, 25:419-428.

HOROWITZ, M. J., BECKER, S. S. & MOSKOWITZ, M. L. (1971), Intrusive and repetitive thought after stress: A replication study. *Psychological Reports*, 29:763-767.

HOROWITZ, M. J., BECKER, S. S., MOSKOWITZ, M. L. & RASHID, K. (1972), Intrusive thinking in psychiatric patients after stress. *Psychological Reports*, 31:235-238.

BECKER, S. S., HOROWITZ, M. J., & CAMPBELL, L. (1973), Cognitive response to others: Effects of demand and sex. *Journal of Abnormal Psychology*, 82:519-522.

HOROWITZ, M. J. & BECKER, S. S. (1973), Cognitive response to erotic and stressful films. *Archives of General Psychiatry*, 29:81-84.

HOROWITZ, M. J. & WILNER, N. (in press), Stress films, emotion and cognitive response. *Archives of General Psychiatry*.

WILNER, N. & HOROWITZ, M. J. (1975), Intrusive and repetitive thought after a depressing film: A pilot study. *Psychological Reports*, 37:135-138.

CHAPTER 6

The basic cognitive model of representational systems, interactive with emotional response and controls as feedback process, appeared in HOROWITZ, M. J. (1972), Modes of representation of thought. *Journal of the American Psy-*

choanalytic Association, 20:793-819, and in HOROWITZ, M. J. (1974), Micro-analysis of working through in psychotherapy. *American Journal of Psychiatry,* 131:1208-1212.

CHAPTERS 8 & 9

The hysterical and obsessional modes of response to stressful life events have been considered in HOROWITZ, M. J. (1974), Stress response syndromes: Character style and dynamic psychotherapy. *Archives of General Psychiatry,* 31:768-781.

CHAPTER 10

The narcissistic modes of response to stressful life events appear in HOROWITZ, M. J. (1975), Sliding meanings: A defense against threat in narcissistic personalities. *International Journal of Psychoanalytic Psychotherapy,* 4:167-180.

Index

363